NATIVE CLAYS AND GLAZES FOR NORTH AMERICAN POTTERS

Oregon volcanic ash imparts a soft, gray, semi-matte, translucent glaze to an earthenware body.

NATIVE CLAYS AND GLAZES FOR NORTH AMERICAN POTTERS

A Manual for the Utilization of
Local Clay and Glaze Materials

Ralph Mason

Timber Press
Portland, Oregon

NATIVE CLAYS AND GLAZES FOR NORTH AMERICAN POTTERS
A Manual for the Utilization of Local Clay and Glaze Materials

Ralph Mason

© Copyright 1981 by Timber Press

All Rights Reserved

Library of Congress Cataloging in Publication Data

Mason, Ralph S.
  Native clays and glazes for North American potters.

  Bibliography: p.
  Includes index.
  1. Clay — North America.   2. Glazes.

I. Title.
TP811.M366   666'.42   81-18493
ISBN 0-917304-02-0   AACR2

Timber Press
P.O. Box 1632
Beaverton, OR 97075
USA

PRINTED IN THE UNITED STATES OF AMERICA

DEDICATION

To my wife Dorothy whose critical pencil did wonders for my syntax.

ACKNOWLEDGMENTS

My grateful thanks to all my friends, both lay and professional, who aided and encouraged me in the preparation of this book, which, like clay on a potter's wheel, had many turnings before it reached its final shape.

INTRODUCTION

Making something useful or ornamental out of clay has a history extending back to our earliest recorded beginnings. Over the thousands of years that man has been working with clay the methods and techniques in use today differ only slightly from those developed before the dawn of Christianity. Sun-dried brick were fashioned and laid up into walls in the Tigris-Euphrates valley of ancient Mesopotamia (now Iraq) 5000 years ago, and artistic and religious objects made of clay are commonly found at many excavation sites of early cultures. Clay very probably has the longest record of continuous use by man of all of the earth's mineral resources.

Although sun-dried brick provided a building material vastly superior to shelters of skins stretched over poles, the attacks of wind and rain eventually reduced them once more to mud. It is interesting to note that many cities and towns in Asia are today resting on huge mounds of mud — the remains of former cities built largely of sun-dried brick. The Etruscans added bitumen, obtained from local oil seeps, to the clay to make it waterproof and thus much longer lasting.

As civilization spread outwards from the semi-arid lands of Asia into more humid climates, the need for fired brick became imperative, particularly so because supplies of bitumen for waterproofing were unknown in the newly occupied lands. An abundance of fuel in the form of wood made the firing of clay possible. It was soon learned that fired clay greatly improved the permanence of structures. Art objects and vessels of fired clay also made their appearance. Originally made of coarse, red-colored terra cotta, the ware slowly changed into lighter colors as better clays and improved methods of preparation and firing were developed. Basically the history of ceramics is the history of developing local materials because clays are usually available in abundance, have a low value per unit of weight and consequently cannot be transported very far economically.

In the American Southwest the art of the potter developed early, probably diffusing out of Mexico nearly 2000 years ago. Although the Pueblo potters are world-famous for their beautifully symmetrical pots, neither the ancient potters nor their modern descendants have ever used the potter's wheel. The Southwest Indian potters use local clays, form their vessels by hand, make their own glazes and pigments, and fire their ware in crude, temporary kilns out of doors on windless days. The perfection achieved is entirely due to the art and skill of the potters who have blended their skills with native raw materials to produce an art form of lasting beauty. It should be further noted that with but few exceptions, the Pueblo potters are women.

In the American colonies local clays were fired at Jamestown, Virginia as early as 1625. During the Colonial period, itinerant potters supplied households with rough earthenware which was usually made on the spot with local clays and fired with wood from nearby forests. Earthenware gave way to stoneware and lead glazes in the early 1700's, but as the toxicity of the lead-coated vessels became known other glazes were substituted.

Shoji Hamada, one of the world's leading art potters, routinely used local, unrefined clay from various sources in the Japanese countryside. The outstanding quality of his work attests to not only the utility but the aesthetic possibilities of native clays. Hamada is the modern exponent of a long line of potters, who, by exploiting the natural characteristics of a local clay and by adapting their own techniques to accommodate its eccentricities, attempted to produce the finest ware possible. Aside from the removal of obvious impurities such as sticks and stones, these potters used the clay as it was dug. In the chapters that follow there will be a discussion on using local clays both in the unrefined and also in the beneficiated state.

In many areas the opportunities for using local raw ceramic materials are excellent, even though the region may not be noted particularly for high quality, white-firing or industrial clays. Information on these local clays is unfortunately widely scattered and difficult to obtain. Sources for some of the more pertinent information have been assembled in the Appendix in the hope that those potters who have mastered the basic skills involved in creating ceramic ware might wish to experiment with new materials, locally obtainable, and possessing qualities that might prove to be uniquely suited to their craftsmanship. Some general suggestions are also given on where to look for undeveloped clay deposits. A potter looking for a new clay deposit is a true prospector and as such he needs all the help he can get. Hopefully some of the information appearing in the section on "Tracking, Testing and Taming Clays" will make the search more productive and interesting.

The names of deposits and mines may change over the years so much dependence must be placed on the legal description. The mystery of the system used to describe the legal location of a property is explained in the chapter on "First Things First".

The overriding problem with attempting to list clay sources of interest to the craft potter lies in the fact that very little interest has ever been expressed by industry or public agencies in small or isolated deposits, regardless of quality. Fortunately large deposits are often excellent guides to other, smaller ore bodies in the vicinity, and the thinner, less economical edges of big mines and quarries are often left unmined.

Listing of clay properties in the various reports issued by public agencies should be viewed with a bit of skepticism. At best the listings can only indicate that at some point in time somebody said there was a deposit at such and such a place — and there probably was. The only problem is that clay deposits are non-renewable, and once mined out are gone forever. Also, when they are paved over they do not sprout up through cracks in the concrete like dandelions. On the bright side, however, it is more than likely that even though a specific property has disappeared, there may be similar material close by.

In the chapter "First Things First" a good deal of attention is given to maps, map-reading, and map-using. Clay deposits are often located way out in the sticks and getting there and back in a workmanlike manner is important. Most people are familiar with the road maps available at service stations and here their knowledge about maps ends. There are many types of maps and knowing about them and how to use them is important if you are to become a prospector-potter.

The chapter "Tracking, Testing and Taming Clay" covers the more important aspects of the complex business of looking for (and recognizing) a raw clay deposit when you see it, understanding the geologic conditions of the deposit, how to drill and sample it, what equipment is needed for field exploration, how to make tests in the field and studio, how to upgrade your clay and lastly how to mine and map your deposit.

"Beneficiation and Processing" is the rather formidable title of a chapter devoted to all of the many steps required to transform freshly mined clay into a product suitable for use in the studio. There are many types and kinds of clay but nearly all raw clays will require at least some treatment before you can use them. Sorting, crushing, fine grinding, concentrating, screening, mixing, blending and sampling are discussed, even though with luck, you may never have to go the full route with your clay.

Ceramic materials other than clay are included in the chapter "Natural Glaze Materials". Minerals used in this service, where to look for them and how to recognize them are discussed.

Listing of clay properties in the various reports issued by public agencies should be viewed with a bit of skepticism. At best the listings can only indicate that at some point in time somebody said there was a deposit at such and such a place — and there probably was. The only problem is that clay deposits are non-renewable, and once mined out are gone forever. Also, when they are paved over they do not sprout up through cracks in the concrete like dandelions. On the bright side, however, it is more than likely that even though a specific property has disappeared, there may be similar material close by.

A selected Bibliography has been prepared and some of the more important entries have been annotated. The literature that deals with clays and ceramics is enormous and ranges from basic pot-making on up to investigations into the space lattices of the clay minerals. Since the mass of reference material is so huge only a very small and highly selective list has been included in the Bibliography. Almost all published works on clay and ceramics have rather extensive bibliographies of their own, and those publications having unusually good ones have been noted.

Since the formation of clay deposits is governed by basic geologic principles some prospecting potters might wish to become more fully informed on just how the clay got to be where it now is. New texts on geology are coming out with increasing frequency. Several of the standard texts on general geology have been included in the Bibliography but the list is intended rather to lead the reader into the general area of the available literature and not to pass judgment on the relative merits of the individual works. College bookstores are probably the best places to purchase these books and thrifty buyers should visit them at the end of the school year when many books are turned in to be sold second hand.

While much information on clays and ceramics has been printed by various state, provincial and federal geological organizations it is usually difficult to obtain. Limited press-runs and a narrow distribution have severely limited the availability of most publicly printed reports. Public libraries may, however, have some of these publications.

In the Glossary an attempt is made to define the special language of geology, mining, beneficiation and processing in everyday terms.

In the Appendix there are some handy tables and charts that are more easily found there than if they were buried somewhere in the text. Also some other information that may prove useful and interesting but which is not essential to the text has been included.

Entry into the business of looking for and developing your own clay can be made at many different levels, and you can also shift your level of interest as you progress. To start with you may wish to simply go out to an established clay pit and start experimenting with some of the pit-run clays. A slightly more venturesome tactic would be to explore in the vicinity of a known deposit, looking for subtle variations in composition. For the prospector-potter a preliminary search of the literature, followed by careful field explorations, sampling and testing may be the way to go. Then there is the dumb luck method where you just put your shovel down in what looks like a good spot and hope for the best. This last method is hardly to be recommended. Clays are quite abundant and deposits, even though hidden, usually signal their presence quite clearly to the observant and informed prospector.

When you want to try a raw clay, even though you have thoroughly tested it, start by using only a small proportion of the new material mixed in with your old, reliable clay. If the new mix seems to work you can gradually increase the percentage of new clay, keeping good records of amounts used, behavior while drying and firing, final appearance, color, texture, and any other factors you feel are important. With luck and careful control over your mixes you just might develop a new and wonderful clay body. Although clays may appear to be shapeless masses of dull, damp dirt when you are forming them, they become rather active socially in the kiln and a lot of complex inner emotions take place as temperatures rise, water evaporates, carbonaceous material burns off and mineral crystals go through fundamental changes. The heat of firing a kiln can best be described as an energy input which activates normally inactive substances. The individual chemicals present in the clay body combine, at high temperatures, to form new combinations which are strikingly different from the original. Fired ware emerging from a kiln is no longer affected by water, is much harder and stronger than before, may be quite resistant to common acids and bases, and in very high quality porcelain ware, becomes translucent. Small wonder, then, that a ceramist must be part artist, part chemist, part mechanic, part prospector, and part scientist.

If you have grown accustomed to the way a certain clay body behaves in the kiln, don't take it for granted that a new clay mix is going to go along with your particular ideas on firing. If you have a complacent, broad-range clay, no sweat, but you may get caught if you try your old pot-boiler glaze which worked so well with the standard clay. The relationship of a clay body to a glaze is much like marriage. The glaze may be a thing of beauty when wedded to a standard body but it may not be a joy for even a moment when married to a new clay in the tempestuous atmosphere of the fiery kiln, even though the body is worthy — of some other glaze.

Although a great deal is known about the general subject of ceramics there is much that is unknown about the performance of individual clays in response to the almost infinite variety of ways in which they can be prepared, blended, formed, fired and glazed. It is this uncertainty, coupled with the anticipation of producing some special ware, that adds zest to the search for, and development of, a new clay.

Partly because clay is so common and so variable, a good, clear-cut definition of what clay is has been hard to come by. Soil scientists, geologists, agronomists, and ceramists have all taken whacks at the problem and come up with different ideas. The following definition may be as good as is likely to come along:

> Clays are naturally occurring rocks, both unconsolidated and consolidated, composed of very fine particles of clay minerals. All deposits of clay contain other minerals, and these impurities are rare in some deposits but abundant in others. The most common minerals are quartz, mica, feldspar, iron oxides and carbonates. Most deposits of clay have as their major component one of the following clay minerals: kaolinite, halloysite, montmorillonite, palygorskite, and illite. Some clay deposits may contain one or more of these clay minerals as a minor constituent.

No guarantee, either express or implied, is conveyed to the reader as to any success he or she may have in the search for and the ultimate results obtained from raw clays. Many raw clays may resemble common mud or dirt when found. The series of field tests in the chapter on "Tracking, Testing and Taming" have been included to help make an on-the-spot determination as simple and speedy as possible.

Nature in the raw is seldom mild. Few, if any, boa constrictors or Bengal tigers have been spotted in North America, but hornets, wood ticks, poison oak, agressive livestock, and last but not least, enraged land-owners, are local equivalents possessing considerable clout. Good visiting manners and a wary eye for natural hazards cannot be emphasized enough.

Happy digging, there's lots of clay fit for firing out there!

CONTENTS

FIRST THINGS FIRST

HOW TO GET THERE AND BACK

I assume that few potters have a good knowledge of the various kinds of maps and how to use them. A good understanding of maps is important to a prospector. Fortunately there are excellent maps available and some time spent studying them before starting out will not only save time and money but make clay prospecting a much more pleasant experience. So let us start with the obvious and go on to the less obvious.

There are three maxims to follow when considering maps: (1) start with general, small-scale maps which cover large areas and end up with specific maps giving detailed information on small areas; (2) know your publisher; a good map is worth its price many times over. You cannot afford to buy a poor one: (3) don't leave home without your maps; know before you go and take your knowledge with you.

Useful Maps

To be useful a map must contain certain basic elements, plus some others that are helpful in providing the special information that the map was created for. Here are the essential features of a good map:

Map scale	A device for indicating how much distance is covered by, for instance, one inch on the map. Scale may be shown by the simple "one inch=one mile", or by a fraction 1/62,500, or by a bar scale.
North arrow	Typically the top of a map is North, but there are many exceptions and a North arrow should appear on every map.
Title and Date	A title tells what, where and sometimes how and why. A date is important; roads, towns and place names change. Some features on old maps may have disappeared.
Publisher	Who printed the map? A land developer, a travel agency, a private corporation, or some government agency? Maps can be misleading if certain information is left off, or added, or shifted a bit. Know why the map was printed.
Map symbols	A map is an exercise in shorthand; space is at a premium and compact symbols are used to say much in little space. There should be an Explanation column which tells you what those funny little doodles mean. Large series of maps may have a separate Explanation sheet.

Figure 1.1 *The essential features of a good map.*

Here is a list of some useful types of maps with some notes on map content and their publishers.

Type	Map Content	Issued By
Road	roads, hiways, towns	oil companies, travel associations
City	streets, hiways, parks	commercial printers
Topographic	contours, waterways, land net, road net, buildings, political boundaries, geographic features	U.S. Geological Survey
Property ownership	property ownership of tax lots	commercial printers
Mineral deposit	mineral deposits, road and land net	state and provincial geology departments, U.S. Geological Survey, U.S. Bureau of Mines, Geological Survey of Canada
Geology	geologic formations, topography, waterways, road net, land net	state and provincial geology departments, U.S.G.S. and G.S.C.
Forest	road net, trails, waterways, land net, geographic features	U.S. Forest Service
Soil	soil types, land and road net, waterways	U.S. Soil Conservation Service

Figure 1.2 *Types of maps useful to the prospector-potter.*

The obvious thing to do first of all is to look at a road map to find out how far it is to the deposit, the best route to take, and the location of nearby towns or camping places such as state or provincial parks. Since road maps are very small-scale you should get a larger scale map of the general area which will show much greater detail and include more information on secondary roads than the general purpose road map. The 1:250,000 topographic map series is a good intermediate map for this purpose. It covers an area measuring about 70 by 105 miles and makes a good base for planning since you can indicate the general location of several likely areas to investigate on the same sheet, and also show those places you have already checked out.

The next level of map you will need will be either a Forest Service district map, which contains excellent information on roads (all of them numbered), or a 15-minute or 7.5-minute U.S.G.S. topographic map. The topographic maps cover areas of about 12 × 17 and 6 × 8½ miles respectively and contain much detail.

As you progress with your field work you may also want to use both a geologic and a soil map. These maps provide information on the nature of the surface materials and rock types that underlie the region. They are most helpful in tracking down other deposits in areas having similar soils and rocks.

Once you have selected a ceramic materials deposit and decide to mine it, you will need to make your own large-scale and greatly detailed mine map. Information on making this type of map is given in the chapter on "Tracking, Testing and Taming".

The familiar road map available at service stations serves as a good general guide to major highways and roads. The overall size of road maps, compared to the area covered, does, however, limit the information about back-country roads, lesser streams and geographic points, and many minor place names.

Detail lacking on road maps can be found on the modern topographic maps published by the U.S. Geological Survey and the Canadian Surveys and Mapping Branch and available from many local suppliers. These maps contain a wealth of information, but much of it is hidden unless you can understand the map symbols and can figure out what those wiggly lines running across the map mean. Here are some of the more common map symbols that you are likely to find on an average "topo" map. Most of the symbols are printed in black, but water-related symbols are usually in blue. (Figure 1.3) A complete list of topographic symbols is usually available at the same place that you buy your topographic maps.

Topographic maps show the elevation of the land surface by means of contour lines, usually printed in brown. The vertical distance between two adjacent lines is indicated near the bottom of the sheet as the "contour interval". Closely spaced contour lines indicate steep slopes, while widely separated contour lines show gently sloping ground. Contour lines are much like the shoreline around a lake — a level line showing equal elevations at all points. If you wish to figure, for instance, how high a hill rises above the valley floor: (1) count the number of spaces between the contour lines from the valley floor to the top of the hill, and (2) multiply the number of spaces by the contour interval shown at the bottom of the map. For example; there are nine spaces between the contour lines to the top of the hill from point 'a' in Figure 1.4, and the contour interval is 40 feet; 9 × 40 equals 360, which, when added to the elevation of the first contour line above point 'a', which is 80 feet, makes a total elevation of 440 feet. The actual top of the hill is somewhat above the 440 contour line, let's say 24 feet, or an elevation of 464 feet. Since point 'a' is lower than the 80 foot contour, perhaps at an elevation of 75 feet, then the difference in elevation from 'a' to the top of the ahill is 289 feet.

Figure 1.5 is a relief model derived from the topographic information shown in Figure 1.4 which shows how the hills and valleys are related to the contour lines shown on the 'flat' map.

Many prominent geographic points will have the actual elevation above sea level shown beside either an 'X' or a triangle. Minor hills are not marked and the height will have to be calculated from the highest contour surrounding the top.

Topographic maps are extremely useful when planning prospecting trips since all of the ups and downs, the heights of the passes and the depths to the stream crossings can be figured out. Topographic maps are also useful in indicating those areas that might be above the snowline during the winter, since weather reports usually give the elevation at which snow is falling.

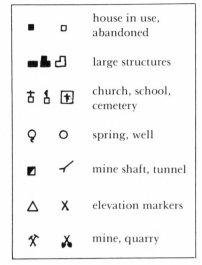

■	▢	house in use, abandoned
■▲	⌐	large structures
♁ ♂	⊞	church, school, cemetery
♀	○	spring, well
◪	⟋	mine shaft, tunnel
△	X	elevation markers
⚔	⚒	mine, quarry

Figure 1.3 *Some typical map symbols.*

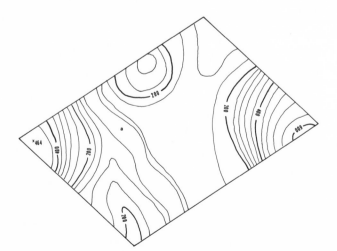

Figure 1.4 *Contours from a portion of a topographic map.*

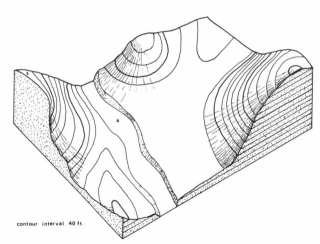

contour interval 40 ft.

Figure 1.5 *Relief model based on the contours shown in Figure 2.4.*

One thing that topographic maps do *not* show, and it is important to keep this in mind, is the network of private logging roads, or other private roads that are not constructed for long periods of use. When using these temporary roads be sure to keep a good road log, using your car odometer and your topographic map so that you do not become lost on your return.

Oddly enough topographic maps do show trails, most of them, anyway. Trails are permanent fixtures, having been there for a long time. The best information on trails and forest roads can usually be obtained from local Forest Service ranger stations. The maps give both trail and road numbers.

HOW TO READ A TOPOGRAPHIC MAP

Now for a short lesson in map reading. Take a close look at Figure 1.6 which is an actual portion of a U.S.G.S. topographic map having a scale of one inch = one mile, and a contour interval of forty feet. If, at this point, you are unfamiliar with legal subdivisions you might like to skip ahead to "Sections, Townships and Ranges" which are discussed a bit farther on in this same chapter before diving into this exercise.

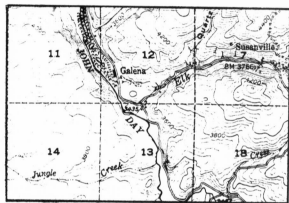

Figure 1.6 *Portion of a 15' U.S.G.S. topographic map.*

Right off the bat you can tell that the area covers six square miles, consisting of sections 11, 12, 13 and 14 in one Township and 7 and 18 in the one adjoining it on the East. Two very small towns, Galena and Susanville, lie nestled in the valleys, one carved by the John Day River, the other by Elk Creek. The presence of numerous mine tunnels and shafts and the special pattern denoting dredged ground along the John Day clearly speak to the "ghost town" and former "gold rush" nature of the settlements.

The area shown on the map is quite rugged, extending from about 3400 feet at the John Day River up to slightly over 4280 feet above sea level in the West half of Section 11. Note that with a 40-foot contour interval, every fifth contour is heavier and indicates a 200-foot difference in elevation.

Some hint as to the dryness of the country can be gained by looking at the symbols used for Jungle, Cress and Quartz creeks. The dash-and-dot pattern denotes intermittent stream flow. Also the three creeks flow down steep canyons, cutting contours at short intervals. Elk Creek has a flatter gradient and the John Day is the slowest flowing of them all. The direction of flow of the John Day is generally northwestwards, the contours paralleling the stream by "pulling away" as the stream sinks lower and lower in its canyon. When contours cross a stream or valley they tend to point upstream, as shown along Jungle Creek in the Southwest quarter of Section 14.

The contorted contour lines throughout the entire map area indicate the ruggedness of the countryside. The tiny, closed circles of some of the contours also give added evidence of the unevenness of the land surface. This type of topography is typical of semi-desert regions where erosion strips away much of the topsoil which would otherwise smooth and round the hillsides as it does in wetter climates.

Most topographic maps cover areas called quadrangles which are bounded by lines showing the latitude and longitude. The U.S. Geological Survey issues topographic maps of various scales: maps with a scale of one inch = approximately one mile cover 15 minutes of latitude and 15 minutes of longitude; maps with a scale of one inch = 2000 feet cover only 7½ minutes of latitude and longitude. The 7½-minute map series have more than four times as much map surface per unit of land area as the 15-minute series. The amount of detail shown on the 7½-minute maps is considerably greater than the 15-minute series.

For general reconnaissance work there is a third series of topographic maps known as the 1:250,000 series with a scale of about one inch = four miles. These maps cover an area bounded by one degree of latitude and two degrees of longitude. These maps cover large areas and are principally useful for planning trips and spotting likely areas to investigate further.

Travel Tricks

These tricks are offered to help you if your maps have failed you. Suppose you have been driving along through the countryside and you can't quite figure out where you are. There are no good natural landmarks and there hasn't been a road sign for miles. If there are power poles along the road, the chances are that they may have a small tag, often colored yellow, tacked on them. The numbers on the tag are location codes which give the exact position of the pole. The top row of figures (Figure 1.7) show the Township and Range, while the lower row gives the section number, pole location within the section, and the pole number. The pole position numbers refer to a grid numbering system for a square mile, or section, with the southwest corner being zero. Each number, starting with zero, indicates the number of 528-foot intervals (equal to one-tenth of a mile) that the pole is located from the southwest corner. The first number gives the number of intervals east of the corner, the second the number north of the corner. This identification system does not indicate whether the Townships are North or South, or whether the Ranges are East or West. In most cases there is little confusion and a glance at a map will resolve any uncertainty.

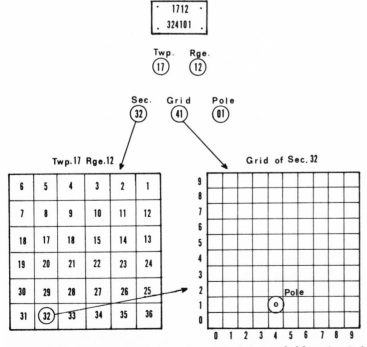

Figure 1.7 *Many utility poles have tags containing coded location information.*

The pole-marking system described here applies to many power poles in the West. Quite possibly other power systems use different markers. A check with your local power company is suggested since they have to have some logical system for locating their poles.

And here is another stunt that may speed your return. When traveling out in the country, either by car or on foot, every time you come to an intersection, or fork in the trail that is not signed: Look Back. Take a good look at the intersection and particularly at the route you came on. On your way back you might be very confused if you had never seen the junction before from the return side.

This idea may just save you from some lost time in getting rescued if you get stuck out in the bush. Before leaving on your trip, run off a copy of the map area you intend to visit, mark your route, destination, and time of return on it and leave it with a friend. Then if you don't show up on schedule, Voila! rescue is on the way.

The Perils of Prospecting

Although it is unlikely that many prospector-potters will be searching for some raw clay more than a hundred or so miles from their studio, it is entirely possible that they could venture into arid or semi-arid areas without traveling very far. Along the entire stretch of the Pacific Coast most of the people live where it rains a lot, but only a few of them realize that very dry climates prevail just over the mountains.

Several things should be borne in mind when prospecting in these wide open semi-desert areas. First, take plenty of water with you; second, distances are often great between gas stations and towns so have adequate food and fuel along; third, weather changes are likely to be much more pronounced. Large differences between noontime highs and evening lows are to be expected on the thermometer, and a real gully washer of a rainstorm can boil up out of cloudless sky in short order; fourth, either stay in motels or organized campgrounds or pick your campsite with exceeding care. Check your proposed campsite well before dark and check especially for its proximity to active ant hills, animal burrows, or game and cattle trails. A camp near a water hole or stock water trough may be plagued with animals coming in for a drink at any old hour, often quite noisily, and hordes of flying insects seem to congregate wherever there is water; fifth, make sure you have permission to camp on the spot you have selected; many areas are not open for camping for one reason or another. Lastly, check your campsite and make sure that it is above and away from any threat of flash flooding. Dry stream beds offer several inducements for camping; the land is flat and usually nice large shade trees are near at hand. Avoid such situations like the plague. Sudden storms in nearby mountains can send torrents of water roaring down watercourses at any time, and many a camper has had to flee with what he or she had on to keep from being swept away. About twenty years ago a survey party met such a fate while camped beside a dry stream bed. All of their camp gear vanished one night and they even had to spend quite a bit of time looking for their Jeep, which was somewhat dishevelled when found down the canyon apiece.

How to Find Yourself in the Woods

THE MAGNETIC COMPASS

On most maps, and on all of those published by the U.S. Geological Survey, the top of the map is North, with East to the right and West to the left. Many maps have an arrow which shows the direction of true North and a second arrow which points to magnetic North. Magnetic North is the direction a compass needle points. The better types of pocket compasses often have a gadget to adjust for this difference, thus making it possible to sight the compass on an object and then to read the true direction on the compass dial directly. The difference between the magnetic bearing and the true bearing is called declination.

A pocket compass is a very real aid when you are out in the field, but it does have one very confusing feature. In the preceding paragraph we said that when you face North, East is to your right and West to your left. Now, look at your compass and you will find that "E" is to the *left* of North and "W" to the *right*. Slowly revolve the compass around and you will see why this is necessary.

One suggestion. If you are not familiar with the use of a compass, better go to a park and try it out before you get lost in the field and then try to figure it out. All too many prospectors have gone just the opposite way from the proper route because they just wouldn't believe what the compass was telling them.

HELP FROM YOUR MAP

If you get out in the hills with a good map, can see two geographic points which you can identify and which show on your map, and have a magnetic compass and a drafting protractor, you can locate yourself in less than five minutes.

Assume that you are completely fuddled by the rabbit warren of logging roads shown in Figure 1.8 and don't know where you are or where the clay prospect that you are looking for is hidden. The first thing to do is to take a compass bearing on one of the two geographic points (point "A" in Figure 1.9). Next plot this same bearing, using the protractor, on the map, extending the line from the point you took the bearing on across the map. Note that this line crosses various roads in Figure 1.9 in at least eight points, but just which one you are on is difficult to determine. Now take a similar bearing on point "B" (Figure 1.10) and plot the bearing on the map. You are located at the point where these two bearing lines intersect.

Make sure that you take careful compass and protractor readings and also check to be sure that your compass has the same magnetic declination set off as the map shows. If you do not have a protractor with you and your compass has straight edges, you can use it to lay off the proper bearing on the map, but it is a bit more involved. Now that you have located yourself on the map it is a simple matter to scale off the distance to the proper turnoff to the clay prospect (in this instance it is 2.8 miles) and you are on your way.

Sometimes when you are lost you can only identify one geographic point. In such cases take a bearing on the point and plot the bearing as you did in the two-point example above. You are located somewhere along this line but are not sure just which of the various roads in the area you are on.

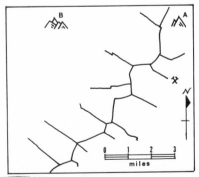

Figure 1.8 *Nothing but a maze of roads and two mountain peaks in sight.*

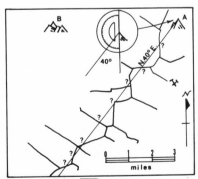

Figure 1.9 *A bearing plotted on point "A". Inset shows how a protractor is used to transfer compass bearing to a map.*

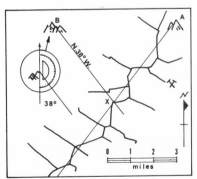

Figure 1.10 *A bearing plotted on point "B". Viewer is located at the intersection of the two bearing lines at "X".*

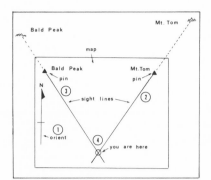

Figure 1.11 *Determining your location by direct sighting on two geographic points.*

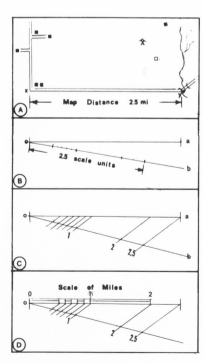

Figure 1.12 *Steps in the construction of a map scale.*

Now take a good look at your trail or road, looking for nearby stream crossings, intersection, turns and other peculiarities which identify the only road on the map having these same features. This particular method requires a firm, flat surface for the map, a protractor, a straight edge, a pencil, and a magnetic compass with one degree markings. Aside from taking the compass bearings, all of the map work can be done in a car if it is raining.

The following method for locating yourself depends upon clear weather (not raining), two points on the map that are identifiable in the field, two plain pins, a straight edge, a compass and a surface that can be kept flat and steady while you take two bearings. First, orient the map to true North, and without moving it, stick a pin in one of the points on the map (Mt. Tom Figure 1.11); second, lay your straight edge against the pin and rotate it until it points directly at the distant geographic feature — and draw a line across the map from the pin toward you; third, do the same thing for Bald Peak without moving the map while doing so; fourth, you are located at the intersection of the two lines.

If you know where you are but don't have a compass and want to orient your map, you can put a pin in the map at the point where you are and another in some identifiable geographic point on the map and, using the two pins as sights, rotate the map until you are sighting past the two pins at the geographic point in the distance. When you have done this, your map will be oriented true North.

Suppose that you have discovered a good deposit of ceramic material some distance from any road or trail and you want to pinpoint its location on your map. Proceed exactly as though you were lost, using either of the two-point location methods described above.

Map Scales

Every map should have some notation, usually a scale, which gives the number of feet, metres, yards, or miles represented by a unit of length — usually one inch on the map. The distance scale is helpful in determining distances between points, road distances, and areas. The scale, when arranged in the form of two or three closely spaced parallel lines that are marked off with appropriate graduations, is called a bar scale.

To measure a distance on your map, take a slip of paper and tick off the distance between the two points. Now place the paper next to the bar scale and read off the distance. This procedure eliminates any errors that may be due to map paper shrinkage or misreading the markings on a ruler.

HOW TO CONSTRUCT A MAP SCALE

Some maps unfortunately get printed without any hint as to the scale used. This can be a real disaster if you must know just where that mine marked on the map is really located on the ground. All is not lost, however, if you can identify two points on the map and can determine the distance between them. For example, in Figure 1.12A the corner (marked "x") which has two houses beside the road and the sharp bend in the same road where it crosses a creek (marked "y") are two good points. The following procedure will give you a correct map scale.

First: Carefully record the mileage on your car odometer at the corner marked "x", and then drive down the road to the bridge at "y", again noting the mileage. Subtract the first reading from the second.

Second: On a sheet of paper draw two lines, o-a and o-b several inches long and meeting at a common point at o. The angle between the two lines is not critical but should be about as shown in Figure 1.12B.

Third: On line o-a mark off a distance equal to the *map* distance between the points "x" and "y".

Fourth: On line o-b mark off 2.5 scale units (the car distance in miles between points "x" and "y"). Try to select a scale whose units roughly equal the distance you have plotted on line o-a. This is easily done with a triangular engineer's scale which has six different scales to choose from. Your drawing should now look something like Figure 1.12B.

Fifth: Now draw a line from the tic at the right end of line o-a down to the tic at 2.5 units on line o-b. Figure 1.12C.

Sixth: Next draw lines parallel to this line at the tics on line o-b at the one-half, one, and two unit intervals. The intersection of these lines with line o-a automatically gives you the true map scale in miles. Figure 1.12C. If you wish to polish the job a bit you can construct a bar scale as shown in Figure 1.12D. You may also wish to subdivide a half-mile unit into one-tenth of a mile sections.

Sections, Townships, and Ranges

Most of the country has been surveyed and divided up into units. These units appear on a topographic map as a grid with lines spaced at six mile intervals. The lines running in an East-West direction are called Township lines, while those running North-South are called Range lines. The squares formed by these two sets of lines are called Townships, and theoretically contain 36 square miles, or sections. The six-mile intervals between the Township lines are also called Townships, and are numbered consecutively both North and South from the Base Line. The intervals between the Range lines are also numbered consecutively both East and West of the Principal Meridian. The intersection of the Base Line and the Principal Meridian is called the Initial Point. Figure 1.13 shows how these two sets of lines are laid out. There are numerous sets of Base Lines and Principal Meridians scattered around the country, and each set is given a distinctive name to identify it. The location of the Base and Meridian lines is shown on

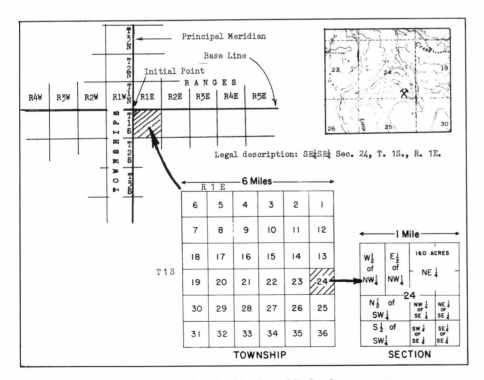

Figure 1.13 *Descriptive elements involved in the public land survey system.*

many maps, including the. U.S.G.S. Index Maps to Topographic Mapping for each state.

The most confusing part in all of this is grasping the fact that a Township is *both* a term referring to a square six miles on an edge, with an area of about 36 square miles, *and* a six-mile *unit of measurement* for North and South distances.

The Township and Range notations are usually printed in red or black and appear somewhere along the borders of the map. Some maps have the numbers of the sections (a section is another name for the one square mile division of a Township), printed in the center of each square; others make you guess. The numbering system for the sections in a Township is shown in Figure 1.13. The abbreviations for Section, Township and Range include: "STR", "Sec., Twp., Rge." or "Sec., T., R.". Subdivisions of sections may be shown either as "NW/4", or "NW ¼" or "E/2" or "E ½".

Suppose you want to locate a clay deposit having the legal description "SE/4SE/4 Sec. 24, T. 1 S., R. 1 E.". This would read "Southeast quarter of the Southeast quarter, Section 24, Township 1 South, Range 1 East." First, look on an index map for topographic maps (all suppliers of U.S.G.S. topographic maps have them) and determine which map has the correct Township and Range values. Second, on the topographic map locate section 24 lying inside the square T. 1 S., R. 1 E., and then carefully divide the section into four quarters with a fine pencil line. At this point you have narrowed the search down to 160 acres. Third, now divide the Southeast quarter into quarters and you have reduced the area to 40 acres which is usually close enough, particularly if the description also mentions elevation, nearness to a road, creek, or some other natural or man-made object shown on the map.

Geologic and Soil Maps

There are two other types of maps, both of which are of critical importance to the prospector-potter in his search for new clay in the field. The maps and map information that have been discussed in this chapter so far are valuable aids in getting to and from places in the field, rather than helping in the discovery of the clay deposits themselves. Although topographic maps will give you an idea of likely places to look, geologic and soil maps will aid you directly in locating the clays you are seeking.

Geologic maps show, by means of symbols and colored areas, the extent and type of the surface rocks. The maps ignore the presence of topsoil so the various formations shown are those of the in-place rocks only. One exception to this rule is in those areas covered by stream or lake sediments. In such cases most geologic maps show these deposits as alluvium and make no distinction between sand and gravel, silt, clay or topsoil. If you are searching for deposits of residual or transported clay, a geologic map will not be of much help. If, on the other hand, you are looking for clays that have been formed by hydrothermal alteration and pigment minerals associated with them, then a geologic map will be of help since the contact zones in which the alteration took place will be shown clearly on the map.

The second type of map is the soil map. As the name indicates, these maps show the nature and distribution of the topsoil. Originally soil maps were published for use by farmers, but more recently they are being used by planners, developers and homeowners. The prospector-potter can also derive much benefit from these maps since they make many fine distinctions between soil types.

Since both geologic maps and soil maps are actually prospecting tools, they are more fully discussed in the chapter on "Testing, Tracking and Taming", which follows.

Mining Claims

It is rather unlikely that you will become so involved in prospecting and developing a clay deposit that you will want to locate a mining claim to protect it for your very own. In the first place, common clays are not locatable in the United States since they, like several other rocky substances, fall under the "common varieties" classification. In the second place, the deposit must be on federally owned land and furthermore federal land that is open to mineral entry (there are all sorts of withdrawals from mineral entry). In the third place, unless you plan on taking out a lot of clay and actually going into business, the bother and expense are probably just not worth it.

If you should decide to locate a claim, the U.S. Bureau of Land Management, which acts as landlord for the public lands in the United States, has published several pamphlets to aid claim locators and these may be picked up at the Bureau's offices.

In Canada much government land is open to mineral entry. Information on the laws governing the location of claims and other rules and regulations may be obtained from the various Provincial agencies listed in the Appendix. In order to stake a claim a prospector's license or its equivalent must be obtained except in Yukon. Claims are usually held by performing at least a minimum amount of work annually. The Mines Branch publication "Digest of Mining Laws in Canada" contains a summary of information on the various prospecting and mining laws. The Canadian Department of Energy, Mines and Resources provides several services that aid prospectors. Among the most important of these are the issuing of geological maps and reports, and special publications on prospecting. These and other publications cover the various aspects of the subject adequately and are revised periodically; therefore those seeking information are urged to order publications instead of asking for replies to questions by letter. Officials of the Department do not select areas for prospectors, advise by mail on the merits of discoveries, nor examine discoveries except when these are included in a research project being undertaken for the purposes of the Department.

The following publications are of special interest to the prospector-potter looking for ceramic materials in Canada: "Prospecting in Canada; Map 900A, showing principal mining areas and producing mines; Map 1250A, a general geological map of Canada; and Map 1252A, a map of Canada showing principal mineral deposits classified geologically. These may be ordered from the Geological Survey of Canada. See the Appendix for further information on Canadian publications and where to order them.

Topographic maps of various scales may be ordered from the Map Distribution Office, Surveys and Mapping Branch, Department of Energy and Resources. Geological maps of local areas can often be obtained from Provincial Departments of Mines, which also provide other services useful for prospectors.

Now let's forget all about getting into the claim location business and discuss what to do if you find a suitable, small clay deposit that has no aspirations to greatness but for some reason or another you have fallen in love with. If you find it in a roadside ditch and a few hundred pounds will satisfy your needs for a long time, there is little need to get very formal about it. Clay banks keep sloughing and ditches fill, so removing a small quantity should cause no problems whatsoever. As always, don't leave a mess. Clay found at other points poses a slightly different problem, and if there is any question at all it is suggested that you talk the matter over with the administering agency, usually at their local office. You may be issued a permit to remove a certain quantity or you may be advised either not to dig at all or please go away, mind your woodsy manners, and don't bother them with trivial requests.

TRACKING, TESTING, AND TAMING CLAY

INTRODUCTION

The information in this section deals with the how and why of clay mineral formation, the origin of clay deposits, prospecting, exploring, developing, and mining techniques, and field and studio testing.

Geologic processes involved in the transformation of rock into clay and the subsequent concentration of the clay into a deposit apply to all areas of the country. An understanding of the basic natural mechanisms which act together to form clay and clay deposits is essential if the prospector-potter is to enjoy any reasonable hope of success.

The factors that change solid rock into plastic clay include: temperature, rainfall, topography, hydrothermal activity and time. All of these are simple, easily understood manifestations of nature but their inter-reactions are both complex and variable. Add to this the great variety of rock types which are the source of the clay and you have a truly formidable jig-saw puzzle. Time plays a most important role in clay formation, as it does in nearly all geologic processes. The clay you dig tomorrow very probably started forming at least ten million years ago.

The literature on clay mineralogy and clay technology is vast and often quite technical. For potters wishing to dig more deeply into these aspects of ceramics, a selected list of references is included in the Bibligraphy. The approach taken in this book is to provide basic information in fairly simple language that will help you in your search for those special clay deposits best suited for your particular needs.

What is Clay?

There seems to be no one completely satisfactory definition for clay. This is understandable since there are quite a few clay minerals, many combinations of minerals and a multitude of uses for both pure clays and those containing many impurities. Although there is general agreement that clays are composed of very fine particles, size alone is not the only criterion. The quality of plasticity plays an important role in clay technology, but not all clays are plastic. The ability to withstand high temperatures during firing is also important, but the range at which clays fuse is wide indeed.

The following definition may be as good as any, particularly for the ceramist and potter: Clay is a naturally occurring, earthy, fine-grained material composed largely of a group of crystalline minerals known as clay minerals. They are hydrous silicates composed mainly of silica, alumina, and water. Several of these minerals also contain appreciable quantities of iron, alkalies, and alkaline earths.

HOW CLAY MINERALS FORM

Clays are quite literally geologic trash, materials resulting from the decomposition of rocks and minerals. They are mixes of all kinds of debris, including not only the clay minerals themselves but a variety of impurities.

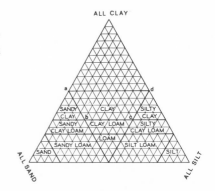

Figure 2.1 *Diagram showing sand, silt and clay relationships. Adapted from U.S. Bureau of Soils.*

Figure 2.1 is a soil classification triangle that has been prepared by the U.S. Bureau of Soils. It is one of many such classifications, but for the purposes of the craft potter looking for his own clay it will serve as well as any other. For many purposes "pure" clay, represented by the area at the apex of the triangle, will be just what you are looking for, but if a more textured body is sought, then a mixture containing some sand and silt might be more suitable. The area bounded by a, b, c and d indicates such a combination of the three factors. Much confusion is expressed by persons who meet a triangular diagram for the first time. Actually it is not only a simple but helpful and ingenious device for showing the various relationships involving combinations of three components. Each "corner" of the diagram has a value of 100 percent of the material assigned to it, with percentages decreasing by 5 percent with each line that lies parallel to the name of the material.

The following table should help to make this a bit clearer.

Percentages of

At point	Clay	Sand	Silt
a	50	50	0
b	30	50	20
c	30	20	50
d	50	0	50

The diagram is useful in two ways: (1) it helps to correlate descriptive terms used in the literature to classify clay-soils with percentages of clay, sand and silt present in them; and (2) the diagram can be used for plotting the composition of raw clays found in the field, and the results of subsequent up-grading. See the section "Field Tests for Clays" and Figure 2.17 in this chapter for suggestions on determining the relative amounts of clay, sand and silt in your raw samples.

Let's take a quick look, before setting out after some new clays, at just how some of this debris is formed, and clay deposits created. There are two main ways in which clay minerals develop: (1) by surface weathering of exposed rocks, and (2) by hydrothermal alteration of deeply buried formations. Clay minerals are also created by other minor geologic processes but they are of little importance.

The formation of clay minerals resulting from the surface weathering of exposed rocks is a long process and represents the final stage in the dissolution of once solid rock. Rocks are composed of assemblages of minerals. The minerals, when attacked by the natural forces of rain, wind, sun, frost and vegetation, react in different ways. The more soluble minerals are chemically altered rather quickly and easily, and this alteration speeds the destruction of the parent rock by opening new avenues for attack. Eventually the rock disintegrates into individual mineral crystals, and these in turn lose their alkalies and alkaline earths by the chemical action of surface and ground water. Under proper conditions much of the non-clay portion of the original rock is removed by weathering or a combination of weathering and erosion, leaving clay minerals which are composed essentially of alumina and silica.

The various feldspars alter readily to clay minerals. Granites, which are much more complexly constituted, eventually are reduced to clay. Many types of rock are candidates to become clay minerals but not all weathered rocks produce clay. Although feldspar-rich rocks are excellent sources for the development of clays, the importance of the original rock type diminishes with the length of the weathering process. Oddly enough it has been determined that different weathering conditions, acting upon identical rock formations, can produce more than one type of clay, and that different types of rock may yield the same type of clay, provided that the weathering process is continued long enough.

The important thing for the prospector-potter to know is that weathering reduces rocks to clay, that weathering takes a long time, and that areas dominated by fresh, geologically young crystalline rocks are poor places to look for clay minerals, while areas of old rocks in humid climates very often have clay minerals in quantity. The one important exception to this rule is that recent volcanic ash which may, under favorable weathering conditions, break down chemically to form montmorillonite-type clays in a relatively short period of time.

Hydrothermal alteration is the other major means by which clay minerals are formed. In this case deeply buried, or sub-surface rocks, are altered by heated ground-water. Hydrothermal alteration, in simple terms, is the action of ground-water containing weak solutions of chemicals, which have been heated by latent igneous activity, upon the surrounding rocks. Not all rocks when subjected to this chemical attack will break down to clay, but some do, and many excellent clays are formed under these conditions. Although most hydrothermal alteration takes place at some depth below the surface, clay minerals may be formed at or near the surface in hot springs and volcanic fumaroles. Clays formed by hydrothermal alteration at depth will eventually be exposed at the surface by erosion of the overlying strata.

Hydrothermal alteration commonly takes place in areas where there has been intensive mineralization as the result of deep-seated igneous activity. Districts noted for concentrations of metallic minerals often have zones of rock that have been reduced to clay.

By the end of either the weathering or hydrothermal alteration cycle clay minerals are almost totally immune to any further chemical attack. This partly explains the ability of high quality clays to undergo high temperature firing without suffering adverse chemical reactions. Lower grade clays, such as common brick and tile clays, have not undergone intense and prolonged weathering and the presence of impurities, chiefly iron, make them more vulnerable to alteration when fired.

HOW CLAY DEPOSITS FORM

There is a very close relationship between the formation of clay *minerals* and clay *deposits*, particularly those deposits which have remained where they were formed originally. These are called *in situ* deposits and, if the geologic processes which formed them have been thorough, the deposits may be of very high quality.

Many *in situ* deposits have, however, been destroyed by one or more geologic processes such as gravity, running water, wind, or glacial activity. Sometimes the transported clay minerals are deposited elsewhere in quantities large enough to be of interest and pure enough to justify working with them. Let's take a look at how some of the more typical clay deposits are formed.

Weathered in situ *deposits*

Deposits of clay minerals formed by weathering must necessarily have some relationship to the ground surface. Deposits on a flat site are generally sheet-like but may vary considerably in thickness. The depth of alteration by weathering is dependent upon the rate of attack by the geologic processes, the time weathering has continued, and the type of rock that has been weathered. The hallmark of deeply weathered areas is the smooth rounding of hillsides, with few if any exposures of rock. If the original rocks were of the proper composition, there may be a clay deposit just below the surface. Figure 2.2 illustrates a typical humid area where weathering has destroyed the surface rocks and produced a deep weathering zone.

If on the other hand the slopes are quite steep, there is the chance that erosion by running water has removed any weathering products, including clay minerals, about as fast as they were formed.

Hydrothermally altered in situ *deposits*

Since this type of clay deposit is typically formed at some distance below the surface the shape, size and purity of the deposit is determined by the geologic structures, rock types and degree of chemical attack. Faults and folds in the rock layers and the nature of the strata greatly influence the pattern of hydrothermal alteration which leads to the formation of clay deposits. These deposits are often rather large and when formed originally extended to rather considerable depths. Many hydrothermally-formed clay deposits tend to be roughly circular or elliptical in shape.

Hydrothermal alteration is commonly present in many mineralized areas so mine workings are often plagued by the presence of plastic clay. This fact is of interest to the prospector-potter when he has access to the mine dump.

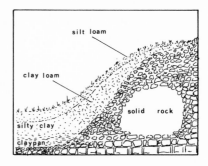

Figure 2.2 *Humid area weathering profile.*

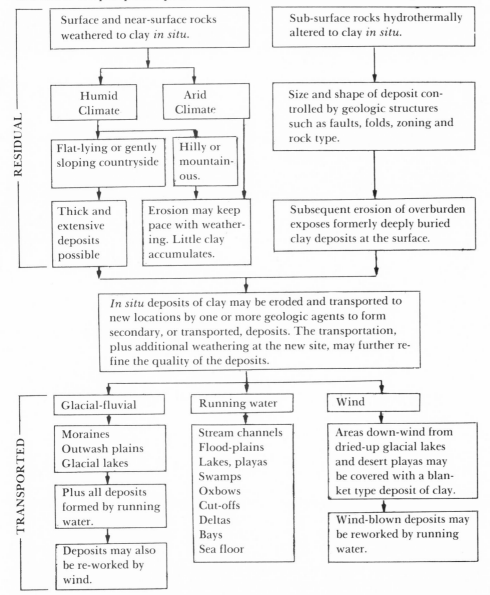

Figure 2.3 *Outline of the more common methods for the formation of clay deposits.*

The erosion of the overburden lying above these clay deposits often makes them accessible from the surface, or near surface. A detailed geologic map of such areas is an invaluable aid in tracking down such exposures. Although weathering plays no part in the formation of hydrothermally altered clay deposits, it may have an effect on the deposit once erosion has exposed it on the surface. If the altered rocks are harder than the surrounding formations, they will be worn away less rapidly and stand out in bold relief, or the opposite may be true. Almost certainly there will be a significant difference in the weathering rate between altered and unaltered rocks, and once this is understood it is relatively easy to locate areas of possible interest.

Secondary, or transported, clay deposits

So far we have been talking about clay deposits that are located at the exact spot where they were originally formed. Most clay deposits of interest to the prospector-potter are those which have been transported, reworked and re-deposited by geologic agents, principally running water, glacial-fluvial action and wind, acting either independently or in concert with each other. All this re-juggling of the original clay deposits results in several profound changes in the nature of the clay and the configuration and extent of the deposit. These will be discussed in some detail a bit later on. Figure 2.3 outlines the more common types of locations for clay deposits and indicates the geologic forces that formed them. One very important guiding principle to be kept in mind in connection with transported clay deposits is that transported clays are carried to their new resting point in a very finely divided state. If the clay was laid down in standing water such as a lake, the clay will be horizontally bedded and will have comparatively good uniformity in all horizontal directions but may vary in texture and quality over short vertical distances. Wind-blown deposits of clay or silty clay which have not been subsequently reworked may have good uniformity both horizontally and vertically since the sorting action of airborne particles is usually quite thorough.

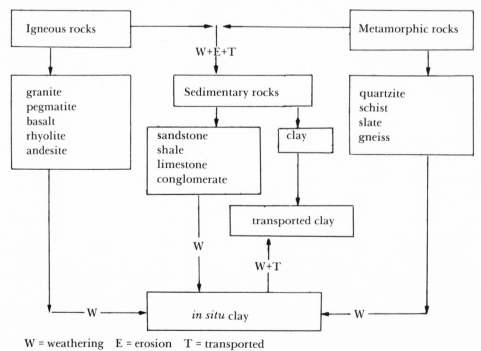

W = weathering   E = erosion   T = transported

Figure 2.4 *The transition of solid rock into clay is accomplished by the combined geologic processes of weathering, erosion and transportation.* **In situ** *clays may be weathered and transported to become transported clays.*

Figure 2.4 shows a simplified, "one way" version of the rock cycle. Here only the progression from solid rock to clay is diagrammed. Actually, of course, the world is not turning to clay. Sedimentary rocks get melted into igneous rocks, or are deeply buried, squeezed and partly melted to form metamorphic rocks — or they get weathered, eroded and transported and become new sediments.

HOW TO LOOK FOR CLAY DEPOSITS

Before getting too involved in the search for a new clay, it might be well to take a look at the various stages of such a campaign. The first step, after doing the necessary reading and records search, is the prospecting for specimens of likely clay. Simple on-the-spot tests will eliminate many that you pick up, but in time you will find a clay that requires a second look. This is the exploratory operation where additional tests are performed and additional sampling done. If your clay stands up to this closer inspection, then you pass into the development period where the size and shape, the feasibility and the economic aspects are carefully determined. The final act is that of production. If you have done the previous steps correctly your clay pit will be successful.

One caution at this point might save you some unnecessary expenditure of effort later. When you are in the field busily tracking down a clay deposit, keep looking out of the corner of your eye to see just how far you have gotten from your car or the nearest road, whichever is the closer. If you find some clay, can you carry it out? Hunting for clay is somewhat different from stalking large game, but you might wish to borrow a thing or two from experienced nimrods. Big game hunters never get far from the road, always hunt above the road, and then chase the game down to the road before dispatching it. If at all possible, plan your field operations so that you can haul your clay and gear down to the road at the end of the day. Gravity is a never-ending help when you have a load to carry downhill.

Another point, don't get carried away with your drilling. Don't drill too deeply, even though you have plenty of pipe and crunchy granola, the drilling is easy and the day is young. Deposits more than a few feet deep require a lot of digging to get at the clay and a lot of dead work filling the hole in again when you are through. The only possible exception to not drilling deeply would be in cases where the presence of clay was suspected and there was a chance that it could be tracked to a nearby bank or steep slope for easy mining.

The Limits to Looking

There are limits to nearly everything, and searching for a new clay deposit is no exception. There is a time to look and a time to stop looking. Figure 2.5 illustrates the problem. Search as long as the chances for finding what you are seeking are good and improving. Quit when the "Quality" curve flattens. There are no sure signals to tell you when "She's deep enough", as the old miners say, but the odds get longer and longer after you have inspected most of the easily accessible deposits and localities and then start searching for clays off the beaten track. "Know before you go" is always good advice, but knowing when not to go is equally important.

This section of the book is designed to help you flatten the "Cost" curve a bit by suggesting some research into possible clay localities before starting out, by helping you to streamline your field testing, thus saving valuable field time, and by providing information that will hone your prospecting and exploration techniques.

One other aspect of the problem is also very important. You may wish to find that perfect clay deposit, but keep in mind that a not-so-good clay may be

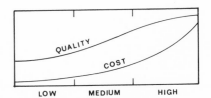

Figure 2.5 *Although the chances for finding higher quality clays increases with the time and effort expended, the cost increases at a progressively accelerated rate.*

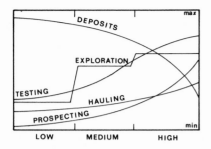

Figure 2.6 *Costs for prospecting, testing and exploring new clay deposits rise with the higher quality of the clay being sought, due largely to the fewer number of the higher type clays and their greater distance from the studio.*

amenable to up-grading. The chapter on "Beneficiation and Processing," and the section in this chapter on "Up-grading Raw Clays" both discuss methods for improving otherwise unsuitable ceramic materials.

A Quick Glance at the Long Search

Figure 2.6 shows in graphic form the principal elements that must be considered in prospecting for and developing a new clay deposit. The following brief discussion of these items will serve as an introduction to a more fully detailed explanation later in this section.

The occurrence of low-quality clay deposits is always far greater than medium-quality ones which in turn outnumber the really high-quality pits. The success rate in finding any of them is in direct ratio to their abundance.

The prospecting effort is at an absolute minimum for low-grade clays since they are numerous and for the most part easily located. The search for better clays requires considerably more enterprise. If a good clay occurs within a reasonable distance of a population center the chances are that it has already been discovered and put into production, thus eliminating it from the list of possible discoveries. Any new medium-quality clays will most likely require a lot of looking for and will be at some little distance from town. The high-quality clays that you may find will be either rather limited in size and thus too small to attract the interest of industry, or they will be poorly located with respect to market, or both. A high-quality clay deposit, even though of modest size, may be of great interest to the craft potter whose tonnage demands are such that the reserves will not be exhausted for years, and the distance from the studio poses no real hardship.

Low-grade clays require only the simplest firing and shrinkage tests. Medium-quality clays, particularly those which have a potential for up-grading, will require a considerably more elaborate set of tests. These clays have a much broader list of possible uses and would require more comprehensive testing. High-quality clays demand a great deal of testing to explore their liabilities and capabilities. Many high-quality clay deposits unfortunately are flawed with impurities in the form of cracks filled with surface debris, veinlets which have introduced chemicals, or horizons where inconsistencies of deposition have created variations in the quality. A proper testing program should explore not only the inherent quality of these special clays but the nature of the deposit as well. Impurities are taken for granted in a common-clay deposit but cannot be tolerated in high-quality clay.

Exploration work at a common-clay deposit normally entails drilling just enough holes to determine whether or not a minimum tonnage of clay is present and to get some representative samples for testing. For the medium-quality clay deposit exploration should be conditioned upon the need to develop sufficient tonnage, to secure samples for thoroughly testing the clay and determining the nature of the deposit, and to provide enough data so that a digging program can be designed if necessary. At the high-quality deposit extensive drilling and sampling must be done to positively identify the quality parameters of the clay, the size and character of the deposit, pinpointing those areas that must be wasted, and providing the basis for setting up a digging program if required.

Exploration programs require considerable planning and should not be started until the ultimate use to which the deposit is to be put has been determined. It is for this reason that the "exploration" line is not a smooth-flowing curve in Figure 2.6, but a series of horizontal levels for each of the three types of clay shown. The degree and kind of exploration carried on at any one pit will differ from any other, even though they might be the same grade of clay.

The last curve that is shown in Figure 2.6 is for Hauling. This has been included only to reinforce the idea that the end product of all of your searching and testing is to develop eventually some clay for your studio. Hauling costs are usually in direct proportion to the distance hauled, although there may be a slight flattening of the curve on a ton-mile basis if large quantities are involved and the haul rather lengthy. The hauling curve shown in the diagram actually curves upward slightly. This reflects the increased distances that most high-grade clays will probably have to be hauled, less the slight saving just mentioned of reduced costs for long hauls on a ton-mile basis.

Figure 2.7 summarizes all of these items in a table. Actually there are two more important steps, Developing and Producing, but discussion of them takes place in the "Exploring, Developing and Producing" section near the end of this chapter.

The above comments should not be considered as arguments for not looking for new clay deposits. Quite the contrary! Do look, but look intelligently, and know that it will take some very careful investigation and a little bit of luck to find what you are looking for.

Quality →	Common	Medium	High
Occurrence	numerous	may be limited	limited to rare
Prospecting Effort	low	may be considerable	may be extensive and expensive
Testing	firing and shrinkage	full series of standard tests	standard and special tests, plus possible tests for glaze fit
Exploration	drill to establish tonnage and quality	a complete drilling program for tonnage and quality, possibly for designing a digging program	extensive drilling and sampling if minimum tonnage found
Hauling	usually short	medium to long	usually long, may be very long

Figure 2.7 *Basic requirements for prospecting, testing and exploring for clays of various qualities.*

Where and When to Look

A considerable amount of sleuthing is required when looking for mineral deposits and clays are no exception. Prospecting takes many forms and none should be overlooked. Keep a sharp eye on man-made excavations such as road-cuts, roadside banks and ditches. Excavations such as post holes along a new fence line or holes drilled for power poles or water wells should be examined. Well drillers can often give information on layers of clay near the surface that they have drilled through.

Grave diggers dig lots of holes, and while it is not permissible to dig within the cemetery, it is quite possible that the clay found there extends outside and lies hidden in some nearby road-cut or steep slope. New subdivisions are excellent hunting grounds for the potter. Lots of dirt is being moved, basements dug, and sewer and water lines laid. Reconnaissance when the work crews have left can often be most rewarding.

Time your clay-prospecting expeditions with various earth-moving activities. In the spring freshly cultivated fields may reveal clays that will be later hidden by vegetation. Water standing in a field, when surrounding areas have long since dried up, may indicate poor drainage and hence the presence of clay not far below the surface. Heavy clay soils often retard plant growth so fields which have patches of stunted vegetation may indicate the presence of clay. (Check with the landowner before entering and digging in his field.) Clay often forms a 'hardpan' or claypan that limits the depth roots will go, and shallow-rooted trees may be easily blown over, revealing clay in the root hole. Go prospecting right after a heavy rainfall which has caused severe stream flooding. The rampaging waters may have ripped away bank-side vegetation and slough, exposing possible clay deposits.

During the rainy season particular attention should be given to landslides. Clays are often the underlying factor causing earth movements of this kind. Abundant water, clay, and even a moderate slope can be enough to cause slippage. You can spot landslide-prone areas by the drunken appearance of trees which tilt at odd angles and the hummocky surface of the hillside.

A sense of time is important if you are going out into the field to search for an old, abandoned clay pit. Heavy rainfall and lush vegetation team together to quickly obliterate even fairly large excavations. Don't expect a large pit described in some reference dated nearly 40 years ago to be easily visible today. Natural processes heal old wounds.

Some Helpful Maps

Although not designing them for use by the potter, the federal government has provided him with two excellent tools in his search for new clay deposits. Prospecting is always an uncertain undertaking and prospectors should avail themselves of every scrap of information they can scrape up. The first of the government tools is a series of soil maps. The second tool is the various geologic maps that have been published since before the turn of the century. Let's talk about soil maps first.

SOIL MAPS

Soil maps, issued over the years by the U.S. Department of Agriculture, Soil Conservation Service, are most useful guides to areas that might have clay of interest to potters. Soil maps are commonly prepared on a single county basis, or some other small geographic unit, and are accompanied by detailed descriptions of the various types of soil. Some of the maps are quite old but public libraries should have copies.

Soil maps differ from geologic maps in that soil maps indicate the nature of the soil mantle to a depth of several feet, while geologic maps largely ignore the soil cover.

Since the soil maps and accompanying bulletins were prepared primarily for agricultural and land-use information, the potter seeking a clay deposit will have to translate the soil descriptions given into terms more useful to himself. Soils tend to change both in texture and mineral composition from the surface downward, so areas covered with just plain 'dirt' may grade into clay suitable for ceramic use in a few feet. To the soil scientist a "silty clay loam" will indicate a difficult soil type for growing certain crops, but to the potter there might well be, a short distance below the surface, a silty clay mixture admirably suited to his needs. It is often helpful to determine the soil type at some specific locality where good clay has been found and then, using the soil map, determine where else the same soil (and clay) will be found.

The newer county soil maps may be obtained in a variety of ways. The local office of the federal Soil Conservation Service or the County Agent, both of whom are usually located in the county Court House or some other public building in the county seat, have copies of currently available soil maps. The libraries at all land grant colleges should have copies that can be inspected. Your local Congressman either has copies at his local office or can obtain them for you. Normally there is no charge for these maps but some local cooperating agencies which have contributed matching funds toward the production of the maps may make a charge to recoup their cash outlay.

GEOLOGIC MAPS

Geologic maps are published in a wide variety of sheet sizes, areas covered, map scales, and map content. The federal government maps tend to cover larger areas, have smaller map scales and may or may not be printed on a topographic map base. Geologic maps issued by state agencies, principally the geology departments, cover smaller areas, have larger map scales and many of them have a topographic base. Nearly all geologic maps are printed in several colors since the complexity of the geologic formations is such that they cannot readily be distinguished unless shown in color.

Geologic maps are of interest to the prospector-potter who is looking for clays formed by hydrothermal processes. They are of little value in the search for residual or transported deposits since most geologic maps focus on solid rock and usually ignore the weathering products derived from them. Hydrothermally altered areas often contain rocks that have been profoundly changed by ascending solutions in the earth's crust. These are readily mappable. Many mineralized districts have extensive hydrothermal alteration surrounding them. Practically every mining district in the country has been intensively mapped and the altered areas are shown clearly.

Indexes showing areas covered by geologic maps published by the federal government are available from the Superintendent of Documents, Washington, D.C., or copies may be inspected at the various state departments of geology. Copies of geologic maps published by the federal government may be ordered from the Superintendent of Documents (check price and serial number, if any). Publications and geologic maps issued by state agencies may be ordered from them after checking the geologic map index to determine the title of the map or publication covering your area of interest.

Many geologic maps are accompanied either by a bulletin which describes the geology and rock types of the area or by a text printed on the map itself. Map legends, or Explanation columns list all of the rock formations shown on the map. In these columns the oldest formations are placed at the bottom and the youngest appear at the top.

The groups of letters appearing on the map are geologic shorthand for the age and name of the formation. They are described in the Legend. The capital letter may be a Q for Quaternary, a T for Tertiary, and so on. The small letters may stand for a wide variety of rock types or formations. Qal is Quaternary alluvium. Refer to the Geologic Time Chart in the Appendix if you want to sort out the various age names.

Figure 2.8 shows two map symbols that you are likely to find on geologic maps. They may vary slightly but a remarkable similarity prevails all over the world. The most important symbol is the one for dip and strike, which indicates the attitude of a geologic formation. The long strike arm shows the compass direction that the vein or formation is headed along a horizontal line. The shorter dip arm, always at right angles to the strike arm, shows the direction that the vein or formation is sloping. The figure beside the symbol shows the degrees of that slope as measured from the horizontal. The dip arm always points down the slope, or dip, of the formation. Down in the lower right-hand corner of the Figure the dip and strike symbol for the inclined beds in the diagram is shown. The symbol has been plotted to agree with the compass direction of the strike of the tilted formation. Also shown is the circular symbol which denotes horizontal

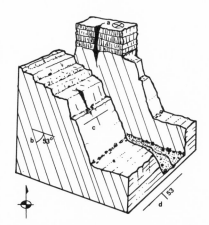

Figure 2.8 *Block diagram illustrating geologic structures and their map symbols. (a) horizontal bedding; (b) the dip of beds and their strike (c) are combined into a dip and strike map symbol (d).*

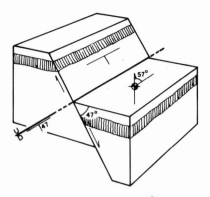

Figure 2.9 *Diagram of a normal fault, with map symbol showing direction of fault, dip of fault and upthrown and downthrown sides of the fault.*

formations, such as those which cap the slanting beds in the far corner of the diagram.

A fairly heavy black line on a geologic map shows the location of a fault. A fault is a great crack in the earth's crust which may dip at any angle from vertical to almost horizontal. Quite often there is movement along a fault, sometimes a great deal of movement. The slippage may have occurred years ago or it may still be continuing. The direction of slippage along the fault plane can be vertical, horizontal or anywhere in-between. In the sketch (Figure 2.9) one of the many possible types of movement is shown. Here the one block has slipped down relative to the other one. The map symbol, shown at the left-hand extension of the fault, tells you several things: (1) the compass direction of the fault, (2) the angle that the fault dips; and (3) if there has been any vertical displacement the upthrown and downthrown movement will be indicated by a "U" and a "D". Note that in this drawing the *bedding* is horizontal, and only the fault plane is inclined.

Faults are of great interest to potters since the grinding action of the movement along the fault may have crushed the adjoining rock and permitted hydrothermal fluids to chemically attack the rock-forming minerals and reduce them to clay. Clays formed by the mechanical grinding action of the fault movement alone are not normally serviceable for ceramic purposes. If substantial vertical movement has occurred along a fault, the exposed face, as shown in the sketch, is called a fault scarp.

If there has been vertical motion along a fault plane after a clay deposit has been formed, the clay that you find on one side may not be available on the other since it could have been too deeply buried, or perhaps elevated and exposed to more rapid erosion and destroyed.

Faults that have sudden movements cause earthquakes, or maybe the earthquakes cause the faults. Anyway a severe earthquake causes lots of damage if it is near where people live, so potters are interested in faults because so many pots, dishes, vases and other ceramic objects get broken — and have to be replaced.

For potters who have a problem wall in their studio or home, geologic maps make great wallpaper. The patterns are unusual, the paper is durable and the colors are wild.

Clays in Humid Areas

TRANSPORTED DEPOSITS

Since many clays have been transported to their present resting place by the action of running water, large river valleys offer excellent sites for prospecting for new clay deposits. All material that is transported by running water is carefully graded as to particle size by changes in stream velocity. The coarser pieces drop out as soon as the current slackens even a little, while the progressively finer fractions are carried away, eventually to be dropped as the stream slows even further.

The sorting action of a stream entering a quiet body of water such as a lake is illustrated in Figure 2.10. In the drawing the water flows from left to right, and as it enters the lake the coarser particles are immediately dropped to form a delta. Successively finer particles fall to the bottom as the current slows even more, and if any clay is present it can be expected on the bottom of the deeper parts of the lake.

Wide valley floors are dotted with both 'active' lakes presently filled with water and an even greater number of old lake beds which have either filled in or have been abandoned by the meanderings of the stream which formerly fed it. It is these latter sites that often provide rich hunting grounds for the potter looking

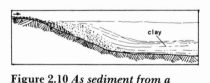

Figure 2.10 *As sediment from a stream enters a lake the particles are sorted by size, with the coarser pieces settling first.*

for new clays. Frequently these old lake beds and slack-water areas have been overgrown with vegetation and covered with organically rich soils. One clue to any buried clays in these situations is the presence of surface water in late spring, when surrounding waters have drained away. Not all standing water denotes the presence of clayey soil since topographic depressions which cut the water table may also trap surface water at times. A topographic map will probably show the scimitar-shaped lakes and scroll-like contours (ridges and swales), of old stream banks. Soil maps also show these features in terms of soil types.

When the parent stream deserts one of its meanders to create a cut-off, one end of the cut-off is usually blocked with sediments while the other may remain open to the main stream for some time. Into this now quiet body of water sediments are deposited, mainly during periods of high water. Coarse materials are dumped near the open end of the cut-off and progressively finer sands, silts and clays settle out toward the far end. Since it may be difficult to determine just which end of the old lake was open the longest some test drilling may have to be done. Figure 2.11 shows the general relationship of the sediments deposited in the cut-off.

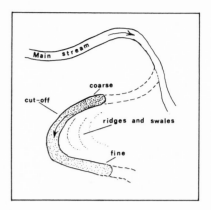

Figure 2.11 *Distribution of sediments in a stream cut-off.*

Along the coastline of the West there are numerous flood-plains which should be sources of clay suitable for pottery. Some rather thick accumulations of clay have formed in those places along the coast which have been sinking slowly for thousands of years. These areas are easy to spot on a map since they often have well-developed bays or estuaries which reach far up the drowned mouths of the rivers and streams feeding into them. It is the fate of most bays to be filled in with sediments and the tidal-flat-to-marsh-to-flood-plain sequence is easy to observe. In these cases old bay muds now are dry land and several miles from the present coastline. When prospecting in these areas stay away from the mouths of stream valleys whose streams very likely dumped their coarser sediments close by as they entered the quiet bay water. An examination of a topographic map should help in selecting prospective areas located at some distance from the stream channels. The water table will be near the ground surface so any deep digging is probably out of the question.

Above the coastal flood-plains and beaches marine terraces have been formed in those stretches along the shoreline where the earth's crust has risen in the recent past. (Other portions of the coast have lowered, as we have mentioned earlier). These terraces are characteristically rather flat areas with steep-sided slopes leading down to the local drainage which is busily engaged in down-cutting its streambed to the level it was before the coast rose. These old terraces are a prime location for finding usable clays. Due to intense weathering some of the clays on the terraces have had part of their original iron content leached away. The deposits are drilled or dug easily.

Of great economic importance are the clays that have formed in deposits which were emplaced immediately following the last Ice Age when great quantities of fine glacial silt brought down by the continental ice sheets and their melt-water streams began to dry up and blow away. Today large areas are blanketed with this material which in geological terms is called a loess, but which is often mapped by soils engineers as silty clay loam, silty loam, or similar terms. This wind-deposited material is much used as a clay source since it occurs at or near the surface, is remarkably uniform and covers large areas. Since its deposition the silt has undergone some modification from weathering and vegetative growth. As a result its color ranges from light gray through tan to light reddish brown. Except for a thin layer of volcanic ash in some localities, the glacial silt forms the uppermost soil layer. The silt normally supports an excellent vegetative cover which hinders field prospecting, but the wide distribution assures ample out-crops along road cuts. Typically the clayey silt makes buff- to red-fired ware.

RESIDUAL DEPOSITS

Residual clay deposits in areas having a humid climate can best be located by selecting likely agricultural areas on soil maps and then examining the land for spots where the vegetation is markedly less vigorous than that nearby. Agricultural areas are easily accessible with literally miles of road-side banks to prospect in. If, in talking with the local farmers, you hear the word "hard-pan", they just may be singing your song. Hard-pan can be compacted clay or shale, and even though the top surface may not look promising due to surface contamination, it may improve with depth.

Residual deposits are widespread in heavily forested areas but the difficulties of spotting likely sites, coupled with the problems of digging through tangles of roots and rocks, make these locations rather uninviting.

The search for hydrothermally altered clay deposits in areas of humid climate is both complicated and simplified by the usually abundant forest cover. Hydrothermal activity seems to be concentrated in mountainous or very hilly areas where volcanic, mountain-building forces and hydrothermal activity are often closely associated. Dense timber on the rugged slopes makes prospecting difficult but changes in soil chemistry caused by the hydrothermal activity may affect either the rate of growth or prohibit certain species entirely. Geologic maps are of great assistance when looking for these types of clays in high rainfall areas since the rock types will be shown clearly. Geologic studies rarely devote much attention to clays in areas of altered rocks since they have had little economic significance, with a few exceptions, in the past. Hydrothermal alteration and metal mineralization frequently are closely related and in many cases the former is responsible for the latter. Mineralized zones in areas with altered Tertiary age volcanic rocks should be checked for clay.

In many instances mercury deposits are excellent guides to hydrothermally altered rocks. The Black Butte quicksilver mine in Lane County, Oregon is a good example of mercury deposition in an altered zone. Nearby Hobart Butte is a huge mass of flinty clay that is thought to have been hydrothermally derived from acid volcanic rocks such as rhyolite and andesite. Just how much effect weathering has had on these two deposits is unknown but very likely the upper portions of both have been exposed to and changed by this process. Clay from Hobart Butte was used commercially for making fire brick for many years. In California several hydrothermally altered clay deposits have been mined, with operations in Mono County at Little Antelope Valley, in Kern County in Jawbone Canyon and at Hart in San Bernardino County. All of these localities are in areas of Tertiary volcanism.

When prospecting for hydrothermally altered clay pay particular attention to the appearance of the rock and soil in road cuts. Sudden changes in color or texture from the "country rock" you have driven past should be investigated. Altered rocks tend to be lighter in color and might be said to have a 'tired' or washed-out look. Altered rocks are often softer and crumble more easily than fresh formations. They just look different.

Clay Deposits in Arid Areas

Before venturing into the arid regions of the West take a look at the section on the "PERILS OF PROSPECTING" in Chapter 1. The hazards are real and in our permissive society it is hard to remember that the forces of nature play for keeps.

Worthwhile clay deposits may occur in arid areas. In the geologic past the region may have been humid and low-lying and ideal for the formation of residual deposits of clay which were subsequently buried by younger geologic deposits, only to be exposed when the countryside crumpled into mountains and the climate changed. Some of these deposits may still be in place, but others have been eroded away and transported to desert basins to form new deposits.

Some desert clays are formed in part by the abrasive action of the elements acting on exposed rocks, followed by eventual chemical alteration in the shallow playas during the wet seasons. Still other clays are formed more or less directly by hot, acid-charged waters acting upon the surrounding rocks in the vicinity of hot springs. Finely divided volcanic ash can be reduced to clay by atmospheric processes.

Some of these clays are of ceramic quality and can be obtained in sufficiently large quantity to make them of interest to potters. Other clays are either inherently "bad actors", such as the bentonites, or contain chemical impurities which render them useless.

TRANSPORTED DEPOSITS

Torrential rainstorms in the desert often produce gully-washers that carry boulders, cobbles, pebbles, sand, silt and clay along at high speed. At the mouth of the canyon two things happen. First, the stream gradient flattens as it reaches the desert floor; then the stream spreads out in several directions since there are no longer any confining canyon walls. With the energy and velocity drop, the stream loses its ability to carry its bed load and as a result boulders are dropped on an ever-increasing pile called an alluvial fan. As the water slows, finer and finer materials are deposited and only the finest particles are carried out into the desert in the muddy water.

Arid regions often contain basins, a depression in the valley floor with no outlet. These basins have shallow bodies of water for several months each year until sun and wind dry them up. The temporary lakes, or playas, can be sources of clay, but approach cautiously for that apparently dry surface may hide some very soft and sticky clay. Clays found in or near playas are often referred to as bentonitic and characteristically have a high shrinkage.

Figure 2.12 *In arid areas little soil develops. Exposed rock, flat valley floors and shallow playas are typical.*

If you visit a playa in the dry season some indication of the dry shrinkage may be readily visible in the form of a network of "alligator hide" cracks which cover the surface. These crusts are composed of the finest sized particles and, depending on the type of rocks from which the sediments were derived, may contain some relatively pure clay. The excessive shrinkage is due to the presence of the clay mineral montmorillonite. Bentonitic clays lose large amounts of water upon drying. Conversely, it takes a lot of water to make the dry clay plastic again, and much swelling occurs. Such material is generally unsuitable for most ceramic purposes unless it is mixed with other clays having either no or very low shrinkage characteristics.

Figure 2.12 shows a typical desert scene, with stark cliffs, narrow, steep-walled canyons, broad alluvial fans at each canyon mouth and the shallow playa occupying the low spot on the desert floor. Figure 2.13 is a cross-section of the same scene.

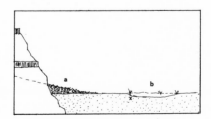

Figure 2.13 *Cross-section of the scene in Figure 3.12. (a) alluvial fan; (b) playa; (x) possible clay deposit.*

During the dry season the surfaces of desert playas are subject to erosion by wind. The finely divided material that had previously been deposited by flash floods is scoured away and deposited at some considerable distance. If the wind-blown silts and clays fall within the same drainage basin in which they originated they will eventually be returned to the playa by running water. Such clays tend to have rather high alkali content since the alkaline earths stay largely within the basin and are merely recycled. If, however, the winds deposit the fines from the playa surface in places lying beyond a desert basin, then the alkali content will probably be much lower since there will be no reinforcement through recycling. In either case, the wind-blown silts and clays will blanket the surface with a uniformly thick layer. Since this material is easily eroded by rainfall and running water, the thickness of the blanket will vary considerably after a few years.

RESIDUAL DEPOSITS

Dry stream beds in the arid regions east of the mountains, although posing the threat of flash floods, are excellent places to prospect for residual clay deposits. Stream banks are frequently washed free of overburden and vegetation so any clay present should be easy to spot. If any hard, flint type clays outcrop in the drainage there is a good chance that pieces can be found in the stream gravels. Careful examination should reveal where the clay came from since the "float" (loose pieces) always migrates downhill from an outcrop. Searching for clay under such conditions calls for exactly the same procedure used by prospectors looking for the "mother lode" in gold country. Figure 2.14 shows a simple example of what may be encountered in the field. High up on the canyon wall an old lake bed has been exposed. The clay which had collected there has slowly been working loose and rolling down the slope to the floor of the dry wash below. Infrequent flash floods have washed some of the lumps downstream and they now lie scattered in a "plume" in the left foreground. (Direction of stream flow is indicated by the arrow.) Work your way upstream until the "float" can be found no more; then sample the canyon walls on either side. In this case a trail of lumps leads up to the deposit on the left. Occasionally the outcrop may be masked by slough from higher up the slope, but you will find no float higher than the line 'x-x' in the sketch and a minimal amount of digging should reveal the hidden clay.

Small irregularities of the surface may reveal the location of a hidden deposit since the clay is most likely either harder or softer than the surrounding rock and will erode away at a different rate, causing an uneven surface.

Sometimes it is necessary to take a look from a somewhat greater distance. A climb up the opposite canyon wall may help you locate quickly the hidden deposit revealed by the subtle changes in the color of the slough on the hillside

Figure 2.14 *"Float" may often be traced to its point of origin.*

where the clay is buried. Good prospectors spend a good bit of their time combing through dry stream bed gravels or scanning the countryside from a high vantage point. Most geologic deposits that are within a shovel's length of the surface have some surface markings that give them away. Look for them. Changes in color, vegetation, and topography are important. Water seeping out of a hillside may indicate a water table resting on clay. A "dust bowl" in arid country could be the site of a clay deposit surrounded by harder volcanic rock. Take a good look, be curious, be informed, be diligent — the clay is out there, somewhere.

Non-Ceramic Clays

In the preceding paragraphs we have been discussing various types of clays and clay deposits that are useful in ceramics. Not all high quality clays are suitable for ceramic applications. Some of them make excellent decolorizers, chemical absorbents, extenders, fillers, carriers or dusting agents. Another special type, known as the expansible clays, must be near the top of the potter's "hate list" of all the clays. These rocks look and act much like clay when worked wet but in the kiln they exhibit an amazing ability to bloat to several times their original volume. Expansible shales can be identified by firing a small ball of material. If the sample swells it should be discarded.

Field Techniques and Equipment

One of the most important field techniques that you will need, must have, in fact, is good outdoors manners. Always remember that *somebody* owns all of the land out there, even if it is miles beyond the end of the pavement. Good manners and just plain common sense are always helpful, but out in the country they may be vital to your health. Private land is just exactly that and you should get permission to enter upon it. If you drive up a lane to a house and there's a barking dog — and nobody comes to the door, a prompt retreat is indicated. An iron-free clay is not nearly as important as a lead-free body.

One cardinal rule for the prospector-potter is to always fill in all holes or, if you plan on coming back very soon, to cover them up. Large and small animals exhibit a very large curiosity about man-made excavations so don't leave booby traps for them to fall into and break a leg.

Vast areas of the West are publicly owned, that is, they are administered by some branch of government, mostly federal. Nearly everyone is familiar with our numerous national forests and national parks and monuments which are plainly indicated on maps. What is not as well known is that there are other large acreages of federal land set aside in Indian Lands, Fish and Wildlife Refuges, Reclamation Withdrawals, Powersite Withdrawals, Military Withdrawals, Grazing Lands and others.

State	Total Acres in State	Total Acres Administered by Federal Government	Percent
California	101,563,520	44,940.392	44.8
Idaho	53,476,480	33,792,574	63.8
Oregon	62,067,840	32,237,579	52.3
Montana	94,168,320	27,608,464	29.6
Washington	43,642,880	12,630,902	29.6

By far the greatest part of all the publicly owned land in the U.S. is administered by the Bureau of Land Management. The Bureau maintains offices in many towns and cities throughout the West at which one can obtain information on the status of local lands federally administered. In many instances there are no prospecting restrictions, but the removal of anything more than test samples might require some type of permit. The important thing is to know the rules and regulations that you must abide by.

WHAT TO LOOK FOR

Along about here you may become aware of a nagging question in the back of your mind: "How will I know a clay deposit when I see it?" When looking in the field for raw clay deposits, you must constantly bear in mind that there is little resemblance between the highly refined commercial product used in your studio and the natural field material. Also, all fine-grained rock and soil are not clay, not all clays may be suitable for ceramic purposes, and even a ceramic quality clay may not satisfy your needs. If you are unfamiliar with the appearance of raw clays, visit several active clay pits. Here you can examine the clay in place, note the soil profile from the grass roots on down to the clay, and the general lay of the land, vegetative cover and other aspects related to the deposit. If there are no active operations in your area, then check the literature and hunt up old pits nearby. The quarries may be a bit shaggy with age but a shovel will usually brighten up a pit face in short order.

THE TOOLS TO TAKE

The old Boy Scout motto "Be Prepared" works equally well for the prospector-potter. Do take proper equipment and don't get over-extended once you get away from your vehicle. Since prospecting for clay is essentially a dirt-digging operation you will need a variety of tools designed to dig, drill and carry it. Figure 2.15 illustrates the more important items that you will need.

The most valuable tool is a long-handled shovel or spade, preferably with a flat blade. The long handle is useful in many ways. You can vault over ditches and streams, reach across watercourses to dig at banks, dig deep holes, and fend off snakes and other crawly things. A shovel blade is a cutting tool and should be treated as one. Clean the blade after each use and oil it lightly.

For very firm or flint-type clays you may need a mattock (also known as a grub-hoe), or a miner's pick. Keep the cutting edges of your shovel and mattock sharp and you will save yourself much energy.

A machete, or corn knife, is almost a necessity and is useful around camp any time. Machetes tend to be a bit expensive. Corn knives are cheaper and can be purchased at most rural hardware or farm supply stores. Buy a scabbard to protect both the blade and yourself or make one from an old fire hose. Keep the blade sharp and you will be amazed at how easily limbs and brush can be cut with it.

The need for maps has already been discussed. A road map, topographic map, and a soil map left back home on the dining room table won't do you much good in the field. Make sure they are on your check list of things to take.

Plastic five-gallon buckets with lids make good clay containers. Get the type that paint or cooking oil are sold in, preferably with metal lids which can be crimped on tightly. A plastic bucket with a tight-fitting lid is also useful for holding small items like maps, lunches, tags, twine and notebooks. Don't fill a five-gallon bucket with wet clay and plan on carrying it very far. A bucket full of clay will weigh about 100 pounds, perhaps a bit more.

Shipping tags, the kind with string ties, help keep your samples straight. There are many ways to identify samples but one fool-proof method is to use the date plus a number for the individual sample. For instance 6-15-79-4 refers to the fourth sample taken on June 15, 1979. The tag requires only those numbers but your notes should be written up as completely as possible.

During the initial testing phase of your campaign you may wish to bring back numerous small samples for checking at the studio. Old bread wrappers, plastic bags or sheets of plastic wrap make good containers for these and they can be carried safely in one of your buckets. A ball of string for tying up the sacks should be carried in a one-pound plastic cottage cheese container which has a small hole for the string punched in the lid.

Flat-lying clay deposits that are not buried too deeply can often be prospected

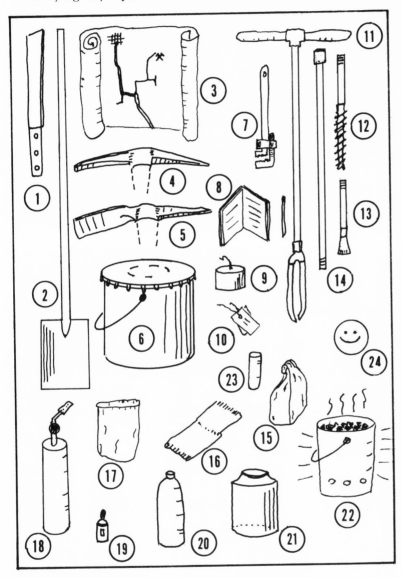

1. Corn knife
2. Long-handled shovel
3. Map
4. Clay pick
5. Mattock
6. Plastic bucket with lid
7. Stillson wrench
8. Notebook, pencil
9. String in container
10. Labels
11. Iwan type soil auger
12. Screw auger
13. Chopping bit
14. Extra length of pipe, 36″
15. Sack lunch
16. Old rags or towel
17. Cloth or plastic sacks
18. Propane burner
19. Dropper bottle with 1:1 HCl acid
20. Water bottle or canteen
21. Glass gallon jar, wide mouth
22. Old bucket, hibachi, or barbeque
23. Test tube
24. Good manners

Figure 2.15 *Typical equipment used to prospect for and test clays in the field.*

and sampled with the aid of a soil auger. The Iwan type pod auger is readily available in most hardware stores and comes in various sizes. The two-inch diameter bit is excellent for sampling but the volume of clay that is recovered per foot of hole is rather small. A three-inch bit weighs and costs a little more but a much larger sample, more than twice as much, can be recovered. Since most of your exploratory drilling will be confined to depths of a few feet, the length of pipe supplied with the auger should be enough. If you need a longer string an extra length of pipe thirty-six inches long, plus a coupling, can be obtained at any hardware store. If you plan on dismantling your auger into its three components — handle, pipe and bit — you will need one 14-inch pipe wrench, otherwise you may simply slip the handle out of its socket and stow the pipe and bit which will have a total length of about four feet.

When drilling in a shale or flint clay, you will make better progress if you use a twist auger, also known as a ship's or coal auger. These bits literally screw themselves into the ground, crumbling it sufficiently for the pod auger to collect a sample. One caution. Don't screw the auger too far into the ground before pulling up on the handles and loosening the clay. If you get in too far you may not be able to reverse the direction of rotation without unscrewing the pipe threads where they join with the bit. If you have a three-foot hole when this happens, you either lose both the hole and the bit or you take your shovel and dig a deep hole to get your tool back.

See the section on "Drilling Tricks" for additional suggestions on making holes. Most tools will work well if you know how to use them — and take care of them.

One item that is *not* included in the equipment shown in Figure 2.15 is dynamite. If you should encounter extremely hard clay you may be tempted to use dynamite. Don't do it. Unless you are thoroughly skilled in handling explosives, leave it alone. Aside from the dangers inherent in the transportation, storage, handling and firing of high explosives, there are the problems of noise and vibration which make the neighbors uptight if not downright unfriendly. If the pod auger won't cut it, and a coal auger won't bite into it you just may have to have your local blacksmith or mechanic make up a chopping bit for you. A chopping bit is nothing more than a straight piece of spring steel about six or eight inches long and an inch and a half or so wide that is welded to a pipe coupling. Screw your pipe lengths into the coupling, remove the wooden twist handle and start chopping up and down, slowly rotating the pipe. Even the most stubborn formations eventually yield to this persuasive treatment.

A large canteen or plastic water container and an old towel or two just about round out the tool list.

You may wish to add a few items for testing purposes, since prospecting and preliminary testing are normally conducted in the field. A two-ounce bottle equipped with a nose drop top and filled with a 1:1 (50%) solution of hydrochloric acid and distilled water enables you to test for the presence of lime. With normal care the acid presents no problems. The bottle should be packed separately since acid fumes are corrosive to metals. Several six-inch test tubes are handy for checking the swelling characteristics of bentonitic type clays. To make crude firing tests in the field you will need some source of intense heat. A propane burner and bottled gas are both compact and easy to use, but if space is no problem you might consider taking along some briquettes and either a barbecue, hibachi or an old bucket with holes punched around the base. The obvious spinoff gained by using the barbecue or hibachi is that it can also be used for cooking in the field.

Another item useful is a one-gallon, wide-mouth, clear glass jug with cover. The use of the jug will be discussed under "Field Tests".

Optional equipment for the compleat prospector-potter might include a compass and altimeter, which would be useful on occasion.

An important principle for all field operations is to take only what you actually need. The above list of suggested equipment is intended as a general guide, but after a few clay-hunting expeditions you will probably add to or subtract from it.

Since time is precious when you are in the field, avoid doing unnecessary work that can be done at home. Pre-labelling sample tags saves field time and bother. Writing up sample descriptions can be simplified by using some form of chart to eliminate repetitious writing of the same terms. When drilling holes with the soil auger, you can save a lot of time if bands of paint are applied every two inches on the pipe, with the foot marks distinguished by another color, instead of measuring depths with a tape. Your corn knife can also help speed the job if you use it to cut the clay out of the auger.

No special clothing is really needed for clay-hunting expeditions, but if you plan on using an auger wear an old sweatshirt or zippered parka — anything but a shirt or blouse that has buttons. Those auger handles make short work of such garments with their open spaces between the buttons. Another plus for sweatshirts is their lack of pockets. When you bend over to twist the auger, the contents of pockets develop an unerring aim for the hole.

DRILLING TRICKS

There are tricks to all trades. The trick in hand-augering is to use your body weight, pushing down on the handles, just as you make a quick half rotation. The weight of the drill is not enough to give it much bite in anything but topsoil. The experienced driller starts a hole with his hands close to the handle socket and then slowly moves them out towards the ends as the drilling gets tougher. This trick saves a lot of unnecessary effort and gets the hole down faster. To pace yourself, drill a hole and then, while your breathing gets back to normal, do a bit of field testing, which can be done sitting down. This way you break up the tedium, don't overdo, and keep your testing and "office work" up-to-date. There is nothing worse than having to write up a lot of samples at the end of a long hard day of drilling when your hands are permanently auger-handle shaped, your back is killing you, it's cold, and it's raining.

A little bit of housekeeping makes the drilling job go more easily. Keep the auger bits sharp, clean and in good repair. At the end of the day wash the augers carefully and give them a light oiling when you get back to the studio. Steel rusts and you want to avoid "salting" your clay with any extraneous iron the next time you use your drill. A pipe wrench is almost indestructible but it is easy to lose around a field project. If it is painted a bright orange or red, that risk is greatly lessened.

A FIELD SAMPLING PROGRAM

The prospector-potter should spend most of his time in the field looking for small amounts of clay and so must concern himself only with a simple sampling program. You should, however, do enough sampling to assure yourself that: (1) the quality of the clay is definitely established; (2) there is at least a sufficient amount of desirable clay to justify further development work; and (3) the deposit can be worked within the financial, labor and time limits available.

Samples can be taken in various ways. If an exposed bank is found, several samples at regular intervals might be taken from top to bottom, and an auger hole might be drilled horizontally into the face to learn something of the extent and continuity in that direction. If the deposit is quite small, only three or four samples might be required to ascertain the approximate dimensions of the deposit and the average quality of the clay. If somewhat larger-sized deposits are sampled, more holes will be required and more samples will have to be tested. To help guard against being misled when sampling, do this: Collect three or four samples and combine them into one, using equal weights or volumes of clay from each sampling point. Then take a separate sample from the approximate center of the deposit. If the test results from the combined sample and the separate sample agree reasonably well, the deposit can be assumed to be uniform in composition. If the two tests show rather wide variations, then there must be some layering or zoning in the deposit which could conceivably affect the clay's characteristics.

Assuming for the moment that you have found a deposit large enough to interest you and the preliminary tests are encouraging, what next? Sit down and consider the cold gray economics before you start digging. How much total effort per unit of clay recovered will you have to expend? How much overburden is there to remove? How far to the road? How many miles to the studio?

If the green light is still lit, it is time to collect some fairly large samples and take them back to the studio for further testing. This testing will be discussed in the next section.

A soil auger is both a prospecting and a sampling tool. It determines not only where, and in most cases how thick, the clay is, but also the drill cuttings provide excellent samples which may be tested individually or combined as desired. Properly done, a sampling program of this kind will provide you with all of the information that you need to make a final determination as to whether the deposit is worth developing. Should larger amounts of clay be needed for testing than can be provided by the auger, they can be obtained by cutting a series of vertical channels down the road-cut; digging several ditches through the deposit at regular intervals; or putting down a series of pits scattered evenly over the area. The objective, as always, is to obtain a truly representative mass of material which will yield test results that can be duplicated in actual use.

Figure 2.16 shows an outcrop of clay in a bank at "x". In this instance the holes at "d" were drilled more or less at random, with the principal objective being to ascertain as quickly as possible if the deposit was large enough to even consider expending any further effort on it. When you are exploring a new deposit, it is always good practice to drill a foot or so deeper than the bottom of the clay to see if there is any more below what might have been the assumed base of the deposit The cuttings from the holes should be mixed with the clay from the outcrop and then tested as a composite sample. This saves time and expense, and if results are favorable more detailed drilling, sampling, and testing can be done.

Field Tests for Clays

Field tests are designed to separate clays from non-clays quickly. Equally important, these tests make it possible to examine more prospects in a given time since the tests take little effort and worthless sites can be rejected early on. Field testing also reduces the number of samples that have to be written up, packaged and hauled back to the studio. Many raw clays when found in the field do not look very much like a usable ceramic material. Some earthy products on the other hand are almost dead ringers for clay. A series of simple field tests can resolve most of these difficulties, and with a little practice a specimen can be checked speedily.

To familiarize yourself with the tests try them on some known clays you have in the studio, next, on some raw clays from a known locality; and then take your kit out into the field and have at it. One of the tests suggested is to heat a small sample over a flame to check for fired color. The sample should be reasonably dry before testing, or if damp, it should be dried out with gentle heat first. Either a

Figure 2.16 *Cross-section through a clay deposit, showing outcrop in bank at "x", and drill holes "d".*

lump of undisturbed material or a small ball or "snake" that has been formed by hand can be used. The sample should be heated until it is red hot, but varying light conditions in the field, plus the uncertainty of whether or not the sample is being fired under oxidizing or reducing atmospheres or combinations of both, make this test far from a precise one. The firing will, however, separate high-iron clays from low-iron white-firing ones.

The presence of lime, particularly in crystal or granular form, is bad news for ceramic ware. Your solution of hydrochloric (muriatic) acid will, when added to a sample in a test tube, bubble vigorously if lime is present. If the temperature is rather low, the test tube containing the sample can be heated gently to increase the chemical reaction. Keep the top of the test tube pointed away from you during the heating since the acid may "bump" and spew out forcefully.

There is no particular order in which the following suggested field tests should be applied. An outline of the tests, which progress from the simple to the complex, is shown in Figure 2.17. Very probably you will not have to make all of

FIELD TESTS FOR RAW CLAYS

PROPERTIES	TESTS	REMARKS
Odor	Breathe heavily on sample, then sniff	Clay will generally give a musty odor.
Color: white, buff, gray	Observe natural color	Refractories: ceramic white-ware, heavy clay products
Reds, browns, greens, yellows	Observe natural color	Heavy clay products
Hardness	Check pressure necessary to scratch dry sample	Requires considerable pressure, *Light color:* high grade ceramic ware and refractories. *Dark color:* heavy clay products and refractories. Requires little pressure, *Very light color:* whitewares. *Dark color:* some ceramic uses.
Texture	Observe presence of pisolitic or oolitic structures*	May indicate bauxite type clay that may be suitable as a refractory.
Plasticity and Shrinkage	Rub moist clay between fingers	Plastic clays can be worked into a definite shape and retain this shape after drying and without cracking.
Swelling	Slowly add dry, finely divided clay to water in test tube	Certain bentonitic clays will swell many times their original volume, forming a gel. Not suitable for ceramics.
Impurities: Iron	Heat a small sample of clay over a flame	Clays containing from 3 to 4 or more percent iron will turn red or brown and are not satisfactory for refractories or whitewares.
Impurities: Calcium Carbonate (lime)	Place a few drops of dilute hydrochloric acid on the clay in a test tube (strong vinegar may also be used)	If clay contains appreciable lime the sample will bubble. A high percentage of lime is not suitable.
Size composition	Place sample in gallon jar, add water and shake vigorously, allow to settle	Observe composition of various fractions

*Rounded masses about the size and appearance of fish eggs. Usually darker than rest of rock.

Figure 2.17 *Outline of suggested field tests for clay.*

the tests on any one clay. If the sample fails one or two tests, there is little point in continuing with your consideration of it as a ceramic material. For example, the presence of bentonite in samples collected in arid regions should be suspected and tested for. Bentonitic clays undergo large volume changes upon drying or wetting, rendering them difficult if not impossible to work with.

After running through the tests shown in the outline in Figure 2.17, you may wish to determine the relative amounts of gravel, grit, sand, silt and clay in a sample. A wide-mouth, clear glass gallon jar is a handy tool for making these determinations. Place about two quarts of sample in the jar, add water, enough to nearly fill it, and shake vigorously for a minute or two or until the sample has completely disintegrated. Let settle for a few minutes and the various fractions that compose your sample should have settled out, the coarser on the bottom, the clay on top. This duplicates, in a crude way, the process used commercially to up-grade clays containing unwanted amounts of sand or other coarse material. This test also gives you a rough idea of how readily the clay can be up-graded, if necessary. You can, by saving the clay samples, make tests in the studio to determine the workability, dried and fired shrinkage, fired color and other properties of the individual fractions or combinations of fractions produced by the jar test.

A simple testing procedure in the field for determining the presence of grit in a clay sample is to grind gently a small piece between your front teeth. It is amazing how sensitive one's own teeth are to minute differences in size and texture. Sound also plays a role here since the noise of crushing the particles between your teeth is readily transmitted through your head to your ears. While performing this test, you might just as well taste the sample. A bitter or slightly puckery sensation indicates that soluble salts such as alum or epsom salts are present, both of which are objectionable since they produce a whitewashed appearance on the fired ware. Now use some water from your canteen to clean your testing apparatus.

When you have completed the series of field tests on a new clay, it might be well to pause for a little and take stock of just what you have. Let's assume that you have found a clay that offers some promise, enough anyway to justify doing some more work on it. You have solid information on the size of your deposit from your preliminary exploratory campaign. Now is the time to consider the accessibility of the deposit. Is it near a road? If you remove a considerable quantity, will there be any problems? Taking a few hundred pounds of clay from a road bank might not present any difficulties but what would happen if you decided that you needed a ton or two? Or 100 tons? How far do you have to drive to get to the deposit, and is it available the year around or only seasonally? If all of these factors seem to pose no real hinderance, then it is time to start your studio tests.

THE LOGIC OF TESTING

Logically the only necessary testing would seem to be the measurement of certain fundamental properties, especially those likely to be important in the various uses of the clays. This will do where a single clay is used in making an all-clay product, such as brick; however, as soon as two clays are mixed, even clays of the same type and with the same characteristics in the raw state, the resulting property values are never the averages expected mathematically. For instance, a shrinkage of about 12 percent might be expected when a mixture of the clays is fired, each with a firing shrinkage of 12 percent, but it usually is either more or less than 12 percent. This is mostly due to the impurities and the effect of the heat treatment on them. Even clays in the raw, dried state seldom have the drying shrinkage rate expected.

To test all clays completely for all uses would be impractical and fortunately is unnecessary. For a general idea of a clay as to type, general properties, and possible use, the testing need be carried only to a certain stage and need be only reasonably accurate.

Because of the general nature of clays and their manner of use over a long period of time, most tests in the past have been wholly empirical or by rule of thumb, and many of the most useful are likely to remain so. Historically, a number of tests and pieces of apparatus, each used with a slightly different approach, have been developed to measure a given property. Often the old, simple method will give about the same information as the latest method, using more carefully engineered equipment. For instance, very fine and accurate means of measuring and controlling kiln temperatures are available, yet the finest china the world has ever seen was produced by Chinese who climbed on top of their kilns, spit in the stack gases, and judged the correct temperature by the rate of change of the spit to steam.

When confronted with a variety of choices, you are frequently wise to adopt the philosophy expressed by Occam's razor which suggests that the simplest solution is likely to be the correct one. If it works, use it.

I once met an old Hawaiian fisherman who was sitting on a seawall with a line cast out into the bay. When asked what he was fishing for, he replied "Anything I can catch". Much the same philosophy can be applied to looking for clay. You go out hoping to find a nice deposit of beautiful clay, but you may end up with some red-firing material useful only for making bricks. Without intending to be the least bit discouraging, I suggest you take a look at the diagram below (Figure 2.18) which shows a hypothetical search for the perfect clay — and what happened along the way. The odds shown are rather long, and quite conceivably should be even longer, but also consider that in running through the various

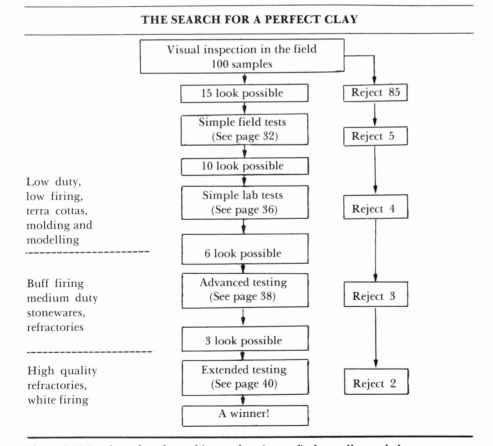

THE SEARCH FOR A PERFECT CLAY

Figure 2.18 *It takes a lot of searching and testing to find a really good clay.*

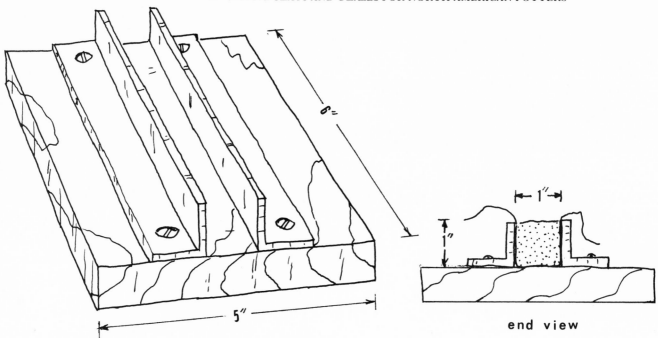

Figure 2.19 *Gauge for incising marks 100mm apart on a clay test bar.*

tests you may discover some perfectly useful clays that are suitable for many purposes.

Try blending two so-so clays, neither of which individually really amount to much. Results may be surprising and could vary considerably with different proportions of the two clays.

STUDIO TESTS

There is no sense in working up a kiln full of ware made from an untested clay and firing it. Almost certainly you are bound to have a big disappointment. Far better to make up some test bars and cones and to place them in the kiln along with some of your regular ware. This procedure applies equally to clays that you intend to use as is and those you plan on modifying.

Test bars will provide some answers about drying and fired shrinkage, fired color, degree of warping and cracking. The test equipment is simple and inexpensive to make. Figure 2.19 shows the essential features for constructing the test bar mold and marking gauge, Figure 2.20. Either aluminum or steel angle stock may be used. Aluminum costs more, is much lighter, won't rust and can be sawed and drilled easily. The marking gauge is constructed so that the razor blades will make two very fine lines on the damp clay surface of the test bar exactly 100 millimeters apart. The object here is to make the determinations of the dried and fired shrinkage as simple as possible. For example, if the green bar shrinks so that the distance between the razor blade scratches measures 94 mm upon drying, then the shrinkage is 100 minus 94 or 6 percent on a plastic basis. The calculation for percent of dry shrinkage on a dry basis is: plastic length minus dry length, divided by the dry length, times 100; or using the above example, 100 minus 94 equals 6, divided by 94 equals .0638 times 100 equals 6.38 percent.

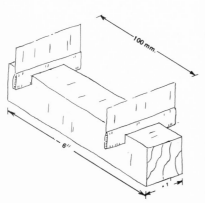

Figure 2.20 *A test bar mold (a); and end view, showing test bar in place surrounded by plastic film.*

The procedure for fired shrinkage is the same as for dry shrinkage. The calculations again may be made either on the plastic or dry basis. If the plastic basis is used, the value is total shrinkage from plastic to fired. For many purposes it is desirable to keep the dry and fired shrinkages separate, hence the usual procedure is to use the dry basis. The formula: dry length minus the fired length, divided by the dry length times one hundred. Figure 2.21 illustrates the relationship.

If you get involved with running large numbers of shrinkage tests you may wish to use smaller test briquettes measuring 1 × 3 × ⅜″, with 50mm gauge marks. The smaller size saves space in the kiln and in storage afterwards.

Plastic length	100mm	
Dry length	–94	
Shrinkage	6	÷ 100 = .06 × 100 = 6% (dry shrinkage, plastic basis)
Plastic length	100mm	
Dry length	–94	
Shrinkage	6	÷ 94 = .0638 × 100 = 6.38% (dry shrinkage, dry basis)
Dry length	94mm	
Fired length	–88	
Shrinkage	6	÷ 88 = .0682 × 100 = 6.82% (fired shrinkage, dry basis)
Plastic length	100mm	
Fired length	–88	
Shrinkage	12	÷ 88 = .1364 × 100 = 13.64 (fired shrinkage, plastic basis)

Figure 2.21 *Relationship between dry and fired shrinkage on both a plastic and dry basis.*

Each bar should have an identifying number. The number can be carefully scratched on the top surface with a fine nail, or stamped with a steel number stamp. Figure 2.22 shows a test bar with the two gauge marks and sample number incised into it. All of the test information should be kept on a sheet together with notes on the location of the sample site, the type of mix, temperature reached in firing, firing schedule, and any other pertinent data such as fired color, warping, cracking and spalling.

Shrinkage in a clay body is caused by several factors. Particle size of the mineral components is one of the more important and the amount of shrinkage varies inversely with it. The kaolinite group of clay minerals has the largest particle size and the montmorillonite group the smallest. The linear shrinkage, both dried and fired, for the three main clay mineral groups is shown below.

Clay mineral group	Drying shrinkage	Fired shrinkage
Kaolinite	3.0 to 10%	2.0 to 17%
Illite	4.4 to 10.7%	9.7 to 14.5%
Montmorillonite	12.0 to 23.0%	20%

Since most clay bodies used in ceramics are mixtures of clay minerals and non-clay minerals (which behave more or less as inert materials), the actual shrinkage is less than the values given above.

So far the tests that have been discussed have given information on the shrinkage of the clay. You will need to develop some knowledge of how the clay performs at specific temperatures during the firing. Standard pyrometric cones having different melting points are used in connection with similarly shaped cones of the clay being tested. The test cones are formed in a standard metal, two-piece mold which is available at most well-equipped ceramic supply houses. A simple wooden base to hold the two halves of the mold tightly together during the forming process is also needed.

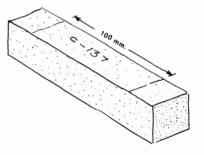

Figure 2.22 *Numbered test bar with incised gauge marks, ready for firing.*

Careful observation of the behavior of the cones during firing reveals when the critical changes occur in the clay.

A pryometric cone equivalent, abbreviated PCE (sometimes p.c.e.), is defined as the number of that standard cone whose tip would touch the supporting plaque simultaneously with that of a cone of the material being investigated, when tested in accordance with the Standard Method of Test for Pyrometric Cone Equivalent of Refractory Materials of the American Society for Testing Materials. Many libraries have the ASTM Designations or they can be ordered from the Society for a small charge.

When PCE cones are used, it is important to remember that both time and temperature are involved. The cones respond (and clay bodies as well) not only to temperature but to the length of the heat soak to which they are subjected. Although opinions differ somewhat, there is a general consensus that clays having PCE values higher than cone 19 are classified as refractory.

Considerable care must be exercised in forming the test cones from your clay, which should be ground fine enough to pass through a 65 or 100 mesh screen. The surface of the mold should be oiled lightly and then the moistened clay is pressed into the triangular, pyramidal groove with a spatula. Some clays may be too friable or too sandy to form cones with water alone and either gum arabic or dextrine may be added as a binder. After drying a bit, the cone is gently slipped out of the mold and set aside to dry before bedding it into the plaque with standard Orton cones of known temperatures. The plaque is formed of a highly refractory clay and may be either circular or rectangular in shape. After stamping holes for the cones, set the plaque aside to dry. The cones are set in the plaque, tilted at an angle of 82 degrees and tamped in with some plaque mix. Standard cones and test cones are set alternately in the plaque. It is wise to make up six or more test cones since they are fragile and several test runs may have to be made before the PCE value of your test clay can be determined.

Just how much testing of new clays should be done is up to the individual potter. If a clay passes the simple field tests and performs reasonably well with the dry and fired shrinkage tests, which also reveal any tendency to warp or crack and give some indication of fired color, then it can fairly be assumed that the clay will serve for average ware production. With this as a basis a potter can then proceed to adjust his clay, as indicated in the section on upgrading, a little at a time in the hope that just the right combination can be arrived at.

ADDITIONAL TESTS ˙

The potter seeking a clay suitable for refractory service, or one who is working with difficult ware designs or ware which will be glazed, will wish to refine his investigations of new ceramic materials and pursue a more rigorous testing program carried to much higher temperatures. The tests discussed so far have been of a general nature and designed to identify rather broad categories of clay types. The following tests are intended to define more narrowly the specific properties and characteristics of clays whose general nature has already been established by the earlier tests.

Particle size

An analysis of the particle sizes present in a raw clay sample is easy to make and provides some information on the type of material being tested. Figure 2.23 outlines some of the compositional possibilities for the various size fractions. A second benefit of a screen analysis is that it permits you to reject certain fractions, and also test individual fractions or combinations of fractions.

A size analysis may be performed either wet or dry, but the wet way seems to be better. For the latter method a sample of raw clay weighing approximately 200 grams is air-dried overnight at 105 degrees Centigrade. A sample of the dried clay

Particle Size	Service
Much +6 mesh	No good as a clay Usually sand. If clay portion is red or brown, good only for foundry sand
Much -6 +20 mesh	If clay portion is light, and washes out easily, clay may be kaolin or fire clay, usable if separated from sand
Small amounts on 6.20 mesh	Brown and red material — common clay
Fair amounts on 60, 100, 200 mesh	Light gray and buff — largely kaolins, fire clays
Very little on 6, 20, 100 mesh	Light colors — soft kaolins
Not over 3% on 200 mesh	Grays, buffs — ball clays
Not over 1% on 325 mesh Mostly -325 mesh	Dark brown, reds — common clays of fine grain

Figure 2.23 *The relationship of particle size to clay composition.*

weighing 100 grams is placed in a vessel with water and stirred until all lumps have dissolved. Allowing the sample to soak for an hour or so is often helpful. The sample is then washed through a stack of either U.S. Standard or Tyler Standard sieves consisting of the following meshes: 6, 20, 65, 100, 200, and 325. A receiving pan under the finest screen completes the stack. The sample is gently washed out of the mixing vessel into the coarsest (and uppermost) screen with a small jet of water from a ¼″ hose. The first screen is removed after all of the undersize material has passed through it and the process repeated with the successively finer screens. Great care should be taken not to touch the finer screens with fingers or stiff brushes. The fractions remaining on the various sieves are carefully washed into vessels, dried and weighed. Since the original dried sample weighed 100 grams, the weight of each fraction in grams gives the percentage of that fraction directly. If reasonable care is exercised in carrying out the above test, it is possible to save yourself a bit of unnecessary drudgery by skipping the drying and weighing of the -325 fraction which will be much diluted by the wash water and, being very fine, probably will take a long time to settle. Weigh all of the other fractions, add their weights together and subtract the total from the original 100 gram weight. The difference will represent the "missing" -325 fraction.

Records of all sieve analyses should be kept. You can make up your own report form, or standard sieve analysis sheets which have a graph grid which enables you to plot a profile of the size distribution are available from engineering supply houses or sieve manufacturers. When either of these is used, it will be possible to make comparisons with various clays whose characteristics have been determined.

For the potter who wishes to pursue the sieve analysis of his samples beyond the -325 mesh point, the path becomes considerably more difficult. Special equipment, best handled by trained personnel, is used. The potter can, however, make a fairly good separation by pouring the thin slurry into a tall graduated cylinder and allowing the particles to settle out. A sample from various levels in the cylinder can be retrieved with a pipette gently inserted to the desired depth. This method yields very small amounts of material for studying, usually with the aid of a microscope. A second method involves the use of much larger volumes of slurry which is placed in a suitable container and allowed to settle for a pre-determined time. Then the upper portion is carefully decanted into a second vessel and the process repeated. This method produces more material, and if water-to-clay ratios, settling times and decantation are standardized, good, re-producible results can be obtained. If enough material is used in the test, the amount of clay in the various fractions will be large enough to carry out firing and other tests.

OTHER STUDIO TESTS

The outline shown below (Figure 2.24) is designed for determining the ceramic properties of clays which may be useful in a wide variety of commercial

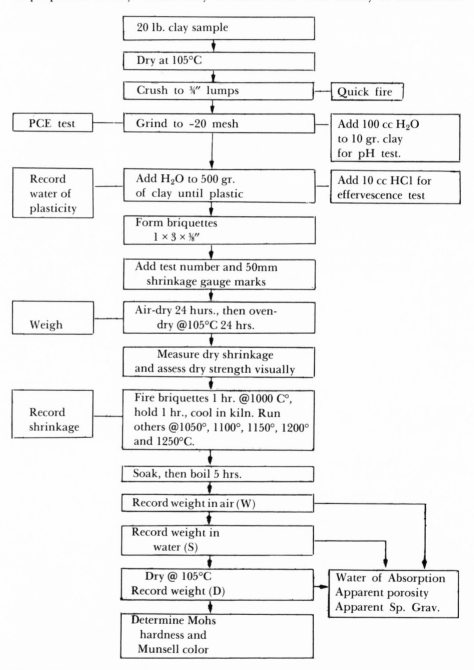

Figure 2.24 *Outline of a series of advanced tests for raw clays.*

products. For most art pottery not all of these tests would normally be required. In the outline the use of briquettes somewhat smaller than the test bars described earlier is suggested. Here the space-saving element is important since normal testing programs involve a great many samples, and the clays have presumably already been checked with the longer test bars. To insure that you will have enough briquettes to complete all of the tests, and to further provide you with a sufficient number so that values can be averaged, you should start off with at least half a dozen identical samples. Having multiple samples to test also will reveal whether the clay is subject to variations in any of its properties.

CALCULATION OF TEST RESULTS

While some of the tests outlined in Figure 2.24 are either familiar to the potter or have been discussed in the preceding section, there may be a few that should be elaborated upon. These tests will be discussed in the order that they appear in the outline.

pH TEST

The pH value of a raw clay sample can be determined by testing the slurry with a standard pH meter used in analytical laboratories, or litmus paper may be used. In the latter case the slurry should be allowed to settle until at least the upper portion of the slurry has cleared sufficiently to avoid masking the color of the paper with suspended material.

WATER OF PLASTICITY

Much ambiguity surrounds this term since it means different things to different people having different end-uses in mind. Water of plasticity can be defined as the percent of water required to develop a workable plastic state. The term "workable" is extremely elastic and acquires precision only when applied to a certain process or end-product, or both. The test can be revealing when clays are being examined for their workability and shrinkage, if you have a single objective in mind. The water of plasticity required to develop a workable body for throwing on a wheel will be greatly different for the same clay destined for casting or dry pressing.

Plasticity is related to particle size, the finer the particle size the higher the plasticity. The shape of the particles also has a direct bearing on plasticity. Clay minerals which are composed of microscopic plates are more plastic than those having more nearly equi-dimensional forms. Since it is almost impossible to obtain pure specimens of clays composed of a single clay mineral, the values for water of plasticity range rather widely. The following table gives bracketing values for the three main clay mineral groups.

Clay Mineral Group	Water of Plasticity (%)
Kaolinite	8.9 to 56.2
Illite	17.0 to 38.5
Montmorillonite	83.0 to 250.0

A clay can be said to have good plasticity if the amount of water absorbed is large and the working range is relatively long. The determination of the water of plasticity of a clay is important in that clays requiring high water of plasticity are subject to greater shrinkage than those needing less water to become plastic.

The following tests are all made on the fired specimens. The tests are useful in determining the character of the fired ware, principally the ratio of voids to impermeable material and the related properties of water absorption and weight. The tests are designed to evaluate the utility of a clay for various applications.

Water of absorption: This is the percent of water absorbed in relation to the dry weight of the fired sample. The amount of water is measured in cubic centimeters, the weight in grams. This is the formula that you use to compute the value:

$$A = \frac{W - D}{D} \times 100$$

A is the water of absorption

D is dried weight of specimen

W is saturated weight of specimen

Apparent porosity: This is the relation of the volume of open pores of the fired specimen to its exterior volume, expressed in percent. The formula is:

$$P = \frac{W - D}{V} \times 100$$

P is porosity of specimen

V is volume of specimen (= D–S)

S is suspended weight of specimen in water

Apparent Specific Gravity: This is the apparent specific gravity of that portion of the fired specimen that is impervious to water. Apparent specific gravity is the ratio of the weight of a given volume of a substance to that of the same volume of water, with water having a value of 1.0. The formula is:

$$T = \frac{D}{D-S}$$

T is apparent specific gravity

Bulk density: Bulk density is the quotient of the dry weight of a fired specimen divided by its volume, including pores. The density is expressed in grams per cubic centimeter. For non-porous specimens, bulk density can be determined readily by weighing the dry specimen, filling a graduated cylinder about half full with water, recording the volume of the water, inserting the specimen (gently, without splashing), subtracting the first reading from the second, and dividing the specimen weight by the remainder. Make sure that no bubbles cling to the specimen during the taking of the second reading. Wetting the specimen before immersion will reduce the bubble-sticking.

The formula is:

$$B = \frac{D}{V}$$

B is bulk density

V is volume (2nd reading minus 1st in cc's.)

The method involving the use of a graduated cylinder is a quick-and-dirty one and is normally sufficiently accurate for most testing. Averaging results from five or more specimens improves the accuracy. Figure 2.25 illustrates the method.

If you have run your clays through the series of tests described above, you will have a pretty good notion of their capabilities and liabilities. Good studio records of the tests, plus your field notes and the test bars and briquettes, make an excellent data bank for future studies of raw clays. The inclusion of some standard clays with your test samples will give an excellent means for comparison which may lead to the substitution of some new clay for an old commercial source.

Several references which explore the testing of clays even more deeply are included in the Bibliography.

Upgrading Raw Clays

At this point we come to a major fork in the philosophical approach to the handling of natural clays. One approach, exemplified by the Japanese potter Shoji Hamada, is to strive to bring out the very best qualities of an unrefined clay and to develop its greatest potential through forming and firing. It goes without saying that this practice is most demanding of the potter's abilities and is probably best left to the very skillful. If you wish to pursue this route, you will have to be very careful in your final selection of a raw clay with which to work, and it will probably require a much greater effort in the field than if you choose to upgrade a raw clay to meet your demands. The rewards to be gained by working with a raw clay that has not been enhanced, except perhaps in the most elementary way, are considerable since you will, in fact, be working within the

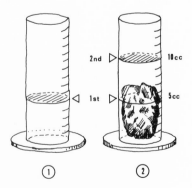

Figure 2.25 *Quick method for determining specific gravity of solids.*

narrow limits of properties possessed by the clay itself, rather than with a clay that has been adjusted to conform to your techniques.

If you do decide to go with an untreated native clay. then more testing must be done in the field to avoid clays which require some beneficiation in the studio. Remember that clay deposits tend to have different textures and qualities with depth, the changes being much more pronounced for transported deposits than the primary or residual type. With this in mind you may be able to select a certain strata or horizon of a deposit which neatly fills your requirements without having to alter it in any way.

On the other hand, most potters believe the real challenge is to discover a new clay and upgrade it carefully to the point where optimum results can be obtained. If you are of this school of thought, see the chapter on "Beneficiation and Processing." Before undertaking any large scale mining or beneficiation, be sure to thoroughly test your clay by firing pieces made from small, up-graded samples.

UPGRADING TECHNIQUES

MIXING

The beneficiation procedures that can be applied to a raw clay are many and varied and are limited only by the resources available to the potter. Basically there are two main types of upgrading: (1) the removal of unwanted impurities, and (2) the mixing of two or more clays. In the discussion that follows the emphasis will be on the benefits that can be obtained by mixing two or more clays together. For a description of the mechanics of mixing and blending see the section on "Mixing, Blending and Sampling" in the chapter on "Beneficiation and Processing".

The typical raw clay is a mixture of several clay minerals, plus some impurities. It is this complexity of composition that sometimes makes it possible, by mixing two or more clays, to develop an entirely new body, or at least one with some new properties. Another benefit from mixing is the assurance that clay from a deposit will remain uniform in composition over the long haul. This can be accomplished by mixing the pit-run material that has been gathered from several points within the pit.

A good clay can sometimes be created by mixing two clays, neither of which has any outstanding qualities. Workability and drying and firing shrinkage may be improved, a better color may show up, and the fusion point may even be lower than that of either of the components. There are no sure guidelines in this area. Due to the complex reactions that take place during firing it is impossible to predict results even when two clays, whose properties are known, are mixed together in a body. Mixtures of clays behave unexpectedly, with failures sprinkled in with successes.

If you embark upon a mixing program, do it methodically, and don't give up after a 50-50 mix is a dud. Try a series of mixes, ranging from 80-20, by 20 percent steps. If one of these combinations shows even a little promise, bracket it with additional tests. For instance, if a 40-60 mix looks a bit better than the others, try a 35-65 and a 45-55, and on the next go-round zero in even closer if tests are encouraging.

Clay mixes have another important advantage, particularly if you plan on working up a fairly large amount of material over the years. By using two or more clays in your mix, you reduce your dependence upon just one source of supply. It may be possible to find a substitute for one or the other of these clays without seriously upsetting the characteristics of the mix, since the new material

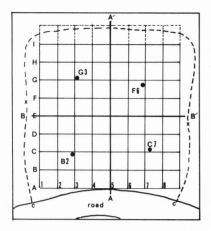

Figure 2.26 *Grid system for identifying sample locations in a pit.*

will represent only a portion of the total. The impact of any change will, of course, be greatly lessened if your carry a fairly large reserve and thoroughly mix subsequent additions into the original mass.

There is another aspect of mixing that is sometimes overlooked. If you find a clay with which you are happy, and the deposit is large enough to see you through a lot of pots, do this: First, check to see if there are any differnces in the quality of the clay, both from top to bottom, and from point to point across the deposit. If you find that these differences affect the quality and appearance of your fired ware, you may wish to devise a digging procedure which will insure the greatest possible uniformity of your feed stock from that pit. This should be carefully considered if you decide to let a contract to have your clay dug for you (see the "Big Dig" section). You may, for instance, wish to waste the top twelve inches of clay and take equal amounts of the remainder from several designated points. The objective is to produce a uniformly acceptable feed-stock with the least possible effort. The best methods for mixing this material will be discussed a little farther on.

The easy way to keep track of where samples came from and where to dig in a pit is to use a grid similar to the one shown in Figure 2.26. The spacing of the grid is optional but an interval of from 3 to 10 feet should be about right. On the ground the corners should be marked with some substantial object such as a stone or post. These can be set back a bit, out of harm's way, and with luck will remain undisturbed during the time the pit is operated. The lines can be either string with spots of paint or rows of short stakes. Since you will be numbering and lettering the *lines* on your plat and also on the ground but sampling and digging from the *space* between these lines, do this: Assign the vertical line number to the space to the right of the line, and assign the horizontal line letter to the space above the line as shown in Figure 2.26.

Exactly the same procedure of sampling, testing, and selecting digging points applies to the second pit which you have selected, on the basis of preliminary tests, as a candidate for mixing with the clay from your first pit. Figure 2.27 graphically illustrates the situation. Both pits tend to vary in quality from place to place so clay is to be obtained from several points in each pit. In the Brown pit the clay is to be dug at four places in equal quantities; at the Hall pit only three places are required, but the center pit is to supply only 20 percent while the other two provide 40 percent each.

This example is complicated. In actual practice a more straightforward routine might be used. It cannot be stressed too strongly, however, that careful testing must be done. The best insurance against erratic behavior in the kiln is feed-stock that has been carefully and intelligently collected. See Figure 2.39 in the "Big Dig" section for large scale digging programs.

There is little point in embarking on a campaign to upgrade a raw clay by mixing it with another one unless detailed and accurate records are kept at every stage of the work. While the work is tedious, unless it is done the result will be total confusion. A carefully conducted testing program can be a most interesting exercise as a pattern of results emerges from the kiln. Another bonus from good lab notes is in your ability to go back and duplicate a certain mix at a later date when you need an identical upgraded clay.

The next step, once you have completed your testing of the various mixes and settled on one or more, is to determine how best to do the actual, full-scale mixing. The first consideration is the size of your operation. Will you be mixing 100, 1000 or 10,000 pounds? If you are at the low end of the scale no special equipment is needed, and even if the method you choose is inefficient, the volume is so small that it makes little difference. The one cardinal point to keep in mind is to use the same basis of measurement that you used in the original testing program. If you used the weight of bank-run material for testing, use the

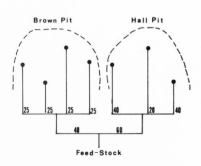

Figure 2.27 *Diagram illustrating possible method for selecting feedstock from two clay pits.*

same when mixing. You can use volume measurements, but errors can creep in due to variations in voids between the lumps. If dry weights are to be used, then all fractions must be equally dry — a difficult thing to achieve in the field but possible in the studio given enough time to bring all the material to the same degree of dryness. Weighing of small quantities can be done on a bathroom scale, although the old-fashioned, practical steelyard, supported by a tripod, is preferable. If the clays are damp and plastic and you have a laboratory grinder with a screw feed, it may be possible to do the mixing by simultaneously feeding lumps of the fractions as equally as possible and then recycling the ground material a time or two to effect a better mix.

Mixing larger amounts of clays requires some mechanical assistance. The portable concrete mixer, charged with a few grapefruit-sized cobbles, can be used to mix dried clays. The clays must be quite dry else they will stick to the walls of the mixer. For quantities of several tons or more the most logical solution is to have a small brick and tile plant run your damp material through its pug mill and recycle it at least twice. Hard, flint-type clays can be mixed by passing them through either a jaw crusher or hammer mill, followed by screening. The clay must be very dry or it will pack against the walls of the crusher or mill like concrete. The drying of this type of clay can be speeded by stage grinding the clay. On the first pass through the crusher or mill set the jaws for a coarse product. After the clay has been allowed to dry the final fine crushing can be done.

The process of mixing your clays has now arrived at the point where final steps must be taken. These will depend upon the type of clays that you are mixing and the methods you have used to mix them together. Slurries will need little, if any, additional mixing; damp, plastic clays should have emerged from the final pass through the grinder or pug mill in a well-mixed condition. Hard, flint-type clays or dry clays will have to be fine-ground before final mixing. See the sections on "Secondary Crushing," "Fine Grinding" and "Mixing and Blending" in the chapter on "Beneficiation and Processing" for details.

SORTING AND WASHING

Many raw clays can be upgraded successfully and sometimes quite readily by the removal of unwanted materials. Other clays contain impurities which are more difficult to remove and the decision then is whether it is worth the candle or not.

Bits and pieces of wood, roots, leaves, or other vegetable material, as well as stones and pebbles should be either picked out by hand or removed by screening. If the clay contains a great deal of sand disintegrate the clay in a bucket or tub of water by vigorously stirring with a paddle. This process, known as blunging, produces a thin, water-clay slurry which is then poured into a separate container, allowed to stand for a time, and then gently poured into yet another bucket. The object of all this is to free the clay of gritty material, which, being heavier than the fine clay, settles to the bottom first. After the mixture in the last bucket has cleared, remove the water, either by siphoning off or by pouring. The fine clay that has settled to the bottom is then saved for use.

Some sand in a clay may not be objectionable. It may even be necessary to have some in a clay mix to produce a body capable of being worked and fired properly. The amount of sand in a raw clay can be controlled in the washing process by varying both the time the slurry is allowed to settle, and the number of times the slurry is poured into another bucket. Only by experiment can the proper procedure be determined.

Some of the arduous work involved in the blunging and decantation steps described above can be eliminated through the use of mechanical aid. Stirrers attached to double-insulated hand-held electric drills will disintegrate the material easily. An old but serviceable washing machine can be used not only as a mixing tub but as a blunger as well. You may wish to avoid lifting and pouring buckets full of slurry by equipping an old washing machine pump with lengths of flexible neoprene hose and carefully pumping the slurry from one container to another. Pumps of this type typically have a rather large tolerance for particles and work well when operated under low head conditions. Also they are not very heavy and if scavenged from an old washer cost nothing. One caution: Be very careful to ground any electric motors and switches used in areas where floors are wet.

AGING

Many clays improve in workability after they have been stored in a damp condition for a period of time. This change is additional to short-term tempering and in some cases is caused by chemical and bacterial development. Some potters, wishing to improve the plasticity of a clay, mix organic matter such as straw or other readily bio-degradable material, together with some detergent containing phosphate with their damp clay. The organic material, in combination with the available phosphate, decomposes in from eight to twelve months. Rate of decomposition is dependent partly upon temperature, nature of the clay (acid or base), amount of moisture and detergent. Some potters add vinegar to help their clays. The addition of straw to clay is interesting in the light of the ancient practice of mixing straw with mud to form sun-dried bricks. In this case the straw was added to improve the structural integrity of the brick and not its plasticity.

This long-term change in a damp clay is known as aging. It is a good argument for having plenty of clay prepared well in advance of need. It is also a good argument for going out and digging your own clay. You can carry a large clay inventory without having too much of a financial investment. The ancient Chinese potter traditionally worked up and stored enough porcelain clay for his son to use during his son's lifetime.

EXPLORING, DEVELOPING AND PRODUCING CLAY

In this section three sizes of mining operation, plus one other, will be discussed. The first is designed for the single potter whose demands for raw clay are modest and whose financial structure is equally inconspicuous. The second type of operation to be explored is a somewhat larger one which might be of interest to several potters working together. The third type of pit may be of any size, but its main characteristic is that it contains clays of rather widely ranging properties which might be of interest for a variety of special applications. The fourth mining operation is of a size that would be of interest to a group of potters who need large quantities of clay over the long haul.

The Single Shovel Scram

In looking at the feasibility of opening up a small pit, the individual potter must wrestle with two major considerations. The suitability of the clay has been roughly determined by preliminary testing. The suitability should be both finite and relative. The clay must be acceptable for your needs and it should be the best clay available within a reasonable distance. The second consideration is one of economics. Will the deposit be large enough to supply you for a minimum period of time? Can the deposit be dug without undue expense? Will an access path or road have to be constructed to the deposit? How much rent or royalty will you have to pay? How far is the deposit from your studio? Can the deposit be worked all year or is it inaccessible during winter months?

If all, or most, of these factors pose no real obstacle, then it is time to address yourself to the next step in opening up your deposit. During the prospecting phase only a grab sample or two were probably taken and tested. In the exploration phase more samples, either from outcrops or from drill holes, will have to be collected. Don't drill any unnecessary holes, but do put down enough to accomplish the twin objectives of (1) determining the minimum amount of tonnage that you will require (and the amount of overburden that may have to be removed), and (2) securing representative samples for studio testing. The samples should be carefully labelled and the holes logged and recorded on a Driller's Log (see Appendix).

Based on the information obtained from your drilling, you should be able to make some tonnage calculations for your deposit. A good, rough factor of two tons per cubic yard of clay in place makes the figuring easy. One common error often encountered in dealing with a cubic yard lies in the misconception that it contains nine rather than twenty-seven cubic feet. To avoid this pitfall try converting linear measurements in feet to yards. For instance: Assume that your deposit covers an area 12 × 15 feet and is 3 feet thick on the average. By dividing these figures by three (to get yards), the dimensions become 4 × 5 × 1 = 20 cubic yards × 2 = 40 tons.

If the studio tests of your exploration samples bear out your earlier examination, you are ready to develop your property. For a small pit, development usually consists of clearing the site of unwanted vegetation and overburden. If the deposit is located away from a road you may have to build a path or road to it. Drainage may be a problem. This can often be anticipated by examining your drill holes. If water collects in them, almost certainly you will have a wet pit. Groundwater may be only a seasonal problem or you may have to contend with it year 'round. If the pit cannot be drained easily, you may have to use a small, portable low-head pump to bail out the water during digging periods. Usually it is wise to erect some sort of fence or barrier around your pit to keep people and livestock away.

You are now ready to begin producing clay from your deposit. If your testing has indicated that the clay is of uniform quality throughout the pit, no special digging pattern or program will be necessary. If, on the other hand, there are differences, then you should consider taking clay from several points and mixing. See the discussion on digging programs in the "Big Dig" section which follows.

The choice of digging equipment will depend largely upon the physical nature of the overburden and the clay. A pick, or mattock, and shovel are standard digging equipment for all but the hardest of flint-type clays. Very hard ground may have to be loosened with dynamite but this operation should be handled by someone who is thoroughly familiar with explosives. Hand tools should be kept in good condition. Sharp-edged mattocks and shovels greatly reduce the physical effort required. All tools should be carefully cleaned after use and oiled if not used again soon. Handles, too, require care. Wooden handles, if exposed to dampness, should be rubbed with linseed oil. A good tool handle should be kept free of nicks and scratches since the rasping effect of these imperfections is detrimental to gloves or human hands.

The final phase of the mining operation is the transportation of pit-run material to your vehicle. Wet clay is heavy and some careful attention should be given as to just how you are going to haul it out of the pit to your car or truck. A rubber-tired contractor's wheelbarrow often works well. Wheelbarrows of this type cannot normally be carried in passenger cars, however, and occupy a lot of space in vans and wagons.

If your deposit is located on a slope above the road and not too distant, you might consider sledding, using an old car hood. This same system can also be used, if your rig has a winch, to haul clay up slopes as well. A child's wagon can be used if a firm path is available. Avoid any dead-weight carrying if at all possible.

RECLAMATION

When you are through mining and before abandoning the site, you will have to either fill in your pit or gently slope the sides so that the excavation presents no physical hazard to people or livestock. Careful planning before you start digging will often save you a lot of work later on when reclamation must be done. Although it is not always possible to back-fill areas that you have excavated as you go along, this should be done whenever possible. It saves an extra handling of waste material and avoids having all the work at the end.

Reclamation work should be "cranked in" as an operational activity and expense, not only for this small operation but for all of the other sizes of mining ventures described in this section.

MEDIUM-SIZED MUD PITS

There are no precise parameters either geologic, economic, or ceramic, for this pit size-classification. Medium-sized mud pits could be operated by an individual or several individuals with only an understanding of general principles binding their separate activities in the same pit together. On the other hand, a medium pit could be operated much like one described in the "Big Dig" section, but somewhat scaled down in size.

The initial phases of "Prospecting" and "Exploring" are similar to those applied to the small single operator pits. Differences appear, however, when the "Developing" stage is reached. Since operations are on a somewhat larger scale, some consideration must be made for the handling of topsoil, the height of pit walls, construction of serviceable access facilities and the eventual reclamation of the pit site.

Depending upon the size of the medium pit and the scale of operations to be conducted within it during the "Producing" phase a decision will have to be made about how the clay is to be mined. It is entirely possible that hand-digging can be carried out successfully, and, in fact, may be the method of choice if (1) the configuration of the deposit is irregular, (2) access to the site is restricted, or (3) the character of the clay changes either vertically or horizontally. In any of these instances, or combinations of them, the inability of mechanical equipment to operate efficiently or even to have access to the pit, plus the need for careful control over digging points, all signal the need for hand-digging. This is not to say that site preparation such as removal of vegetative cover and overburden cannot be done with power equipment where possible.

For pits where there are no physical or geologic prohibitions against the use of power equipment there may still exist a gray area where no clear-cut economic advantage between power and hand methods is discernible. If the digging is contracted for, the exact costs are easy to determine and can be equitably assessed. There may be a problem of cash flow where out-of-pocket expenses may have to be met long before any benefits are derived. Hand-digging requires less outright cash but much individual effort by members of the group. The assessment of the "worth" of these individual efforts sometimes leads to friction. There is also the problem of coordinating times for work parties, the determination of how much should be dug and when, and the value of each member's equity in the clay in its various stages of production in the event that there is a change in group membership.

Try to keep your mining operation as simple as possible. For short-term digging programs or for operations involving limited tonnages, the purchase of expensive mechanical equipment is not advised. Far better to rent or lease digging equipment or contract the entire job than to saddle your project with high amortization costs conditioned on small reserves.

One further consideration in arriving at just how much personal effort you should be putting into mining your own clay revolves around the relative amount of time that you should be devoting to work in the studio compared to work in the pit. A potter does not improve his skills by swinging a pick, but by swinging a pick he may have a better clay and better clay may make a good potter even better.

Perhaps the guiding principle should be one of using mechanical aids as much as possible without compromising the quality of the clay.

The "General Store" Pit

This is the pit that has something for everybody. Sooner or later you will run across a clay deposit that has large variations, both with depth and also horizontally, not only in fired color but in texture and other firing characteristics. The iron content is not consistent over any great distance, the sand-clay ratio changes with depth, and parts of the deposit have sprinklings of mica, magnetite, calcite or other minerals in various percentages.

If you have been looking for a nice, dependable, consistent and uniform deposit your first reaction upon discovering a "General Store" pit is to beat a hasty retreat. A second look, after a bit of deep thinking, may convince you that here you have many clay mixtures all in one place, some of which may be just what you want for some special ware someday. In fact, by doing some experimental mixing and testing, you may discover that there are even more interesting combinations than your original sampling indicated.

"General Store" pits may be composed of either residual, transported or hydrothermally altered clays. Deposits that show marked color changes, have iron-stained veinlets, or include bands of clay that have obvious textural differences almost always signal the presence of a material with ceramic properties which change rather abruptly over short distances. Some residual deposits may have a considerable thickness of rather uniform clay near the surface, but there may be a pronounced change in its nature with increasing depth, as the base of the weathering zone is approached. Often there is a transition zone in which completely weathered rock, which has turned to clay, changes into fresher and fresher material until solid, unaltered rock is reached. In this area there may be layers which have widely differing firing characteristics.

When the deposition took place under turbulent conditions, transported deposits can have a mixed-up assortment of clays. Many of these deposits are far too jumbled for ceramic purposes, but on occasion deposits with mixed but usable clays can be found. Often the margins of deposits that were deposited during flood times are less disturbed and more orderly, in a rumpled sort of way, than the central portions where stream velocities were greater.

Clay deposits that have been formed by hydrothermal alteration sometimes exhibit wide variations in clay compositions over rather short distances in any direction. Look for narrow veinlets of mineral that have intruded into the clays. These were at one time avenues for the introduction of chemical solutions and the surrounding clays may be affected. Color and textural changes should also be noted, just as with residual deposits.

Careful sampling is a must in "General Store" pits, with holes more closely spaced than normal and with greater attention to shorter vertical sampling intervals. Keeping good records of your drilling, sampling and testing is a must, and ready access to test bars for inspection may save you much effort when you need that special clay.

The Big Dig

All of the discussion on tracking, testing, and taming new clays so far has been aimed at the needs of the individual art potter whose demands for bulk material are modest. If a group of potters decide to band together to develop some native ceramic materials, then the scope of operations must be broadened with respect to minimum acceptable tonnages required. Greater expectations require more intensive sampling, more testing and larger reserves of raw material.

ECONOMIC CONCERNS

Since dollar signs cast very long shadows, careful attention must be paid to the costs involved in searching for, developing, testing, digging, transporting and possibly beneficiating raw ceramic materials. It may come as a complete surprise to many potters to discover that raw clay in an undeveloped deposit has almost no monetary value. Value is added only as energy is expended upon it, whether the energy be human muscle, gasoline, chemicals and fuel for testing, or the consumption and use of supplies and tools. The expenditure of energy, then, determines the length of the shadow of the dollar sign.

Figure 2.28 outlines the succession of steps and the main activities that normally are undertaken as you open up a new clay pit and put it into production. Each of these steps is discussed in the following pages.

	STEPS TO TAKE
Prospecting	Take a grab sample and field test.
Exploring	Make arrangement with landowner. Search for additional outcrops, or drill. Field tests, followed by pattern drilling, studio testing, calculation of possible reserves.
Developing	Get lease from landowner. Square up deposit area. Drill additional holes to define area. Construct several cross-sections. Calculate reserves, stripping ratio.
Producing	Check with state, federal agencies. Let out a digging contract. Design a digging program. Arrange for shipping to studio. Plan for final disposition of pit.

Figure 2.28 *Basic steps leading up to the production of clay in large quantities.*

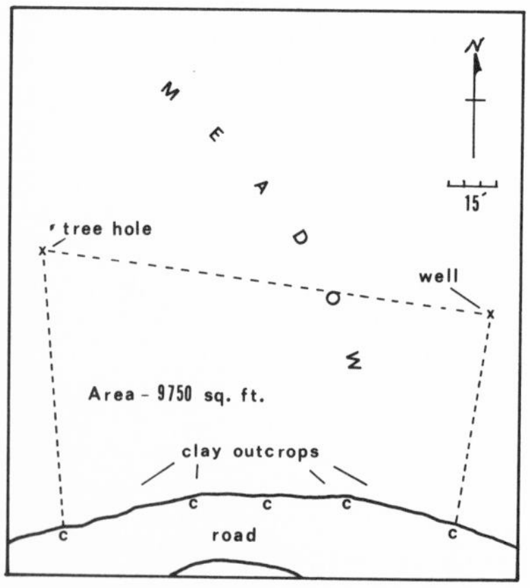

Figure 2.29 *A clay prospect with clay exposed at three points; in roadcut at "c", in tree hole and in old well.*

PROSPECTING

Let us assume that a likely clay deposit has been discovered in the course of your prospecting activities and from outward appearances seems to be large enough for some group project.

A layer of clay was found cropping out along a road bank for a distance of 120 feet, Figure 2.29. In searching the meadow north of the road an old hand-dug well was found that showed the same clay strata just below the surface. A tree-hole, developed when a wind-felled tree became uprooted, also revealed clay. These four points indicated the possibility of a continuous body of clay lying within the envelope defined by the four points.

Now, before proceeding any further take a little time out to make some preliminary field tests on clay gathered from along the road and at the well and tree-hole. If these tests look good, you are ready to drill.

EXPLORING

For deposits located on generally flat or gently sloping land the size and shape can best be determined by drilling two rows of holes at right angles to each other, Figure 2.30. Here a line A-A' has been staked out midway between the four exposures in a north-south direction. Drill holes are then put down at 15-foot intervals, starting at the edge of the road and continuing northward until the edge of the clay is reached. At the mid-point on line A-A' a second line is laid out at right angles and holes are drilled, starting at the center, outward in both directions until no more clay is struck. Half-interval holes are drilled at the end to determine more precisely the margin of the deposit.

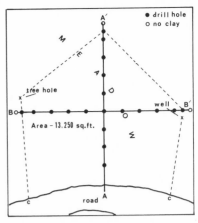

Figure 2.30 *Exploration of clay prospect shown in Figure 2.29 by two rows of drill holes.*

One good rule-of-thumb when exploring, particularly with a drill: Never project the continuation of a deposit more than one-half the distance between your series of evenly spaced holes.

At this point the envelope line, drawn through the last holes in each line that hit clay, now encloses an area of 13,250 square feet. When drilling these test holes, bear in mind that you have several objectives. One: The holes are drilled to determine the presence of clay, the thickness of the overburden, and the thickness of the clay. Two: The cuttings from the holes become a sample, or series of samples, for field and studio testing. The first samples should be taken at intervals of about one foot of depth or upon encountering color changes as the hole is drilled. If no significant variation is found in these samples, a composite sample of the entire hole can be taken from then on. You may find upon testing, however, that the top- or bottom-most portions of the deposit vary from the main body and that you might wish to exclude them from mining later on. Once you have satisfied yourself about the nature and quality of the clay in your deposit there is no need to sample each and every hole. Just drill the hole to see if the clay is there and move on to the next one, recording only the thickness of overburden and clay. The objective now is to find out if there is enough clay to bother with.

Each drill hole should be numbered and that number, plus the date, should be used to identify the samples. A driller's log should also be kept, with depth of overburden, thickness of clay, and, if samples were taken, the sample numbers and the thickness of clay that they represent. A typical form for a Driller's Log is included in the Appendix.

Residual clay deposits, derived from large, deeply weathered rock formations, can be sampled at greater intervals than those deposits which have formed in areas in which rocks of several types have weathered. The color of the sample taken from a drill hole is often related to its composition. Once this relationship has been established it may be possible to skip some studio testing.

Transported deposits, if laid down in fairly large basins, are generally of uniform composition over large horizontal distances but may change vertically rather quickly. Again color, and quite often texture, are excellent guides to changes in composition.

A METHOD FOR CALCULATING RESERVES

The following table, Figure 2.31 has been prepared to make it easy for you to calculate rough estimates in the field of the reserves of clay that you have discovered in the course of your drilling campaign.

Although a drill hole technically "samples" a cylindrical body of the earth, it may in some cases make more sense to assume that the drill hole occupies the

Depth	Spacing of Holes					Cubic yards per acre
	8 ft.	10 ft.	12 ft.	15 ft.	20 ft.	
3 ft.	5.58	8.73	12.56	19.63	34.90	4,840
	7.11	11.11	16.00	25.00	44.44	
4	7.45	11.64	16.76	26.18	46.54	6,453
	9.48	14.81	21.33	33.33	59.26	
5	9.31	14.54	20.94	32.73	58.17	8,067
	11.85	18.52	26.67	41.67	74.07	
6	11.17	17.45	25.13	39.27	69.81	9,680
	14.22	22.22	32.00	50.00	88.89	
8	14.89	23.27	33.51	52.36	93.08	12,906
	18.96	29.63	42.67	66.67	110.52	
10	18.62	29.09	41.89	65.45	115.35	16,134
	23.70	37.04	53.33	83.33	148.15	
Area of circle	50.26	78.54	113.10	176.72	314.16	—
Holes/acre (square-centered)	680.00	436.00	302.00	194.00	109.00	—

Figure 2.31 *The volume of earth, in cubic yards, represented by holes drilled at various intervals and to selected depths. The upper of the paired figures represents volumes of cylinders with diameters equal to the spacing shown. The lower figures are for hole-centered squares with sides equal to the same spacing.*

center of a square. The diameter of the cylinder and the length of a side of the square will be determined by your spacing of the drill holes. In the table the volumes represented by various diameters of circles, or edges of squares, are both shown in cubic yards; the volume for the cylinders appears above the volume for the prisms. To convert the figures for cubic yards to tons simply multiply by two, which will give a close enough figure for estimation.

Also shown are the number of cubic yards per acre for various thicknesses. At the bottom of the table the area in square feet is given for circles of the five diameters shown, and the number of square-centered holes per acre required for various hole spacings. An acre contains 43,560 square feet. Legal dimensions for an acre usually measure 66 x 660 feet, but for estimating purposes it is sometimes handy to visualize an acre as being about 208 feet square.

Figure 2.32 shows the volumes of a cylinder and a square prism having equal lengths, with the diameter of the cylinder equal to an edge of the prism. Tonnage and grade calculations for a deposit that has been drilled on a grid are generally based on the square-centered hole method. This system is simple and accurate and includes the entire mass of the deposit with the grid lines. The cylinder-centered hole method is used for randomly spaced drill holes, and the tonnage of each cylinder pretty much depends on the maximum diameter that can be assigned to it with confidence.

With more than twenty samples in hand it is now time to retire to the studio and do some more testing. If your new-found clay stands up to rigorous studio testing it is back to the field for the final steps in your mining program.

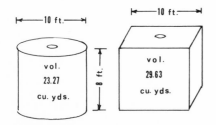

Figure 2.32 *Comparison of the volumes of a cylinder and a square prism having equal length and with the diameter of the cylinder equal to an edge of the prism. See Figure 2.31 for other values.*

DEVELOPING

In Figure 2.33 the area is assumed to contain a sufficiently large body of clay to accommodate a square measuring 120 feet on an edge. Two test holes are drilled at the northwest and northeast corners to make sure that there is clay there and then holes at 15-foot intervals are drilled along the west, north and east sides. This effectively boxes in the deposit which now covers at least 14,400 square feet.

CALCULATING STRIPPING RATIO AND TONNAGE

Drawing some vertical cross-sections through your project at this point will greatly assist you not only in understanding the size and shape of your deposit but in calculating the thickness of overburden and clay and the waste:ore stripping ratio. Figure 2.34 illustrates a typical cross-section through a deposit. Each square represents two feet in distance and four square feet in area. To construct the cross-sections, do this: (1) On engineering graph paper, either 8x8 or 10x10 divisions to the inch, plot the thickness of the overburden and clay that was

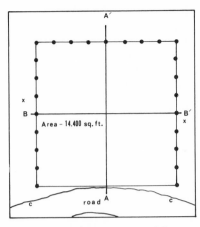

Figure 2.33 *Clay prospect with area squared and drill holes evenly spaced around perimeter of deposit.*

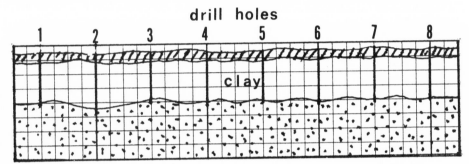

Figure 2.34 *Cross-section showing eight drill holes penetrating a clay horizon. Each grid division is two feet.*

encountered in each drill hole along the line you have selected for the cross-section. In the example shown there are eight holes and the thickness of overburden and clay are tabulated below (Figure 2.35). The thicknesses are totalled and divided by the number of holes to arrive at the average figures, in this case the average overburden thickness is 1.18 feet and for the clay 5.98 feet. In actual practice you would probably want to construct cross-sections along each of your lines of drill holes and average all of them for greater accuracy.

Hole No.	Overburden	Clay
1	1.2 ft.	5.8 ft.
2	1.0	6.5
3	1.2	5.9
4	1.1	6.0
5	1.2	5.8
6	1.2	5.9
7	1.3	6.0
8	1.2	5.9
TOTAL	9.4	47.8
Average	1.18	5.98
Stripping ratio: 5.98 ÷ 1.18 = 5.1		

Figure 2.35 *Method for determining the average thickness of overburden and clay, and stripping ratio of overburden to clay for cross-section shown in Figure 2.34.*

These calculations indicate a stripping ratio of overburden to clay of 1:5.1, which is well within the normal limits for this type of mining operation. This means you will have to remove one ton of waste for every 5.1 tons of clay that you mine.

A few additional calculations are now possible and certainly necessary. By averaging the thickness of the clay struck in your drill holes, you have determined that the average thickness is almost six feet. Determining the weight of a cubic foot of undisturbed clay is a bit of a bother. For practical purposes the round figure of 150 pounds is probably close enough since the water content will vary from month to month, and its presence or absence can change at least ten percent of the total weight.

The volume and weight of the deposit then is determined as follows: Area in sq. ft. × average thickness in feet = 14,400 × 5.98 = 86,112 cubic feet. Multiplying this figure by 150 pounds per cubic foot, and dividing by 2000 to reduce the product to net tons yields the following: $86,112 \times \dfrac{150}{2000} = 6458$ tons. This is a lot of clay.

You will also have to move 1274 tons of overburden at least once and possibly twice, depending on the future disposition of the site when you abandon it.

THE NAIL MAP

Here is a low-cost, easy to construct visual aid and planning tool to assist you in keeping track of your drilling and sampling. If you later decide to develop and mine your deposit, it will help you in carrying out your mining program. A clay deposit is an irregular, three-deminsional solid which may be difficult to visualize without some device which allows you to view it from many directions and to make measurements of the deposit that would otherwise be either difficult or expensive in terms of time and money.

A Nail Map consists of nothing more than an appropriately sized and shaped piece of ¾″ plywood covered with engineering graph paper and studded with finishing nails inserted to mark the location of your drill holes. Each nail is driven into the plywood until its top reaches the scale elevation for that point. Thickness of overburden and clay are shown with bands of paint on each nail. Figure 2.36 illustrates a typical nail map. Since horizontal and vertical scales are the same, it is easy to calculate both areas and volumes that are enclosed by three or four nails. The thickness of overburden and clay lying within areas bounded by selected drill holes can be averaged as shown in Figure 2.35.

To improve the visual aid feature of the nail map place strips of cardboard, cut flush with the tops of the nails, along each row of holes. The clay profile can then be plotted on it. If the cardboard cross-sections are faced with the same type of graph paper that was used to cover the base, the plotting of the overburden and clay can be simplified; see Figure 2.37.

Each drill hole or sample point that is plotted on the nail map can be referenced by using the lettering and numbering system shown in Figure 2.26.

Although we have called this device a nail map there is no reason why lengths of coat-hanger wire, balloon sticks, or small wood dowels cannot be used. Coat-hanger wire already has a coat of black paint which can be used to indicate overburden. By selecting strongly contrasting fast-drying paint colors — red for clay and white for the country rock lying below the clay — and by holding the map at eye level, you can get a clear picture of what the deposit looks like from any number of directions. This "x-ray" view is possible long before you have excavated the first shovel-full of dirt, and can indicate just where you should be

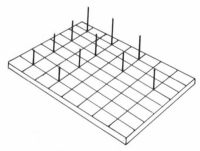

Figure 2.36 *A nail map, showing grid lines and a few nails in place.*

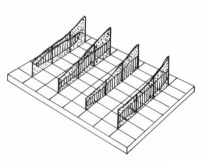

Figure 2.37 *A nail map with four cross-sections in place along lines of nails representing drill holes.*

concentrating your drilling or sampling efforts to give you the necessary information; see Figure 2.38.

A nail map is a working map. The location of all drill holes and sample points is plotted on it, together with details of the surface configuration, the overburden and the clay. As your development and mining proceed, this work is also plotted on the nail map. When areas are mined out, the nails representing those drill holes are removed and on the base graph paper the date that mining took place is noted. If these notations are kept up to date, you not only have a running inventory of your un-mined reserves but you can figure out your rate of depletion as well.

If your pit has drainage problems, your nail map may save you time and trouble since you can do a lot of dry engineering to determine the best method before digging any ditches. See the section on "Levelling" for some ideas on how to determine the surface elevations of your pit and the proper way to slope your drain ditches.

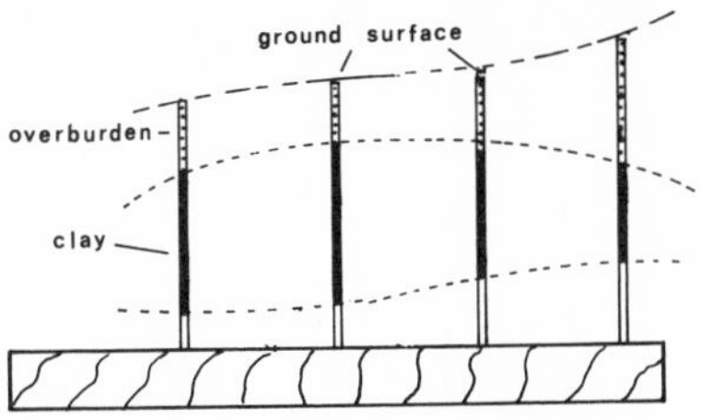

Figure 2.38 *Eye-level view of one row of nails representing drill holes in a nail map.*

LEVELLING

Unless your clay pit is located on absolutely flat ground, it is important to know just how it slopes so that you can plan your digging program, hauling and drainage. There are several ways you can determine the surface configuration of the pit area. Here are some of the simpler methods. The carpenter's level can be used in conjunction with a homemade level rod. The rod is a piece of 1×2" lumber about 8 feet long with a cloth or steel tape attached to the face. The zero end of the tape is at the bottom of the rod. Select a convenient height for the level. An old stump with a 12-inch square of ¾" plywood nailed to it in a horizontal position forms an excellent base, but a sturdy post will also do. Make sure the plywood surface is level in all directions, since the carpenter's level must also be dead level. At a convenient spot nearby establish a bench mark and assign it an elevation of, say, 1000 feet. Set the rod on the bench mark, sight over the top of the carpenter's level, and read the figure on the rod which appears in the line of sight. Add this value to that which you have assigned for the bench mark. This elevation now becomes your "height of instrument", or HI. Now place the rod at each drill hole or other points that are important and record the rod readings. When all of the shots have been made, subtract the rod readings from the HI and you have the elevation of your points. Be sure to catch the highest and lowest points in your pit area.

If the distance between the carpenter's level and the rod is so great that you can't read the figures on the rod, have the rodman slide a card or pencil up and down the rod until the level line is reached, and have him call out the figures.

A pocket transit or Brunton's compass can be used in place of a carpenter's level, or you can rent a builder's transit which has a low-power telescope and is mounted on a tripod.

If you have a drainage problem, you can figure out, after your levelling, where to put the ditches, which should have a gradient of not less than four inches per 100 feet of ditch. Make the slope of the drain ditch as steep as reasonably possible to prevent damming and siltation of the channel.

PRODUCING

After you have mapped your deposit and determined how you can provide access to it and drain it, you are ready to discuss digging costs with a dirt contractor or perhaps a local farmer who has digging equipment. The timing of the operation may affect costs. If the work can be done during slack times rather than during the peak season, and over a fairly long period of time rather than on one specific date, the cost may be lower.

Another item to consider is the manner in which the clay will be dug. Do you want it taken at one point or several? Do you want the entire thickness dug in one operation or can it be scalped off in layers? The answers to these questions will depend on the variation, if any, discovered in the clay during your sampling and testing work.

A DIGGING PROGRAM

To insure the most homogeneous feed-stock possible from a clay deposit some systematic digging program must be devised and adhered to. There are several advantages in doing this. First, any variations in composition and quality of the clay are pretty much averaged out by the built-in mixing resulting from the digging program. Second, if the digging work is contracted out, it is not always possible to be on hand when the work is done. It is vastly simpler to indicate just how and what you want dug — and to be able to check on it later. Third, if your operation is a do-it-yourself cooperative affair with various people digging from time to time, a digging plan is the only way that any consistency of product can be hoped for. A properly designed digging program should be considered to be a grown-up version of the original sampling program that you conducted earlier. Although the quantities are vastly larger, the accuracy should be at least equal, if not superior to, your smaller studio samples.

Three digging programs are shown in Figure 2.39. In "a" the digging area has been divided into quarters and clay is to be taken simultaneously from the four points marked "x", with the excavations advancing in the direction of the arrows. In "b" four panels have been laid out and digging is scheduled to proceed in opposite directions in alternating panels. This digging design can be adjusted to situations where unequal amounts of clay are to be dug from several points in the same pit. The panel widths are altered to meet the requirements of the mix and no further calculations are needed during the life of the operation. Also the number of panels can be changed easily to accommodate the number of digging points.

For a deposit having an overall acceptable quality but with variations over short distances the program shown in "c" is suggested, since the digging sequence, proceeding from 1 to 4, provides a good distribution of digging points at all times. Other programs can be used for special situations but every program should be carefully designed to provide the most uniform mixture of clay

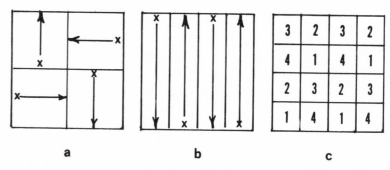

a   b   c

Figure 2.39 *Three digging programs. Digging in "a" and "b" starts at point "x", with all four panels being advanced simultaneously. In "c" work starts in the four squares marked "1", and proceeds to "2", "3,", and "4".*

possible. A good digging program is the first step in assuring a constant quality feed-stock for your studio.

As the digging proceeds, the excavated clay from the various points should be placed in one pile, care being taken to make it cone-shaped by dumping each addition on the center of the pile. If large quantities are mined, the entire pile can be reworked several times with a front-end loader or a trench hoe to further mix the material when it has all been dug. For smaller quantities the cone should be divided into pie-shaped segments and each wedge removed as completely as possible with a hand shovel before starting on the opposite one. For intermediate quantities the use of garden tractors and tillers to rework the clay pile is suggested.

The method of hauling is also important. Can you accept dump-truck loads of five or more yards at a time, or must the clay be sacked or shipped in containers? Where and how will you store the clay once it is delivered? These factors should be thoroughly explored before committing yourself to having the work done.

One final caution. Be sure that all parties understand precisely what will be done with the clay pit once your clay has been removed. There are county, state and federal regulations that might apply to your operation, so inquire before you start.

Some thought might be given to air-drying the clay in the field, possibly in an old barn or shed, before shipping to storage or the studio. In addition to the saving in weight, which might be 10 percent or more, there is a possible saving if the clay has to be up-graded. Dry clay can be pulverized and converted into a slurry easily, thus permitting the separation of unwanted factions. Some clays, when wet, are rather difficult to mix with water and require much handling before a slurry is developed. Clays that have been allowed to dry may not regain their original plasticity immediately after being moistened again, but given time the problem usually resolves itself.

One argument against storing dry clay is the loss of the possible benefit to be derived from aging, which was discussed earlier under Upgrading Techniques.

MINING COSTS

Trying to estimate mining costs is like writing your name on a waterfall. Mining cost centers can be identified, however, with a fair degree of accuracy. Figure 2.40 outlines the principal items and activities that enter into a small open-pit operation. The cost figures shown are close to 1979 costs and will have to be adjusted. They do point up where your money might go. The recoverable tonnage figure of 6458 tons is the same that was calculated in the final phases of the "Big Dig" operation.

In Figure 2.40 you will note that a mining cost per ton of $23.80 has been arrived at. When you are planning your own mining operation, you might want to consider working with your figures from the bottom up. Determine the maximum amount you can afford to spend on your own clay and then distribute the individual costs. If you find that the total of the unit costs adds up to more than you can afford, better look for another pit.

No two clay deposits ever have exactly the same problems or costs. Each one is unique and determining costs will depend on many variables. There are often trade-offs possible in any mining program. For instance, the amount of drilling, sampling and testing that will be required can vary widely. A large deposit with uniform clay will need far less of these three items than one that varies over short distances, is irregular in outline or has to have a lot of drainage expense.

The cost of the haul from pit to studio or storage site varies directly with the distance. You can afford to spend more on mining if your hauling charges are less, and vice versa.

The stripping ratio will be different for each pit. If one pit has a lot of overburden, its removal may cost nearly as much per ton as you will pay for mining the clay. In another pit the stripping ratio may be more favorable but the construction of a short access road is an added cost factor not required at the first pit.

Storage of mined clay is a fairly straightforward expense item but consideration should be given to stockpiling the raw clay out in the open, rather than in the dry. Clay is practically indestructible and the loss rate from pilferage or theft is low indeed. Storage costs can be controlled somewhat by renting only enough space for a minimum supply for your studio. Add new material from time to time, but don't have the entire mine shipped to storage all at once.

Beneficiation expenses may be considerable, or, if the clay can be used more or less pit-run, this item can be eliminated. Sometimes the careful selection of a mining program, coupled with bulk mixing at the pit, will offset much of your beneficiation cost. The trade-off here is that you may save money by having the work done with power equipment on a fairly large scale, but the money for having this done will have to be spent well in advance of using the clay.

Miscellaneous expenses include, but are not limited to, items such as liability insurance (if you go to mining on your own), legal fees for drawing up a contract with a land-owner and perhaps a digging contractor, supplies for taking and testing samples, and unanticipated contingencies which crop up in the best managed operations.

As a general principle try to keep your investment costs as low as possible for as long as possible. You can afford to spend money on prospecting and testing, which are small budget items, but don't plunk down big dollars for mining and hauling until you have to. Buying money is not only expensive, but committing large chunks of cash for a pile of clay deprives you of any financial flexibility for a long period of time.

Almost certainly you will be getting your clay from private land and will have to enter into some kind of arrangement with the owner. If conditions warrant, and the land-owner has the capability for digging your clay, there are several

	Travel	Testing	Drilling	Mining & Royalty	Hauling	Storage	Beneficiation & Miscellaneous	¢/ton	Total Cost
Prospecting	4*	10						14	$904
Exploration- Development	8	20	25					53	3423
Mining	8			300				308	19,891
Hauling					1000			1000	64,580
Storing						5		5	323
Beneficiation & Miscellaneous							1000	1000	64,580
TOTALS ¢/ton	20	30	25	300	1000	5	1000	2380¢	$153,701
$ Cost	1292	1937	1615	19,374	64,580	323	$64,580		
Cumulative									
cost/ton	.20	.50	.75	$3.75	$13.75	$13.80	$23.80		
$ Cost	1290	3227	4837	24,211	88,791	89,114	$153,701		

*values shown are in cents per ton of recovered clay

Figure 2.40 *Identification of cost elements involved in producing 6458 tons of clay from a captive pit. Cost figures used are for purposes of illustration only.*

excellent reasons for having him do so. First, the costs will be known in advance of mining. Second, the owner will dig the clay, and perhaps even deliver it for you. This spares you all of the problems connected with landlord-tenant relations, and you take possession of the clay at point of delivery. Third, reclamation of the pit will be up to the owner, and any problems relating to drainage, wandering livestock and access roads will be his also. As noted above, give careful attention to when you want the clay dug and delivered.

In the event that you do become an operator, you will need a contract with the land-owner. You will probably have to pay a royalty on every ton you take, and may even have to pay a minimum monthly rental which is normally applicable to future royalty payments incurred during that year. Many items can be included in a mining contract but keep it as simple as possible. When dickering over the royalty keep in mind that un-mined clay, or any industrial mineral for that matter, is worth only a few cents per ton. The value grows as you expend energy on it, and that energy is provided at your expense, not the land-owner's.

A land-owner is entitled to a fair return on the sale of his clay but it should be pointed out that in some cases the removal of the clay from sour agricultural land may actually improve the tilth of the soil. If a clay deposit is unusually thick, and a lot of clay is removed, the resulting pit represents a considerable value. Pits may be used as stock ponds, solid waste disposal sites or basement excavations for structures. Other sites can be smoothed over, covered with the topsoil originally stockpiled off to one side, and returned to productive agricultural use. Careful planning on how the abandoned pit is to be disposed of may save much money in the long run.

THE TAX MAN COMETH

Mining is a self-defeating operation. The harder you mine the faster you run out of ore. Unless you have developed a very large deposit and your demands are modest, you should, shortly after you get your mining program underway, start prospecting for, exploring and developing another pit to take its place. If you can find another closely similar pit you might want to consider, in the closing stages of your first pit, a mixing program, using increasing amounts of clay from the second pit so that the transition will be as smooth as possible.

If your combined mining and ceramic operation is of such size that you may excite the attention of the tax man you certainly should explore the ins and outs of mineral depletion allowances with a tax attorney. Non-renewable resources that you mine enjoy certain tax benefits, since you are in a very real sense consuming your raw material capital. You will have none left unless you make proper allowances for developing new sources.

BENEFICIATION AND PROCESSING OF GLAZE MATERIALS

INTRODUCTION

This chapter could just as easily be titled "Problem Solving", for that is the main thrust of what is to come. The problem is to figure out how to take a raw chunk of mineral suitable for glaze material, grind it into a powder and remove as many of its impurities as possible, all at the same time. The solving of the problem has a long and interesting history, and even today, with all of our wonderful technology, we still use some methods and equipment that closely resemble those in use about the time that calendars were invented.

Beneficiation and processing is a nuts and bolts activity requiring expenditure of ingenuity, imagination and just plain muscle power.

In the discussion that follows there is always the danger that the device or method described will be understood by the reader to be the *only* one to use. This, of course, is far from the truth. Examples are given, in part to explain what the problem is, and how it can be solved, and in part to provide a point of departure from which you can perfect your own equipment and system. Don't be awed by the state of the art. Much has been accomplished, but so much remains to be done.

Principal topics to be investigated in this section include the selection and identification of raw ceramic materials; separation of waste from ore; primary and secondary crushing; concentration; fine grinding in both dry and wet modes; procedures for preparing iron-free, low-iron and high-iron materials; the art and practice of screening; and mixing, blending and sampling. In addition to the definitions which follow, most of the specialized and perhaps unfamiliar terms are listed in the Glossary. If you really get deeply involved in beneficiation and processing you may wish to refer to some of the published literature which appears in the Bibliography.

Should You Grind Your Own?

Before plunging into the business of beneficiating and processing your own ceramic materials it might be well to pause for a moment and consider some of the pros and cons.

First, a sufficient quantity of ore should be ground to keep you in stock for a considerable period of time since it might be difficult, if not impossible, to duplicate it when you run out. (However, see the section on "Mixing and Blending" at the end of this chapter, before throwing in the towel).

Second, if the task of grinding the ore may prove too burdensome and time-consuming you might be better advised to purchase commercially prepared material instead.

Third, depending on your needs, you may find that the storage of rather large quantities of finely powdered material is both a nuisance and is too demanding of space.

Fourth, after doing all the hard work of collecting, beneficiating and grinding you may discover that you just don't need all that much material, have gotten sick and tired of using it, and are wondering what to do with enough glaze to cover every pot west of the Rockies.

Fifth, are you prepared to keep your material identified as you take it through the various operations? Good labels and detailed records are a must.

There is a real thrill and much satisfaction in doing it yourself, but it should be tempered with common sense. Have fun but don't overdo it.

Definitions

Beneficiation simply means the improvement in the quality of a mineral product. This improvement can be as simple as sweeping away unwanted overburden when digging out the ore, dunking the specimens in wash water, or separating pieces of ore from the gangue. On the other hand it can involve more complicated procedures such as grinding, screening, jigging, tabling, blunging, settling, magnetic separation and so forth.

The processing of minerals refers to the actual equipment and its operation that is employed to accomplish the beneficiation. Processing equipment includes, but is by no means limited to, crushers, rolls, ball mills, jigs, screens, washers, gold pans, and magnetic separators. A few of the time-honored devices useful in transforming a raw chunk of mineral into a pure, finely ground product are described in the sections that follow.

All of this sounds rather formidable, but each step is simple and straight-forward and you are basically dealing with one problem at a time. Beneficiation takes place all the way from the initial discovery, or if mining of the ceramic material, on down to the final sweep through the finely powdered ore with a magnet to remove any tramp iron. Similarly processing, which starts with the first blow of your pick or hammer out in the field, progresses through a wide variety of treatments in different devices, until you have a pulp that has passed through your finest sieve.

The combined action of beneficiation and processing increases the purity, decreases the volume, and reduces the particle size of the original material. Several flowsheets have been prepared to help guide you through the various steps. As a last resort turn to the Index where, with luck, the item in question may have been included.

Here is a beneficiation "road map" that charts the progress of raw ore on its way to usefulness (Figure 3.1). Many ceramic materials will certainly not need all of the tender loving care outlined here. Some may only have to be squashed down a bit for use while others may require the full treatment. Don't take your material through all of the buckets unless it is really necessary.

No two ores respond to beneficiation and processing in exactly the same way, and no two operators achieve exactly the same results, even with identical equipment. Here is a hypothetical example of what might happen to 100 pounds of ceramic material containing 45 percent of a sought-after element when it is given a series of treatments designed to improve the purity of the final product. Figure 3.2 shows the almost perfect mirror image developed in the relationship between the rising purity of the ore at various stages of beneficiation and the shrinking volume as more and more low-grade fractions are discarded. Also shown is the reduction in particle size with each stage of crushing and grinding.

The Metallurgical Balance

This same relationship can be approached from a mathematical standpoint in an exercise known as the metallurgical balance. This sounds terribly complicat-

RAW ORE
Mining, digging, collecting
Hand sorting
Washing
Primary crushing
Screening
Hand-sorting
Washing
Magnetic separation
Secondary crushing
Screening
Magnetic separation
Concentration
Polishing
Washing
Magnetic separation
Fine grinding
Screening
Magnetic separation
FINISHED CONCENTRATE

Figure 3.1 *Principal steps in beneficiating and processing raw ore.*

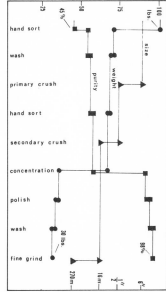

Figure 3.2 *Diagram showing the effect of beneficiation and processing on ore.*

	Concentrate			Assumed		Discard				
	Weight of ore	% Purity	Weight of Metal	% ore Weight Loss	% of Metal Loss	Weight of Reject	% Purity	Weight of Metal Loss	Ratio Metal: Ore loss	Operation
A	100.00	45.00	45.00	—	—	—	—	—	—	Original
B	70.00	51.43	36.00	30.00	20.00	30.00	30.00	9.00	1:3.3	Hand-sort
C	31.50	97.14	30.60	55.00	15.00	38.50	14.00	5.40	1:7.2	Concentration
D	31.19	97.85	30.52	1.00	.25	.31	26.00	0.08	1:3.9	Polishing
E	30.57	98.82	30.21	2.00	1.00	.62	50.00	0.31	1:2.0	Washing
Loss 69.43		Loss 14.79				69.43		14.79		

Notes:
1. Weight of ore = weight of ore (A) — weight of reject (B), etc.
2. Percent purity = weight of metal, or metal loss, divided by weight of ore, or reject.
3. Weight of metal = metal weight (A) × (100 — % metal loss (B)) etc.
4. Percent ore weight loss — assumed.
5. Percent metal loss — assumed.
6. Weight of reject = weight of ore (A) × % ore weight loss (B).
7. Weight of metal loss = weight of metal (A) × % metal loss (B).
8. Ratio of metal: ore loss = weight of reject divided by weight of metal loss.

Figure 3.3 *A metallurgical balance.*

ed but really isn't. Figure 3.3 shows how the balance is organized and the notes below it explain how the various values are arrived at. No "higher math" is involved. As in so many things it's the bottom line that counts and this table is no exception. Against a loss of 69.43 pounds of ore which contained a non-recoverable 14.79 pounds of the sought-after metal, the purity of the original ore has been improved from 45 percent to 98.82 percent.

The principle of the metallurgical balance, which in simple terms means that in any milling process all of the material entering the milling flowsheet must be accounted for when the process is complete. Note that the loss of 69.43 pounds of ore (Column 1) is balanced by the gain of an equal amount in the weight of reject (Column 6), and the loss of 14.79 pounds of metal (Column 3) equals the amount gained in the weight of metal lost (Column 8). Some assumptions, or limits, have to be established as you go along. You can sacrifice some of the weight of metal in your original sample and gain a higher percentage of purity by pitching out low-grade chunks during the hand-sorting phase. Or, if a lower purity product will serve you adequately, you can retain more of the low-grade while hand-sorting and not be quite so fussy during concentration. This latter course will give you more product than the first option. You can decide which way you want to go and just how much material to discard at each step if you work up a metallurgical balance before you get all geared up. You can tinker with the figures until the desired result is obtained, but your ore and metal losses on the concentrate side must equal those gained on the discard side.

There are a few pitfalls and a trick or two that help in setting up the parameters for your beneficiation and processing work. The big hang-up is in knowing how to judge how much good metal or mineral you are tossing out while hand sorting. Disseminated ore is always a problem, but massive high-grade mineral is simple. One check on your ability to sort out disseminated ore is to crush up several lumps of reject, weigh, and then pan and weigh the concentrate. Divide the weight of the metal concentrate by the weight of the reject and you have the percent of metal in the ore that you are discarding.

The metallurgical balance is most helpful in spotting potential bottlenecks in your flowsheet. If you elect not to hand-sort very much ore, then you may have insufficient crushing and grinding capacity, since more ore per unit of contained metal will have to be processed down through the concentration step.

If you use the principle of the metallurgical balance, you not only can keep tabs on your operation but save much time and energy by operating in a more efficient manner. A metallurgical balance is very similar to an audit of a set of books.

A careful analysis of the calculations in the Metallurgical Balance example will probably raise some questions as to why certain practices were followed. For instance, the rather high (30 percent) metal content of the discarded material during hand-sorting seems wasteful. In defense it might be argued that disseminated ores are tough to sort and unavoidable losses are the rule. A metal content of 30 percent, however, is high and quite possibly better beneficiation practice would have been to discard only lower-grade ore and less of it. This in turn places a heavier load on the crushing and concentration departments, but if the ore was difficult to obtain it might well be worth it.

It might also be questioned whether or not the polishing step was worth the effort since the purity of the concentrate was only raised by 0.71 percent. Here the objective was to remove an objectionable mineral coating which no other process could do. And finally, the washing resulted in the loss of a whole pound of metal and only raised the purity less than one percent. Sacrifices of this kind are costly in terms of the weight of the finished product and are only bearable when the very highest purity possible must be sought rather than the volume of the product. Some glaze formulations are adversely affected by small amounts of impurities or combinations of impurities, even though the sought-after metal oxide content may be sufficiently high to satisfy the requirements of the formula. Ceramic material concentrates, unlike feed stocks for metallurgical plants are used *in toto*, that is, what goes in stays in, and the waste material cannot be slagged off and removed once the final process starts. Any sacrifices of concentrate to upgrade the purity must be made *before* they are used ceramically.

THREE TYPES OF ORE

Processing rocks and minerals is very much like dealing with people; they all vary somewhat and their response to treatment is in direct relationship to the manner in which they are handled. Three distinct types of raw ceramic material are illustrated in Figure 3.4. While all three will have to be crushed, ground, and beneficiated to some extent, the approach to the treatment of each differs markedly. It is critical in all beneficiation and processing procedures to understand as fully as possible what you can expect from any upgrading that you do. In the three examples given here the end products have little resemblance to each other if the same fineness of particle size is ignored.

The disseminated chromite ore is typical of much metal oxide ore. Mineral grains of various sizes are strewn throughout the matrix, often in a heterogeneous manner. Primary crushing may separate some of the larger chunks of mineral but much of the finer-grained material remains locked up in even the smaller pieces. The illustration (1) shows the incipient fractures which open up when the ore is crushed. Clearly hand-sorting will neither upgrade the original ore very much nor be very saving of the metal content. The second problem involves the chemical nature of the chromite crystal itself. The mineral chromite is composed of a molecule of chromic oxide, Cr_2O_3, and iron oxide, FeO, of which the chromic oxide amounts to about 68 percent of the weight. From this it is apparent that even if the ore is concentrated to the point where no waste is left, the metal content cannot be more than that figure. Actually, due to the fact that

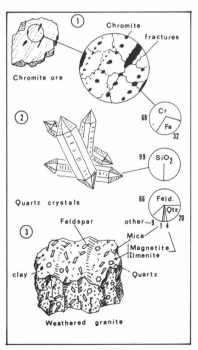

Figure 3.4 *Three types of ore.*
(1) Disseminated; (2) pure crystals;
(3) Mixture of coarse crystals.

some of the Cr_2O_3 in the chromite crystal may undergo an exchange with either iron or aluminum when it is crystallizing, the available chromic oxide may be far less. Since practically every chromite deposit in the country has been investigated and reported on, the purity of the ore when concentrated can be determined. Essentially the same information is available for all other metal oxide deposits.

The second mineral consists of a group of very pure quartz crystals. Simple washing in conjunction with crushing and grinding should be all that is required to produce a maximum purity product. Inevitably there will be trace amounts of some other elements but these should pose no real ceramic headaches. Water-clear crystals of calcite, a mineral composed of calcium carbonate, are often chemically quite pure, as are several other non-metallic mineral crystals. Beware this same platitude when it comes to feldspars, however. Although the individual crystals may be of almost theoretical purity, it cannot be assumed that all feldspars are alike. They aren't. A quick look at the glaze minerals listed in the Appendix shows that there are numerous feldspars, with a variety of compositions. Feldspar is a wastebasket term that is useful in many instances, but for ceramic materials the identity of the individual mineral could be important. Feldspars as a group are almost a complete glaze formulation in themselves and if a batch of the mineral, gathered from a certain point works well, stick with it, even if you can't identify the specific feldspar mineral.

Unbuttoning a Rotten Rock

The third example is really a rock rather than a mineral, but it contains several potentially useful ingredients, namely quartz, magnetite, ilmenite, clay, and a feldspar.

The rock is a deeply weathered granite in which some of the feldspar has degenerated to clay. Because it is quite rotten, crushing and grinding will be easy. Since you are dealing with a veritable super-market filled with useful minerals you will be as busy as a juggler trying to keep any of the goodies from going down the drain. Some careful planning will be necessary and you will probably need a lot of extra buckets. Here is a general plan of attack, although variations, based on individual needs and conditions, are many.

After primary crushing pick out as much of the feldspar as possible. If the quartz crystals are large enough, sort them out also. Crush the feldspar and quartz separately and pan to remove impurities. After secondary crushing of the remaining material remove any magnetic fraction and then pan, saving all of the wash water in a tub or large bucket. This panning should eliminate both quartz and feldspar that was not removed by sorting earlier, plus mica and some clay, leaving ilmenite in the pan. Now gently stage-grind your mixture of quartz and feldspar which you have retrieved from the washtub by screening. At this point the tub should contain a slurry of clay and some mica, plus a small amount of other minerals. These will be dealt with in good time.

Wet grinding is probably best for the quartz-feldspar fraction since the slightly softer feldspar can be continuously removed. Avoid grinding too fine at this point. If grinding in the wet way, add a bit more water along with the feed than you would normally. This will flush the material through the mill more rapidly. If dry grinding, screen the batch frequently. Should you be able to use a mixture of quartz and feldspar in your formulation then there is no problem at all, just grind them together. No practical method exists for making a perfect separation of quartz and feldspar in your formulation then there is no problem at all; just grind them together. No practical method exists for making a perfect separation of quartz and feldspar under studio conditions, so after you have recovered as much feldspar and quartz as practicable, discard the rest.

Any films of clay that might have been clinging to the feldspar crystals have by now been washed or ground off and all of it should be in the wash tub. The mica, most of it at least, can be removed by filtering the wash water through your finest screen. You will also catch any non-clay grains at the same time. The clay slurry can now be allowed to settle a bit before decanting and drying. You may wish to grind the ilmenite fraction, which had been left from the panning operation earlier, down to only the –40 +60 range to act as "seed" in combination with rutile glazes.

The composition percentages for the weathered granite shown in the "pie chart" should not be taken as the standard for all granites. Granites not only have a fairly wide range of percentages of the various minerals in their make-up but the degree of weathering directly affects the amount of clay derived from the feldspar. Deeply weathered granites may eventually become mostly clay. If you decide to take a granite apart there are two things that make the job easier: (1) pick the coarsest-grained granite that you can find; and (2) find the most weathered specimens possible. After that it is simple.

Constructing a Wall Flowsheet

You may have found the above discussion about unbuttoning a chunk of weathered granite somewhat confusing. Here is a suggestion that may make things easier and more understandable. On your studio wall hang a rather large piece of wrapping paper. On a 3×5 file card jot down the weight of your raw material and list the minerals you can identify in it. Tape the card at the top center of your big sheet. Keep adding cards for every step in your beneficiation process, recording what you did (such as "hand crushing", "panning",) together with the fraction ("feldspar", "quartz") and the weight. Arrange the cards on the sheet and add heavy lines from one card to another with a felt-tip pen. Figure 3.5 is an example of what your wall flowsheet should look like.

If you make up a wall flowsheet you will be able to keep track of your operation, and can use the figures to construct your metallurgical balance (see Figure 3.3) and update it at every stage. Study the results after each step and decide what you are going to do next. There is no sense in laying out a beneficiation program and following it blindly through to the bitter end when changes in mid-flowsheet are clearly indicated by the metallurgical balance you are developing.

When you have finished with your program make a page-sized replica of your wall flowsheet and file it away together with the 3×5 cards for further reference.

Know Your Minerals

Before you start your own beneficiation program for some raw mineral that you want for glaze material, make sure that what you are about to polish up a bit is really what you think it is. If in any doubt about the identity of a specimen either check it out with one of the numerous excellent mineral identification books that are readily available. (a list is included in the Bibliography but there are many others just as good), or lug it down to your friendly state geology department for an identification.

There are several good signposts to help you in your search for metallic minerals. First, they are almost always considerably heavier than common rock. Second, high-grade ore minerals look like a million bucks. They make you feel good just to hold them in your hand. Low-grade or disseminated (salt and pepper looking) ores are tougher to figure out since individual grains or crystals may be so small that identification by other than an expert is difficult. Here a gold pan is handy. Crush the sample, wash it carefully in your pan and then take a hard look at what is left in the bottom of the pan. The concentrate should resemble the solid ore fairly closely.

For non-metallic minerals such as quartz, calcite, and feldspar the search is simplified since all of them are excellent crystallizers. Size of individual crystals may range from tiny specks to many inches across. Color is no real help, quartz may be water-clear, cloudy, or many colors, calcite likewise. Feldspars tend to have characteristic colors but still may vary. Albite and anorthite are usually white but may be colored also. Orthoclase may be white but is typically a distinctive flesh color. Mineral crystals are usually very pure and should require no beneficiation other than hand-sorting, reduction to proper size, and a quick rinse.

BENEFICIATION AND PROCESSING

Hand-Sorting

Hand-sorting ore from an old mine dump or from your own prospect is the simplest and most useful beneficiation step in the entire up-grading program. It takes a bit of hand, brain, eye coordination practice, but once you get the hang of it, the job goes along speedily. You can soon tell by the color, lustre, cleavage or fracture whether the lump is waste or ore. At the same time your hand hefts the lump and either confirms your visual appraisal or refers the whole matter to your brain for binding arbitration. A bucket of water in which to dunk doubtful specimens is most helpful. A nice, clean and wet rock is a lot easier to identify than a dusty or muddy one. The real pros only dunk half of a rock — keeping their hand and glove dry. You'll be glad you did by the end of the day.

If you are sorting rather small pieces, it is best to wash the whole works first. Use a fairly heavy mesh screen and dunk small quantities at a time in a tub or bucket, or hose them off with a fairly strong spray. If you toss the washed rocks on a flat surface, they will drain quickly and can be sorted readily while still damp. One last suggestion on hand-sorting. If you can possibly avoid sorting reddish or brownish ores in the late afternoon, do so. The late afternoon light tends to be heavy on the red side and it imparts a bothersome filtering effect when red-brown colors are involved. The same holds for painting red barns and houses. It's amazing how many skips you can make in that beautiful sunset light.

Here are two flowsheets (Figs. 3.5, 3.6) of suggested steps to take if you decide to beneficiate either soft or hard minerals for use in a glaze formula.

See the Appendix for a list of glaze minerals and their Mohs hardness values.

Primary Crushing

After you have hand-sorted the good ore from the waste, bring the good ore to your studio for the next step. The first thing you should know is that there seems to be no easy way to have the ores that you have obtained in the field yourself reduced to the requisite fineness by commercial grinders. The reasons are quite obvious when you stop to think about it. Most commercial mills usually grind for their own account and their equipment is designed for their purposes. Custom grinders can grind material to their customer's specifications but the minimum volumes that they handle on any run are far and away above the maximum quantities that an art potter, or group of potters would be likely to have at any one time. It isn't the actual grinding that fouls things up, it's the set-up and cleaning of a lot of materials-handling equipment that kills the deal.

Crushing of minerals is a fairly straightforward operation. Like the old convict joke "It's making little ones out of big ones". Figure 3.7 outlines the various options available for crushing small (5 pounds) and medium (up to 50 pounds) quantities of both soft and hard ores that must be reduced to powder in either an iron-free, low-iron, or high-iron state. "Soft" ores are here defined as

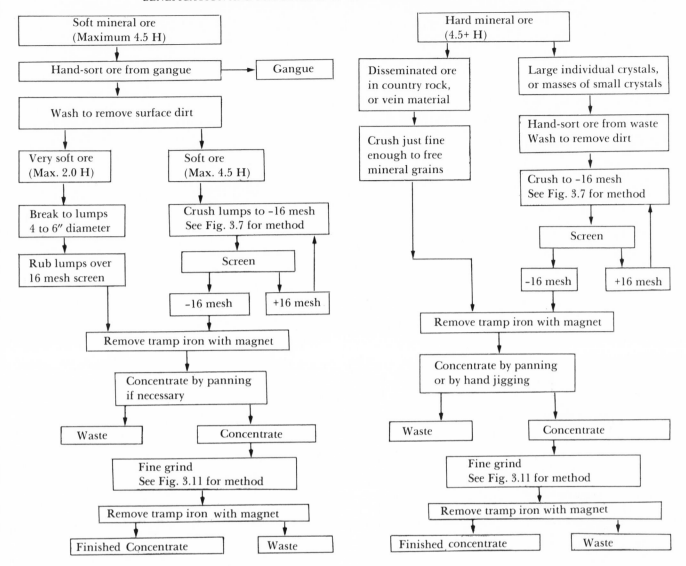

Figure 3.5 *Flowsheet for beneficiating soft minerals.*   **Figure 3.6** *Flowsheet for beneficiating hard minerals.*

having a maximum Mohs hardness (see Appendix 3) of 4.5 and "hard" ores, anything above 4.5. The designation "low-iron" has been arbitrarily set at one percent Fe_2O_3 maximum, which will satisfy some and deeply offend others, but no figure will make everybody happy.

Let's take a look at just what can be done in the studio to pulverize solid lumps of ore until they become powder. If your lumps of ore are large they should be broken up with a miner's pick into pieces not over six inches in diameter. You may wish to do this outside, since you will need a lot of clearance overhead for a full swing with a pick.

Once the larger lumps have been broken up, the two or three pound pieces remaining may be further reduced by striking with a square-faced geologist's hammer, or stone mason's hammer. The blows should be directed at a point near an edge and the force of the blow should be away from the center of the mass so that a chipping and spalling action results. This can often best be accomplished by holding the lumps in one hand and using short, quick blows with the hammer held in the other. The fragments resulting can then be cracked by direct blows into even smaller sized pieces.

During the primary reduction process you should keep a sharp lookout for any

		IRON-FREE	LOW-IRON	HIGH-IRON
SMALL QUANTITIES	Under 4.5 Hardness	(1) Break up chunks of ore with miner's pick into 6 to 8 inch lumps (Rub ores with a maximum hardness of 2, over 16 mesh screen) (2) Crush with hammer into one-half inch maximum size pieces **For ores having a hardness of 2 to 4.5** (3) Crush between iron-free stones to -16 mesh (4) Remove any tramp iron with magnet		(3) Crush between any tough and hard stones to -16 M.
	Over 4.5 Hardness	(1) Break up with miner's pick and sledge into 4 inch lumps (2) Crush with hammer and chisel into one-quarter inch pieces (3) Crush between iron-free stones to -16 mesh (4) Remove any tramp iron with magnet		(3) Crush between any tough and hard stones to -16 M.
MEDIUM QUANTITIES	Under 4.5 Hardness	(1) Break up with miner's pick into 6 inch lumps (For ores with a maximum hardness of 2, rub lumps over 16 mesh screen) (2) Crush with hammer into one-half inch pieces (3) Remove any tramp iron with magnet		(3) Crush with large roller on steel plate to -16 mesh (4) Remove iron with magnet
	Over 4.5 Hardness	(1) Break up with miner's pick or sledge into 4 inch lumps (2) Crush with hammer and chisel into one-quarter-inch pieces (3) Remove iron with magnet		(3) Crush with large roller on steel plate to -16 mesh

Figure 3.7 *Methods for crushing minerals having various hardnesses and iron content.*

gangue that might be exposed by the new surfaces developed. Although individual, solid crystals of a mineral are usually quite pure, some ores are composed of many small crystals which have grown together, often trapping non-ore materials in their midst. Hand-sorting, by picking out the ore crystals before fine grinding, is relatively easy and one of the best ways to up-grade the quality of your ore.

A good, sturdy, and fairly heavy chunk of rock makes an excellent anvil upon which to crush your material. Obviously this is not always a convenient way to go in the shop, but out in the field you can often reduce your raw ore quite readily in this manner. Many laboratories where minerals and ores have to be reduced by sledging resort to a section of log about 18 to 24 inches long and from 10 to 18 inches in diameter for an anvil base. Usually the up-ended section of log is capped with a heavy iron or steel plate an inch or so thick. It is amazing how much shock a chunk of wood like this will absorb. Some shops wrap a sheet metal guard around the top of their log-anvils, leaving one side open for the sledge and for sweeping off the fines. The guard extends above the top of the log about six inches and greatly restricts the broken materials from flying all over the shop. A length of old garden hose about four feet long can be hairpinned around chunks of rock to hold them in position. This beats using your hand. If the tenants in your building object to the racket from your crushing try slipping several layers of insulating wall-board under your log or rock anvil — or do your crushing after-hours when the neighbors have left the building.

Just how fine you should crush your ore during the sledging, or primary stage depends on what type of grinding equipment will be used in the secondary stage. In general the hard ores should be crushed finer than the soft ones. Ores that must be reduced to fines in an iron-free or low-iron condition should not be crushed with iron or steel tools any more than necessary. Ores where iron is no problem can be crushed much finer. Since the effort to crush smaller pieces diminishes rapidly it makes little sense to use the same eight pound sledge that was used to break up a twenty pound chunk to smash up pieces to a half-inch size or less.

Before proceeding with secondary crushing and grinding a strong magnet should be passed over the crushed material to remove any tramp iron. The ore should not be lying on a metal plate during this operation, since any tramp iron would cling to the plate rather than the magnet. This is also a good time to remove any pieces of gangue that may have appeared during crushing. It might also pay to wash your ore to remove dust and dirt introduced during processing. An easy way to accomplish this step is to place the crushed material on a quarter-inch mesh screen held over a bucket. Any fines washed into the bucket can then be saved and panned along with your fine ore at the end of the secondary grinding stage.

A word or two about safety before leaving primary crushing. Many ores and minerals are quite hard and brittle. When striking them with a sledgehammer directly or with a hammer, and either a moil or chisel, great care must be taken to guard against flying chips and pieces of rock. Wear shatter-proof goggles or an industrial type face mask, and heavy gloves and clothing. Do not at any time use a regular carpenter's claw hammer to pound either on the ore or on a heavy chisel or moil. Carpenter's hammers are not designed for this type of service and chips may fly off from the face. Use instead either a geologist's or miner's pick, a ball pein hammer, with or without a chisel, a four pound, short-handled sledge called a "single jack", or a long-handled, eight pound sledge called a "double jack". Ordinary cold chisels used by mechanics or somewhat heavier ones made especially for mining purposes can be used. Keep the burr that forms on the head of the chisel ground off since pieces of the metal tend to fly off from time to time when struck and the rough edges of the mushrooming cap can also inflict cuts through careless handling.

This brings us to the end of the primary reduction stage and the beginning of the secondary crushing activity. Up to this point your ore is probably still readily identifiable since individual pieces are large enough to retain recognizable characteristics. Once secondary crushing begins, however, it will be difficult to tell one ore from another since they will become too fine and will look very much alike. Be sure to label each batch of ore carefully, and keep a record of what it is, where it came from, any analyses of its metal content and other pertinent information.

Secondary Crushing

VERY SOFT ORES

Very soft ceramic materials (up to Mohs hardness of 2) can be reduced to a fineness that is either directly usable or ready for fine grinding in one operation. Talc and typsum, with a Mohs hardness of 1 and 2 respectively, are examples of material that you may wish to incorporate into a glaze formulation some day. Such minerals, having a maximum hardness of 2, can be rubbed over a board covered with ordinary steel fly screen. Any oversize material left on the screen can be readily crushed to the proper size by rolling as described in the section on soft ores which follows.

SOFT ORES

Soft ores (Mohs hardness of 2 to 4.5) present few problems and the emphasis here should be on the ease with which the work can be done, keeping in mind the amount of iron that can be tolerated in the finished product. After the primary crushing has been done and pieces about half an inch or less in size have been produced there are several ways to go. If a smooth surface, such as a concrete floor or wood floor that can be covered with a steel sheet about one-quarter of an inch thick and approximately three feet square is available, the ore can be crushed by using a water-filled or concrete-filled steel lawn roller. This method is quick and dirty, not recommended when iron-free materials are required. Ores crushed by this method should have a strong magnet passed over them, particularly for the first few times that the steel roller and plate are used since inevitably much loose iron scale will be dislodged. The ore must, of course, not be left on the metal plate when the magnet is used.

Here is a neat trick when using a magnet. Before you start, carefully wrap your magnet in a small piece of plastic kitchen wrap. When you are through simply strip off the wrap and all the iron goes with it.

Frequent screening of your ground ore will speed the work and lessen the effort involved as further crushing is required for only the larger lumps. If a lawn roller is not available you can make a crusher by filling a five gallon pail with concrete.

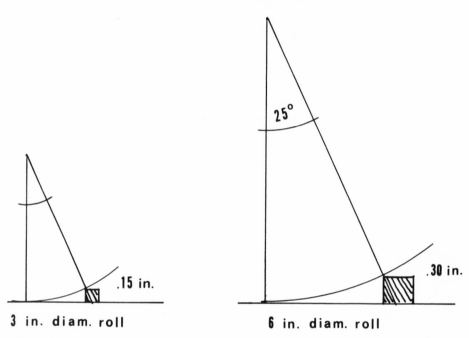

3 in. diam. roll   **6 in. diam. roll**

Figure 3.8 *The size of a particle best suited for roll crushing varies directly with the diameter of the roll. Optimum nip angle is about 25°.*

A pipe inserted through the ends of the pail will serve as an axle. Other alternatives, such as a section of pipe, shafting, or any cylindrical object that is harder than the material to be crushed, can be used.

In choosing the size of roller you use always match the maximum-sized particle to be crushed to the size of the roller. Figure 3.8 illustrates the problem. The most efficient angle of contact, or nip angle, is approximately 25 degrees. If a six inch diameter roller is being used, then the maximum-sized piece to be crushed should not be over about one-quarter of an inch across. Lump and roller size vary directly, so with a three inch diameter roll particles half as big (one-eighth of an inch) as those used with the six inch roll can be crushed most efficiently. The minimum roll diameter:particle size ratio should not be less than 24:1.

For larger quantities of crushed, soft, iron-free mineral the use of a stoneware vessel such as a pickle jar ten or twelve inches in diameter and weighted with damp clay might do the trick. Two people, rolling the jar between them over the crushing floor, will speed the production without having to resort to some pivot or axle arrangement for solo crushing.

Once you have reduced your ore to one-eighth of an inch or less in size you may find it more convenient to transfer your operations to a bench. Here a metal sheet measuring about 10 by 20 inches and at least an eighth of an inch thick can be fastened to a piece of three-quarter inch plywood and attached to the bench, leaving, if possible, an overhang of about an inch at both ends for slipping a shallow pan or heavy plastic sheet under to catch the fines when you are ready to screen. Short sections of steel shafting, or steel pipe filled with lead, can be used to complete your crushing on the bench. Do not use galvanized pipe since zinc will wear off and contaminate the ore.

HARD ORES

In principle, the secondary crushing of hard ores (those having a Mohs hardness of 4.5 or greater) is done in much the same manner as was described for the soft ores. However, the greater hardness poses several problems.

First, the Mohs scale of hardness numbers give little hint of the true difficulty of crushing the ore. A mineral with a hardness of 2, such as talc, can be scratched readily with your fingernail, while quartz, hardness 7, will scratch glass and steel. In addition, some minerals, although hard, tend to be brittle or cleave readily but most are exceedingly tough and cleave poorly.

The second difficulty is that hard minerals limit the implements that can be used to crush them.

At each stage in their treatment hard minerals must be reduced to finer sizes than the soft ores and the preferred method is by striking quick, sharp blows which induce spalling and shattering. Efforts to crush hard ores by abrasion methods will quickly wear away the surfaces of the equipment and also introduce disproportionate amounts of unwanted tramp iron or other contaminants.

The use of commercial jaw crushers or rolls for crushing chunks of very hard minerals which must be prepared in either an iron-free or low-iron condition should be avoided. Very hard minerals such as quartz can shave off bits of metal from the mill surfaces. This tramp iron cannot be removed with the aid of a magnet since the wear surfaces are almost always made of manganese steel which is non-magnetic.

Hard minerals which occur as disseminated grains in the rock should be released by crushing the ore just fine enough to free the individual grains. This operation is conducted in conjunction with concentration which is discussed in the following section. Frequent screening should be done to save unnecessary crushing and equally importantly, give you a little break from rather strenuous activity.

After breaking up the larger chunks with a sledge or miner's pick to lumps not over four inches in diameter, further reduction can be done with a moil or heavy chisel and single jack. All of the pieces at this point should be able to pass through a quarter-inch mesh screen.

Iron-free ores should be crushed to -16 mesh between iron-free stones, using one of the methods described under "Historic Hand-Grinding Devices" in the Appendix.

Low-iron ores can be crushed with the same equipment, or with stones having only minor amounts of iron-bearing minerals. High-iron ores can be crushed between any tough, hard stones. The –16 mesh product from all three of these operations should be treated with a magnet to remove any grains of magnetite.

This completes your primary and secondary crushing operations. Your ore is now ready for either some additional reduction in grain size or concentration.

Concentration

At this point some decisions on how to proceed must be made. If your ore, which is now reduced to one-sixteenth of an inch or smaller, is sufficiently pure for your purposes, then fine grinding is the next step and it is discussed in the following section. Purity of the ore can usually be determined by visual inspection, aided with a 14 power hand lens. Any impurities should be easily visible, since the contrast between ore and waste minerals is usually marked. If impurities are present they may occur as whole grains of unwanted material, or you may have grains which are composed of two minerals, one ore and one waste. If whole grains of waste are mixed with whole grains of ore then concentration is indicated. If, on the other hand, there are many two-mineral grains, or hybrids, then finer crushing is needed to separate as many of them as possible before concentration. Figure 3.9 is a flowsheet of these operations.

Mineral concentration is the up-grading of a raw ore by various procedures which remove unwanted minerals. The end product is called a concentrate. The unwanted fraction is variously referred to as "tails", "tailings" or simply "waste". The original ore is called "heads", or sometimes "feed-stock".

Concentration methods are many and varied, but here only hand-sorting, panning, jigging, and magnetic separation will be considered. The basic concept of concentration is to take advantage of differences in the physical properties of the minerals found in an ore and to use these differences to effect a concentration of the mineral sought.

Concentration is your last chance to upgrade your ceramic material before you use it in the studio, so perform the various steps with great care.

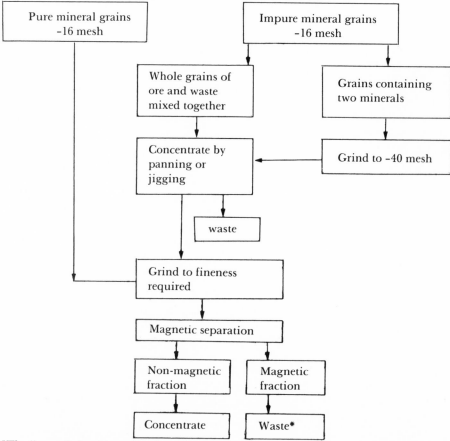

*The "waste" should consist of nearly pure magnetite which may be useful in achieving special effects in ceramic bodies.

Figure 3.9 *Flowsheet for processing ores from –16 mesh to powdered concentrate*

WASHING AND PANNING

If your ore was reasonably pure when you started to crush it the chances are that a simple washing to remove junk introduced during the crushing is all that is required. Such material is usually lighter than the ore and will either float off or can be washed away easily when placed in a prospector's gold pan.

If you are uncertain about how to use a gold pan take a look at the short description in the Appendix. A gold pan is simplicity itself but the combined factors of gravity, centrifugal force and hydraulics perform a near miracle in separating minerals having slight differences in specific gravity.

The pictures always show the old prospector squatting beside a stream with his gold pan tipped into the water and his rifle handy by. It is less romantic but infinitely more comfortable to use a tub or large dishpan half full of water and a low stool. With practice you can pan a batch of ore in a few minutes. Save your concentrate from each panning and then repan the combined concentrate to make sure you have it clean.

If, on the other hand, your ores contain a mixture of materials, some of which are not desired in the final product, several methods can be used to concentrate the ore you want. Perhaps a very careful panning will make the required separation, or will separate a fair amount of usable material, and leave a mixture of ore and waste in the wash bucket. This unsorted material should be ground a bit finer and panned again since the grinding will break up any hybrids present.

HAND JIGGING

For larger quantities of ore than can conveniently be handled by panning you can resort to hand jigging. In its simplest form hand jigging requires only a tub of water, a circular testing sieve and a small scoop. Hand jigging is performed by moving, with the sieve partly filled with ore and held partly submerged in the water, in an up-and-down motion. A short, quick down-stroke is followed by a somewhat slower up-stroke. Keep the top rim of the screen above the surface of the water. After several strokes the heavier ore fraction will have settled to the bottom of the sieve and the waste material can then be scooped off. If you do not have a testing screen you can make a crude frame 10 to 12 inches square and about 3 inches deep. Cover one end with screen supported by half-inch mesh hardware cloth or wires.

After you have jigged all your ore, clean up your jig concentrates in the gold pan. If you are working with either iron-free or low-iron materials, dry them thoroughly, spread thinly on a non-metallic surface and once again run a powerful magnet over them. Undersize jig feed will pass through the screen in the bottom of your jig and collect in the wash tub or bucket. These fines can be collected and panned when your jigging is completed.

The optimum screen size will depend upon the grain size of the jig feed. The screen mesh should be smaller than the feed, but not too much so, since good jigging action depends upon a forceful uprush of water with each down-stroke, and very fine screens tend to hinder this movement.

Screening

Screening is a time-consuming operation and one that must be done with a considerable amount of care. Done properly, screening will reduce the amount of effort required in crushing and grinding and produce a final product that consists of grains conforming to the size parameters that you have determined.

The screening of ores is more of a science than an art, though tricks learned by experience are most helpful. Screening is done for several reasons:

First, it removes material that has been crushed or ground to the required fineness by the reduction process.

Second, by removing this finely ground material, the cushioning effect between the grinding medium and the ore is reduced, thus making the grinding action more effective.

Third, by removing properly sized material from a mill or other grinding device, space is provided for adding fresh material to be ground.

Fourth, a rough separation may sometimes be made of the various minerals in an ore by virtue of their differences in hardness or original grain size.

Usually the objective of screening is to produce a product having a rather narrow specified range of sizes. For instance, you may require a ground material to simply be no larger than that which will pass through a 100 mesh screen (often written –100). On the other hand you may need a product that is –100 but no finer than that retained on a 270 mesh screen (–100 +270), or even a mixture consisting of 30 percent –80 +100, 40 percent –100 +150 and 30 percent –150 +270, with all of the over-size and under-size material being discarded. The need for such size fractions could arise from the discovery that the subtle differences in chemical composition of these screen sizes imparted special properties to a glaze formula, or that you required some closely controlled sizes of your ceramic material for special textural effects.

Screening, then, makes it possible to tailor your ground material to your specific needs. Remember, though, when you select certain fractions and discard others that you may be skewing the chemical, physical and ceramic characteristics of the original material. If you are working with pure, mineral crystals this effect is greatly minimized and the benefits of screening are negligible.

A range of sizes for ground quartz is an excellent example. Quartz is no stranger to ceramic mixes, where it may make up as much as 75 percent of the materials used in the manufacture of structural clay products, for instance. The size distribution of the quartz grains plays a role in the properties of the clay material. A clay body containing fine-grained quartz will require more clay to make a good body than a material that has quartz particles evenly distributed in a large number of sizes.

THE SCREENING PROCESS

The practice of screening, when properly done, imposes a certain discipline on all of the preceding grinding steps and equally importantly it makes it possible to prepare ground ceramic material that precisely meets your requirements. After going through all of the agony of crushing and grinding your ceramic materials, don't jinx the whole deal by skimping on the screening.

Basically, screening is simply an attempt to get a lot of irregularly shaped objects of various sizes squeezed through a hole that you have provided for them. The key word here is "opportunity". You must provide not only a lot of holes but a lot of opportunities for the particles to come in contact with those holes. This is where the art of screening comes into play. To provide the optimum opportunity for a particle-meets-hole situation a great deal of motion must occur.

The motion given to the screen or sieve during the screening process should be a combination of quick side-to-side movements and equally quick up-and-down motions. The latter can be accomplished by tapping the sieve rather smartly down on the bench or table top. A metal washer about half an inch in diameter, placed on the screen, speeds the work when using coarser mesh screens, but only a fibre washer should be used on very fine screens if at all. The sliding action of the washer greatly improves the screening action.

All this activity imparts a certain energy to the otherwise inanimate particles, and if enough opportunities are made available for those particles of the proper size they will fall through the holes. Problems arise when grains get hung up part way through. They effectively block the holes and reduce the number of opportunities for passage of the right-sized pieces. Here is where the sliding action of the washer solves the problem by sweeping them away. The brisk rapping on the bench-top either convinces the reluctant right-sized pieces to go on through or pops the oversize ones back up.

Once you have finished with any of your rather fine mesh screens it is a good idea to brush them lightly on both sides with a one-inch wide paint brush. This helps to remove any grains that might still be caught in the mesh and cleans the screens generally. Care in handling and storing the finer mesh screens is mandatory since the screen is easily damaged. Although minor repairs can sometimes be made it is usually impractical in the long run.

When screening very fine, dry materials there may be a problem with dust. Since finely divided materials can disperse widely, keep other ceramic products in the area well covered to avoid possible contamination. From a health standpoint a dust mask should always be worn when handling dusty substances.

SCREENING EQUIPMENT

There are a great variety of screens available and some thought should be given to the proper selection of your screening equipment. Screens are made from plain steel, stainless steel, galvanized steel, copper, brass, bronze, phosphor bronze, aluminum, neoprene and polyester. In addition to a wide range of space openings, there are choices in the diameter of the wires used in woven screens. Although most screens are woven it is also possible to buy punched and slotted plates made from brass, steel, stainless steel and aluminum.

Even though there is a wide spread in the cost of the various screens, your concern should be based on the service that you intend to put the screens to. For dry screening, the use of plain steel might be indicated, but for wet use only non-rusting metals or plastics should be employed. Very hard minerals will wear soft metal quickly and screens with harder wires should be used. If short runs are all that you anticipate, you can get by with the cheaper screens and toss them at the end of the project.

Equipment for sizing and screening ores includes a wide variety of items such as heavy woven wire screens with a mesh opening of half an inch or more, on down through hardware cloth of various meshes to fly screen, filter screen and standard testing sieves with meshes as fine as 325. Although a bit less durable than metal screens the use of women's nylon stockings has found its niche in the screening business. The nylon net often found as a household item is also useful. These last two items are somewhat limited as to the size of opening that they can cover, but given some support by means of metal screens, they can be very serviceable.

Commercially built screens or sieves (when of large diameter they are called riddles) are available in a variety of sizes and meshes and are quite expensive. They are designed primarily to provide a standard sizing mechanism for the size control and identification of material where precise particle size is critical. Standard testing sieves are available in two series, the Tyler Screen Scale and the U.S. Standard. The various meshes are listed in the Appendix. Figure 3.10 illustrates this type of screen.

For most art pottery uses it is not necessary to go to the expense of acquiring the commercial screens. Coarser meshes can be approximated by using ordinary hardware cloth readily available at hardware and most garden supply stores. Fly screen is made out of steel, bronze, aluminum and plastic and should serve adequately for screening material in the 16 mesh range. Finer screens can usually be purchased by the square foot from industrial suppliers (see "Screen Equipment and Supplies" in the telephone directory). These screens can be fitted into a

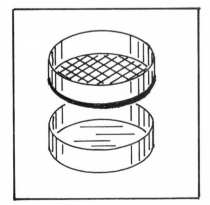

Figure 3.10 *A standard testing screen and pan.*

rough box made to suit your own needs, or attached to the bottom of an old pan, bucket or can. The finer screens may require additional support from coarser screens if the opening is very large. Years ago very fine materials were screened through woven cloths of fine weave, collectively referred to in the industry as "lawn". The modern equivalent is the nylon stocking and nylon net discussed above.

With a bit of imagination and some effort one can obtain a fair selection of screening material at little cost. First of all, figure out those industries that use screens in their processing. There are lots of them, and every one probably has some worn out, broken or outmoded screens that can be picked up for little or nothing and salvaged for your purposes. Here are a few suggestions for where you could look: Mineral concentration plants, rock crushers, flour mills, dairies, sewage treatment plants, paint manufacturers, canneries, manufacturers of air, water and oil filters, and many chemical processing plants. If you are not too proud, a visit to the local garbage dump and junk yard can be productive.

The actual opening between the parallel wires of screen fabric is called "space", or "clear opening". Size designations for screen openings are of two kinds. If a single figure, or fraction, is given in the "space" column in a listing, it refers to the net distance between the wires in both directions (for cloth with square openings). If two figures, such as 16×16 are given in the "mesh per lineal inch" column, the figures refer to the number of openings per running inch. These two systems can be confusing. For instance, a screen with a 1/16" space is equal to 0.0625", while a screen with 16 openings per inch equals 0.0345". The nearest equivalent to a 1/16" screen would be a 12×12 with an opening of 0.060.

Many screens are available in several diameters of wires for the same space opening mesh. Heavier wires give added strength and resistance to wear but reduce the net opening area. A 12×12 screen with 0.041" diameter wire has an open area of 25.4% while the same screen made with 0.060" wire has 51.8%. The cost per square foot varies directly with the diameter of the wire used, the larger the diameter the higher the price.

Screens are usually made to exacting standards, both as to quality of materials and workmanship, and the precision of the size of the openings. All screens should be handled and stored with care to protect the integrity of the size of the openings.

WET OR DRY SCREENING

Screening, like crushing and grinding, may usually be accomplished either wet or dry. If wet grinding and screening are done there will be a certain, inescapable amount of mud around. If you go the dry route then there is bound to be some dust. There are several points to consider before deciding whether it will be wet or dry screening. If you ground your ore wet then it makes good sense to wet screen. If your ore has any soluble elements in it then dry milling and screening are indicated. If the ore minerals are all insoluble, but some of the gangue is soluble, then you may effect a certain amount of beneficiation by wet grinding and screening. Wet screening is hard on steel screens and unprotected wooden frames but will not harm commercial brass frames and copper, bronze or stainless steel screens. Quite probably you may have to dry your wet-screened material, particularly if it is to be blended with other ingredients in a glaze formula. Almost certainly your wet ore upon drying will cake a bit and have to be run thru a sieve before you can use it. If you decide to screen dry, make sure that your ore is really dry.

UP-GRADING BY SCREENING

Although the screening process is normally conducted to sort grains on a size basis only, there are times when this operation will achieve a certain degree of separation based upon relative hardness of the grains. If the crushing or grinding is interspersed with frequent screenings, and there is a distinct difference in the hardness of the grains, it will be found that the softer fraction will be finer than the harder one. The separation will never be perfect but in some cases this method has its merits.

Separation of the various minerals in your ore by screening may also take place if there are rather wide variations in the original size of the mineral grains in the chunks of ore. Small grains of pyrite or magnetite, for instance, may be interspersed with much larger quartz and feldspar crystals. It may be possible, when crushing, to free the small grains from the mass without producing too many fines from the larger crystals. If the crushing and screening is done carefully, most of the small-sized grains will be sorted out without too much loss of undersize material produced from the ore minerals.

OTHER METHODS AND DEVICES

If you have the money and wish to acquire more sophisticated equipment for concentrating your ceramic materials, small laboratory scale concentrating equipment can be purchased new from supply houses. Alternatively you can scout around colleges and universities that once taught mining engineering, or old private mineral testing laboratories for out-dated or discarded equipment. Nearly all of the mining schools have closed and many of the assayers and laboratories catering to the mineral industry have folded. There must be some dust-covered concentrating equipment out there somewhere.

POLISHING

When the crystals of ore are coated or at least partly covered with waste material, you should use polishing techniques to concentrate the ore. After crushing the ore just fine enough to free most of the ore mineral crystals or grains from the rock matrix, place a suitable quantity of the ore in either a mill jar if the ore is iron-free, or in stoneware or steel gallon cans if the ore is low-iron or high-iron. Do *not* add any grinding media. Run the mill for an hour and inspect the contents. In most cases the tumbling action of the individual grains will rub off the soft "skin" which can then either be removed by dry screening, or rinsing with water. If all of the coating has not been removed at the end of the first stint of milling, you may wish to extend the milling time a bit and inspect the charge again. This procedure does not reduce the grain size appreciably but it does "polish" the grains and remove impurities.

Mill jars are laboratory-scale grinding devices made of porcelain or stoneware. They very much resemble stoneware pickle jars but are commonly only a few inches in diameter and six to eight inches long and are equipped with tight-fitting lids. See the section on "Iron-free Grinding" and "Mill Jars and Stoneware Jars" a little farther on in this chapter.

Occasionally you may encounter a mineral that is coated with calcium carbonate, which is the principal ingredient in the mineral calcite and limestone. If polishing in a mill fails to remove the calcium readily you can leach the coating away by immersing the crushed ore in a bath of weak (50 percent) hydrochloric acid. Warm the bath slightly to speed up the chemical action. The chemical reaction of the acid on the calcite will produce bubbles. When the bubbles stop coming to the surface, one of two things has occurred. Either the calcium carbonate is all gone or the acid has been neutralized. An inspection of the mineral grains will determine which has happened. If the acid has been neutralized repeat the process until the calcium carbonate is removed. Wash the ore thoroughly in several pans of fresh water before proceeding with your ore treatment.

Fine Grinding

Fine grinding is the next step in the beneficiation and processing program. At this point your concentrate should be reasonably free of impurities and in the -16 to -40 mesh size range. Other than the removal of tramp iron, there will be little opportunity for further concentration and your objective is to reduce the grain size to meet your requirements as efficiently as possible.

During the preceding crushing and concentration of your ore you have inevitably produced a certain amount of fines. Set them aside for the time being and incorporate them with the finely ground material when you have completed your grinding. Individual sieve fractions rarely have the same chemical, physical, and ceramic properties that the entire concentrate has. See the section on "Mixing and Blending" for further information.

WET OR DRY GRINDING?

The choice between grinding wet or dry depends upon several factors: (1) dry grinding is usually preferred if iron-free materials are required since the removal of tramp iron with a magnet is almost impossible with damp concentrates (but see "Separating magnetic fines"); (2) grind dry if there is the possibility that wet grinding may pick up some iron in solution from tools, utensils and other ferrous objects used in the grinding process; (3) low-iron or high-iron materials can be ground wet unless they are soluble in water or, (4) develop an electrolytic action when in contact with metal utensils. Dry grinding tends to produce some dust; wet grinding involves a fair amount of water and can get a bit messy.

Before you start fine-grinding your concentrate it is best to plan ahead and determine whether you will grind wet or dry all the way through. Remember that you will be screening at intervals and this will have to also be done wet or dry to match your milling style.

DRY GRINDING

Fine grinding can be done either wet or dry, but for small batches doing it dry seems preferable since less equipment is needed. If you decide to grind dry, then make sure your stock is *dry*. If it isn't then fine screens will "blind" and the surfaces of your grinder will tend to cake. Figure 3.11 indicates the possible methods available for iron-free, low-iron, and high-iron materials that are to be ground in small or medium quantities. The boundaries for the quantities are rather flexible but those for the amount of iron permissible are not. A few program notes to accompany the above chart are perhaps needed.

IRON-FREE GRINDING

Iron-free grinding can be accomplished either by using some age-old hand methods, or by employing modern hand-operated equipment or mechanical devices. The choice will hinge upon the amount to be ground, the availability of suitable stones for hand grinding, the amount of time and energy you wish to expend, and in the case of the mechanical equipment, the amount of money you have to commit.

The purity and quality of the end-product resulting from either approach will not be greatly different if reasonable care is taken at every stage of the operations. Iron is introduced into the finished product in three main ways: (1) iron-bearing minerals associated with the ore being ground; (2) iron-bearing minerals associated with the natural grinding stones, and (3) tramp iron introduced inadvertently during the crushing and grinding process. Some iron-bearing minerals, such as magnetite, are attracted to a magnet and may be easily removed after secondary crushing. Other iron-bearing minerals may, in the primary or second-

		IRON-FREE	LOW-IRON	HIGH-IRON
SMALL QUANTITIES	Under 4.5 H.	Remove any tramp iron with magnet Grind in porcelain, agate, or glass mortar and pestle Grind in mechanical muller equipped with mullite mortar and pestle		Grind in iron mortar Grind with iron buck board and muller Remove iron with magnet
	Over 4.5 H.	Remove any tramp iron with magnet Grind in porcelain, agate, or glass mortar, or use mill jars, or grind in mechanical muller equipped with mullite mortar and pestle		Grind in iron mortar Remove iron with magnet
MEDIUM QUANTITIES	Under 4.5 H.	Remove any tramp iron with magnet Finish reduction in battery of large mill jars	Grind in battery of mill jars or stoneware jars with lids Remove tramp iron with magnet	Grind in gallon cans with steel ball bearings
	Over 4.5 H.	Remove iron with magnet Finish reduction in battery of large mill jars	Grind in battery of large diameter stoneware or hand-thrown stoneware jars with lids	

Figure 3.11 *Methods for fine-grinding –16 mesh minerals having various hardnesses and iron contents.*

ary crushing stages, be removed by panning but once the particles are finely ground this is no longer possible.

Small quantities of iron-free mineral can be hand-ground in a standard laboratory mortar and pestle made of agate, glass, or porcelain. Also mechanical mullers equipped with a mullite mortar and pestle are available.

When using hand-held mortars and pestles be sure to apply a lot of pressure with a gently rolling motion. Note that the face of the pestle has a curvature slightly greater than that of the inside of the mortar. The rolling motion traps, or nips, the particles between the two surfaces, and with strong pressure they are further reduced in size. The use of a leather sail-maker's palm is suggested to protect your hand. Some pestles come equipped with wooden handles which afford a somewhat better grip.

Mortars and pestles made of agate, glass, or porcelain are both hard and tough but care must be exercised not to strike the mortar and pestle together or to drop them, since they may either spall or break.

When you start to grind some ore add only a little bit, grind it for a minute or two and then discard it. This will remove any contamination that may have remained from previous use. The equipment should be rinsed and dried immediately after use.

If you decide to grind slightly larger quantities you may want to take a look at the "Historic Hand-Grinding Devices" section in the Appendix. These cost little to make but require considerable amounts of energy to operate.

Larger quantities can best be ground in mill jars made of porcelain with tight-fitting lids and charged with porcelain grinding balls, or cylinders which are commercially available. An economical substitute for these cylinders is the old-fashioned porcelain electrical knob formerly used in home wiring. These

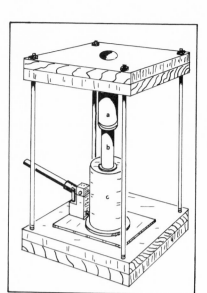

Figure 3.12 *Press for extruding ceramic grinding media cylinders; (a) pipe nipple threaded into pipe flange on underside of top; (b) wood dowel plunger; (c) hydraulic jack.*

cylindrical insulators are both hard and very low-iron. Look for them at flea markets, old houses and at garage sales.

Another source for low-iron or even iron-free grinding media is the porcelain salvaged from old-style plumbing fixtures. The sides of ceramic toilet tanks can be cut into rough cubes with the aid of a tile-cutter which can be rented from any do-it-yourself flooring or tile shop. The cubes will slowly wear away but they will be contributing only tiny amounts of silica and aluminum to your mix. It is suggested that you run your mill charged only with these cubes for half an hour or so to knock off the edges and corners, after which the attrition rate will be greatly reduced.

Some thought might also be given to forming your own grinding media. Although the composition of the media will be more or less dependent on the nature of the material to be fine-ground, the formulation should be such that no deleterious metallic elements are used that could wear off and contaminate the pulp. Figure 3.12 illustrates a device that could be built from readily available materials to extrude the ceramic cylinders from a section of steel pipe. The device consists of a stout framework to house a hydraulic, hand-pumped jack, and directly above it a heavy wooden top. A pipe flange is attached to the underside of the top and positioned directly beneath a hole leading to the center of the upper side. A length of steel pipe is threaded into the flange. Threaded rods support the top and also resist the thrust of the jack during extrusion. A hardwood dowel with a diameter just slightly less than the inside of the pipe is placed on the jack plunger and inserted into the lower end of the pipe.

The ceramic mix is rammed tightly into the pipe from above and the jack then pushes it out. The extruded cylinder is cut into lengths about 25 percent longer than its diameter. The diameter of the ceramic grinding cylinders depends on the size of the grains to be ground (see "Secondary Crushing" and Figure 3.8).

A BATTERY OF MILLS

A substantial quantity of material can be reduced in mill jars if a rotating device, capable of holding several mills, called a battery, is built. Figure 3.13 shows the general arrangement of the mills, rollers, and drive pulley. The central roller, driven by the large diameter pulley, turns both mills, one clockwise and one counter-clockwise. Diameters of the mills, rollers and pulleys will depend on your individual set-up. See Figure 3.16 for suggestions on producing proper rotational speeds, and the section on "Milling with Mill Jars" farther on in this chapter. In any event the rollers must be large enough to permit the mills to rotate without rubbing against each other.

The battery can be housed in a simple but sturdy wood rack which has bearing-holes in both ends to accept the stub axles of the rollers. A quarter-horse electric motor has sufficient power to turn the whole works.

Mill jars are available in sizes ranging from about three inches in diameter by six inches long up to fifteen inches by sixteen inches, and in capacity from half a pint up to six and a half pints.

When using this system, coarse ore is ground with relatively heavy grinding media in the first mill, ore partly reduced by the first mill is ground in the second mill with smaller media, and successively finer ore and lighter media are used in the remaining mills.

SEPARATING MAGNETIC FINES

The removal of finely divided particles of magnetite or tramp iron from ore that has been fine-ground may, like crushing and grinding, be done either wet or dry. For small quantities of dry material the small horseshoe-shaped alnico

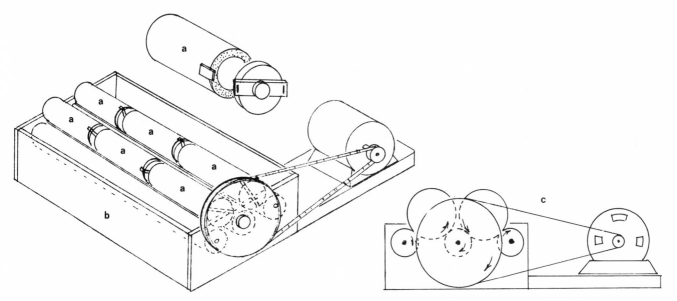

Figure 3.13 *A battery of mill jars. (a) mill jar with locking lid; (b) battery with six mill jars; (c) end view showing rollers, drive pulley, motor, and mills.*

magnet, wrapped in kitchen plastic film, can be used. Larger quantities will require somewhat more elaborate equipment to speed the work. Lengths of bar or rod magnets attached to a simple wooden or plastic frame can be used like a rake to stir the pile. If large quantities are to be treated the use of small-sized commercial electro-magnets, powered by direct current, are suggested. Large, powerful disc-shaped permanent magnets, or magnetic pulleys over which a thin belt passes, may also be used.

Wet slurries can be treated for the removal of magnetic particles in much the same manner as was outlined above for dry processing. As long as permanent magnets are used no special precaution need be observed. If a rack containing rod or bar magnets is used it can be rotated slowly while suspended in the bucket or jar containing the finely ground ore, or placed in the wooden trough through which the pulp is flowing from the grinding mill. An alternative method is to suspend the rack of magnets in the bucket and agitate the slurry mechanically for a period of time.

The use of electro-magnets is *not* recommended for wet processing unless industrial type equipment is used and elaborate precautions taken to avoid the shock hazard.

When using either the wet or dry method bear in mind that tiny particles of magnetic material may have a hard time fighting their way through the thick slurry or dust on their way to the magnet, so take your time, move the magnet slowly so that it passes quite close to every particle in the mass.

LOW-IRON GRINDING

Low-iron grinding of ores is performed in much the same way that iron-free reduction is accomplished. You can use the same equipment employed for iron-free grinding or, if you plan on using hand-operated grinding devices, you can have a much wider selection of stones since the presence of minor impurities, chiefly iron, can be tolerated. If you decide to use your grinding equipment for both iron-free and low-iron grinding be sure to carefully clean all of the working surfaces when you switch back to iron-free grinding. Furthermore, grind some ore to purge the equipment and toss it before you start a production run.

MILLING WITH MILL JARS

Low-iron ores can be prepared in the laboratory mill jars described above, but instead of using porcelain balls for the mill charge you may substitute quartzite or flint pebbles which are much less expensive. The pebbles need not be perfectly rounded since the abrasive action in the mill will tend to true them up and impart a polish of sorts to them. If the addition of silica poses no problem you might consider using some of the non-crystalline forms of quartz such as agate or chalcedony as your grinding media. With any kind of luck you will end up with your ore nicely ground to a fine powder and have a handful of polished semi-precious gemstones to boot.

The use of commercial laboratory mill jars for low-iron grinding, as suggested above, is not absolutely necessary. Inexpensive and reasonably simple covers for sealing regular stoneware jars or crocks can be devised which will act as a good substitute for commercial mill jars. You can adapt the old wood turner's trick of gluing two pieces of wood together with a sheet of paper in between. The object is to make certain that the contact between the rim of the jar and the underside of the lid is sufficiently tight to prevent material from escaping. First grind down the high spots on the rim of the jar with fine abrasive.

Now add your mill charge, and carefully wipe off the rim of the jar. Apply glue to the rim of the jar, place a paper ring on the glue and then add glue to both the upper surface of the paper and the contact area of the wood lid, pressing the lid down firmly. After a grinding run gently insert a thin knife blade into the edge of the paper and work your way around the rim. The paper will split apart after a bit, freeing the lid. If the lid proves stubborn dampen the glue line with water. Either the paper will weaken or the glue will soften, assuming that water-proof glue is *not* used.

Another method for affixing the jar lid is to drill a small hole in the center of the lid and another in the center of the bottom of the jar. Run a small bolt or threaded rod through the bottom hole up through the jar and through the hole in the lid. Some sort of gasket, fashioned out of an old truck tire inner-tube or automotive gasket material, can be used. After filling the jar, tighten the nut or nuts on the end of the rod and you are all set. If the two holes through which the bolt passes in the lid and jar bottom leak dust during the grinding operation they may be caulked. A small piece of chewing gum should suffice.

By now it has probably occurred to you that you can throw your own mill jars and pierce the bottom and lid before firing. This is the preferred route to travel since drilling stoneware does take a bit of time. Figure 3.14 illustrates the assembly arrangement of jar, lid, gasket, bolt and reinforcing plywood disc. Dimensions of the jars you thow are a matter of personal choice.

CHARGING AND OPERATING MILL JARS

Once you have your mill jars ready for grinding, you should pay rather close attention to the proper amount of material that you introduce into them, and equally importantly, the speed at which the jars will be rotated. You should keep careful records of the weights and kind of ore that you add to the mill, the weight and type of the grinding media, the time spent in grinding and the revolutions per minute of the mill jars. There are some well established parameters for the ratio of ore to grinding media, total mill charge, and the revolutions per minute of the mill, but you will undoubtedly have to fine-tune your own milling operation to produce optimum results and only good records will help you to do this.

Here are the general procedures for charging grinding mills and for determining proper speed of rotation. As a general rule you should add to your mill about two-thirds as much ore as grinding ball or pebbles. The ore should occupy

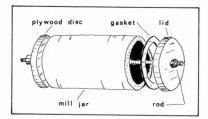

Figure 3.14 *Hand-thrown stoneware mill jar with lid-clamping device.*

approximately one-fourth the volume of the mill. Although there are obvious differences in the rate at which ores of different hardnesses will be reduced to the required fineness, this should have no bearing on the amount of ore placed in the mill. Too much or too little ore added to a mill has a great impact on the overall efficiency of the grinding operation. The variable will be in the amount of time required to effect the proper grinding.

The way to determine the proper amount is to calculate the volume of the jar in cubic centimeters, divide this figure by four and use it as the basis for the mill charge. A simple plastic or metal container can be made that will hold this volume when level full. The ore can then be weighed and entered in your records before it is placed in the mill. As has been mentioned earlier, all ores should be perfectly dry before attempting to grind and screen them.

Much research has been conducted on the proper speed of rotation for grinding mills. Actually the concern is more properly directed to the action of the material in the mill, which of course responds to the speed at which the mill is turning. The mill should revolve just fast enough to cause the contents to cascade down over the load as it creeps up the side of the mill. Too fast a rotation may cause the load simply to revolve with the mill due to centrifugal force. Too slow a motion and the load will climb up part way and then slip down as a mass, with no grinding action. Quite often you can tell when the mill is revolving properly by listening to the clicking sound of the balls hitting against each other as they run "down hill" — something like roulette. Since it is quite impossible to peer into a mill jar once the lid is in place, and since the speed of rotation is fairly critical, I suggest the following. Instead of affixing the regular mill jar lid, prepare a disc of heavy, rigid, water-clear plastic, drill a hole in the center to accommodate the bolt and use it as a temporary lid while you observe the grinding action in the mill.

Figure 3.15 gives four views of the end of a mill that is rotating at various speeds. In 'a' the mill is turning so slowly that the load merely climbs up the side of the mill and then slides down again with very little grinding action. In 'b' the mill is turning at the proper speed and the load is tumbling or cascading down over itself, crushing the ore with every bounce. In 'c' the mill is turning faster than it should and the load is climbing way up the side of the mill and free-falling, or cataracting, down to the bottom, performing less useful work then it did in 'b'. In 'd' the mill is rotating so rapidly that centrifugal force prevents any movement of the charge, hence no grinding.

To get your mill or battery of mills, operating at peak efficiency do this: (1) determine the speed at which the mill load will cling to the surface of the mill all the way around (as in Figure 3.14-d). When this point, known as the critical speed, is reached, there will be no noise coming from inside the mill; (2) reduce the speed to 60 percent of the critical speed; (3) grind for one hour, at the end of which time screen the ore and weigh the various fractions; (4) vary the speed by 10 percent, both faster and slower and repeat as in step 3. Somewhere in this range you should find an optimum rotational speed.

Adjusting the speed of rotation of the ball mill can be done in several ways. You can install a variable speed pulley on the motor that drives the belt to the rollers or attach a circular hardwood block to the face of a vee-belt pulley mounted on the motor shaft. Start the motor and, using regular lathe tools, turn a vee-belt groove in the block. If the pulley is too large, that is, it drives the mill too fast, turn it down to a slightly smaller diameter and test again. Eventually you will be able to get the speed just right.

An alternative method, or one that can be used in conjunction with the first method, is to attach a large diameter wooden pulley on the driven end of the belt. In this instance the pulley would have to be turned down to size either on a wood

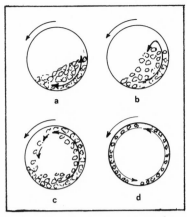

Figure 3.15 *End views of mill jars rotating. (a) too slow, with charge sliding; (b) properly, charge cascading; (c) too fast, charge cataracting; and (d) much too fast, charge held against mill with no grinding action.*

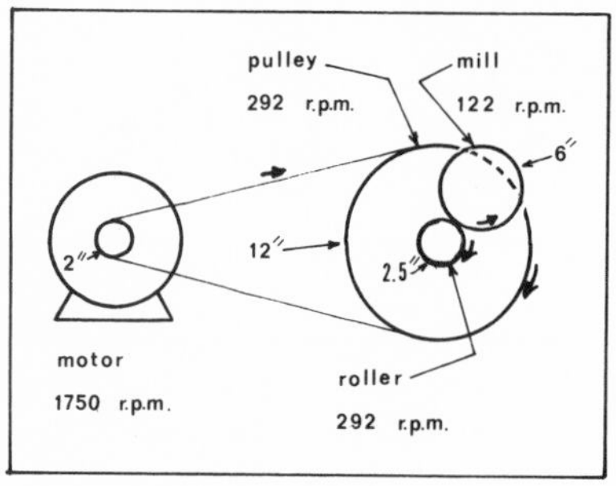

Figure 3.16 *Speed reduction by means of pulleys.*

lathe or temporarily attached to the motor pulley. The mathematical solution comes out this way: Divide the diameter of the drive pulley by the diameter of the driven pulley multiplied by the revolutions per minute of the drive motor equals the r.p.m.'s of the driven pulley. For example, you have an electric motor which turns at 1750 r.p.m. and is equipped with a two-inch diameter pulley. The driven pulley is 12 inches in diameter. Then:

$$\frac{\text{Diameter of drive pulley } 2''}{\text{Diameter of driven pulley } 12''} \times \text{r.p.m. of motor } 1750 = 292 \text{ r.p.m.}$$

The 12 inch pulley is solidly attached to the roller than turns the mill. The roller is 2½ inches and the mill 6 inches in diameter, so repeating the process we have:

$$\frac{\text{Diameter of drive pulley } 2.5''}{\text{Diameter of driven pulley } 6''} \times 292 = 121 \text{ r.p.m. for the mill.}$$

The final r.p.m. shown for the mill may not be the correct speed for your set-up but the diameter of each of the three pulleys can be changed to give the correct rotational speed. Figure 3.16 is a schematic of the arrangement discussed above.

The mill contents should be screened at intervals of about one hour to avoid over-grinding the ore and to reduce the cushioning effect of the finely powdered material. New ore is then added to replace the material removed.

OTHER GRINDING EQUIPMENT

If your ore is rather soft you might want to try a laboratory grinding mill which is a close cousin to the household meat grinder only it grinds finer and costs more. With much perseverance such a mill will grind about ten pounds of ore an hour. The next step up, both in cost and productivity, is a laboratory pulverizer mill which is actually a smaller hammer mill revolving at 10,000 r.p.m., accepts feed as coarse as one-quarter of an inch, and turns out a very fine-mesh product. It will grind approximately 50 pounds per hour, depending on hardness of the material.

HIGH-IRON GRINDING

Grinding ores, where the presence of iron creates no problem, can be done in several ways: (1) Small quantities can be reduced with the old-fashioned cast iron buck board and muller. This is an "armstrong" method but it works. Both the buck board and the muller are heavy and clumsy, but the ore does get smashed down in short order. (2) Gallon cans can be used for ball mills and steel shot, ball bearings, quartzite pebbles, or any hard lumps can be used for the ball charge. Gallon cans are the favorite medium used by rockhounds when they tumble semiprecious gems. Depending on the hardness of the ore to be ground and also on the quantity, you may elect to add to your battery of gallon can mills, using equipment described above for turning mill jars.

The preceding section on fine grinding has outlined some of the more common and easily achieved methods for reducing a variety of minerals. With the application of some ingenuity other systems for fine grinding can be devised, or improvements made on those now in use. The appearance on the market of new materials and equipment opens up new possibilities for processing ores that were undreamed of twenty years ago.

No matter which system for fine grinding you adopt or which material you happen to be grinding be sure that you grind *all* of the batch down to the requisite fineness. If you discard even a small over-size fraction you will most certainly alter the composition of the batch and make it difficult to match when you grind another later on. Unless you are contemplating a one time only use of the material you are grinding and have ground approximately what you will be needing you should mix each batch with the others until all of the material is ground. If this is done and careful rolling and quartering is adhered to each time you prepare a sample, then you are assured of the greatest possible uniformity for each sample.

WET GRINDING

Wet grinding has some advantages and some disadvantages when compared to dry grinding. The addition of water makes possible the removal of material that has been ground to the proper size even as the grinding process continues. With the use of water, new material to be ground can be added during the milling operation. Dry grinding, in contrast, is a batch process, requiring dismantling of the mill, emptying the charge, screening, and reloading. Much industrial grinding is done in the wet way since water provides a cheap and easily controlled transport mechanism throughout the entire milling operation. Other things being equal, it is probably more efficient to grind wet, but unless a considerable quantity of material is to be reduced, the tooling-up expense and effort will probably outweigh the savings. Material that is soluble in water cannot be ground wet and any ores that must be kept in either an iron-free or low-iron state cannot be wet ground in an iron or steel mill.

If the idea of wet grinding appeals to you and you have a studio where the presence of certain amounts of errant water and some mud will cause only minimal problems, the following suggestions may be helpful.

Since damp floors and electricity make for a deadly combination be sure that your electric motors are mounted where they will be dry and make certain that all are electrically grounded. Strange as it may seem, those ordinary vee-belts have been known to carry electric currents when threaded over a metal pulley mounted on a motor. Switches controlling motors and lights should be located in dry areas.

MILL-FEEDING MECHANISM

Figure 3.17 illustrates one method for introducing feed to a wet mill and for continuously removing material that has been ground. Note that the steel pipe used for holding the cover in place also serves as a supply pipe for the raw feed. Outside the back end of the mill a ¾″ to ½″ pipe reducer is threaded on the pipe and provides a shoulder to help in clamping the lid. A half-inch pipe nipple several inches long is threaded into the reducer and a 90 degree ell and another nipple about six inches long is added. The six-inch nipple (a) requires a closure at its end and a narrow V-shaped slot. This crank-like appendage is the automatic feeder which scoops up a little raw feed with each revolution. A suitable container is placed behind the mill and positioned so that the end of the "crank" just misses the bottom as it rotates. The size of the slot will have to be determined with experience. A small hose should be rigged to drop make-up water into the container to replace that removed by the feeder crank. The mill should rotate in a clock-wise direction, as viewed from the front end of the mill, to keep the pipe threads tight. A half-inch wide, V-shaped slot (b) cut in the pipe at a point just inside the back wall of the mill lets small amounts of feed drop in with every revolution. It will take a bit of cut-and-try to balance out the proper rotations for the mill, size of the feeder crank slot and the amount of make-up water.

At the discharge end of the mill a quarter-inch thick disc of plastic serves as a grate. A central hole, slightly over one inch in diameter, to take the three-quarter inch pipe, and several holes about an inch in diameter, and about one-half inch in from the periphery, are drilled. The latter holes are covered with a screen of the proper mesh size you want your ore, and mounted inboard. If the screen is quite fine it should be protected from the contents of the mill by one or more discs of heavier screen. A gasket may be required between the front rim of the mill and the cover, but small leaks are no real problem and usually seal themselves when

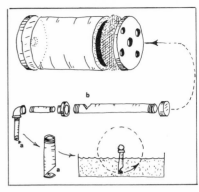

Figure 3.17 *Feeding device for mill jar. Feed enters notch at "a" as it passes through feed box, and discharges inside mill through notch "b". Screen "c" covers discharge ports.*

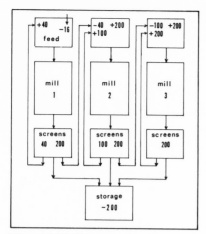

Figure 3.18 *Flowsheet for three mills running in tandem for stage grinding.*

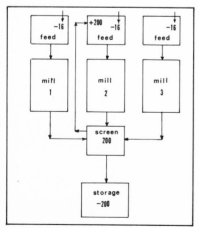

Figure 3.19 *Flowsheet for three mills running in parallel with common feed.*

grinding starts. A pipe cap, or some three-quarter inch lock-washers, such as those used on electrical conduits, provide the tightening mechanism for holding on the lid.

STAGE GRINDING

If you plan on operating several mills, so that you can stage-grind your ore, even greater efficiencies are possible, since baby-sitting several mills takes no more time than looking after one. Figure 3.18 shows a flowsheet where three mills are run in tandem for stage grinding. The product coming out of Mill #1 is washed over 40 and 200 mesh screens. The +40 mesh fraction is returned to the feed box for the #1 Mill, the –40 +200 mesh material is dumped into the feed box of the #2 Mill, and the –200 mesh pulp goes into the finished product storage container. The #2 Mill product is screened through 100 and 200 mesh screens, with the +100 mesh fraction returned to the #2 Mill feed box, the –100 +200 mesh material goes to the #3 Mill feed box and the –200 mesh pulp goes to storage. The #3 Mill's product is screened over a 200 mesh sieve and the +200 mesh material is recycled back to the #3 Mill feed box and the –200 mesh goes to storage. This flowsheet allows the removal of finished material at three points, preventing unnecessary over-grinding and making it possible to increase the amount of raw feed into the #1 Mill. The screen sizes shown in the flow sheet can, of course, be changed to suit your particular needs.

Figure 3.19 is a flowsheet of the same three mills but this time the "plumbing" has been changed a bit. Each mill has the same feed and their common product is screened through a 200 mesh screen. The +200 mesh material from all three mills is recycled into one of the mills, and the –200 mesh is sent to the storage container. The parallel arrangement may be more efficient than stage grinding if the feed material is already rather fine or the ore is soft and easily ground. You can switch easily from tandem to parallel, and back again if you find that one flowsheet is more efficient than the other. Three mills are shown in these flowsheets but there is no reason why you can't use only two or as many as half a dozen. Things get pretty complicated it the number of mills is more than three or four, however.

There is no law that says that all of your mills must be the same size. In fact, there may be good reason for using a larger #1 Mill in the tandem flowsheet since part of its output goes directly to storage and is not handled by the #2 Mill. In the parallel milling flowsheet the #2 Mill could also be the largest in the circuit since it handles the recycling load from all three mills.

Don't worry if the initial output from your mills has a considerable amount of oversized material. A fairly high recirculating load is standard practice for commercial grinding mills since it is more efficient than turning out a high percentage of finished product on the first pass. The theory here is that if most of the product has been ground to the proper size in the first trip through the mill there must be a lot of material that has been ground much too fine as well. The removal of finished material at the earliest opportunity should be a prime consideration in any fine-grinding operation.

Both of these flowsheets are very flexible. If one of the mills goes "down" for some reason or other, you simply by-pass it if you are tandem grinding, or ignore it when in the parallel mode.

When starting a stage-grinding operation get your coarse ore mill running smoothly first and begin collecting the feed for the second mill. Then get the second mill humming and you will have enough feed for it, and so on. Be sure to screen each mill's product and distribute the fractions to the proper containers.

Much labor and fuss and muss can be saved in handling slurries of finely ground material if use is made of some old water pumps salvaged from washing machines and dishwashers. For low pressure duty these pumps work well and since they have rather lenient space tolerances between impeller and casing there should be a minimum of blockages. It is a good idea, however, to pump clean water through the system when you have finished a run. Otherwise some of the material may dry and harden to something resembling concrete. Simple pinch clamps applied to neoprene tubing make good valves for regulating the flow of water or slurry. The pump impellers "slip" a lot anyway and constrictions in the line should have little or no effect on them. These pumps can also be most useful if you are grinding hard, flint-type clays. The finely ground material can be fed into a series of 5 gallon buckets and allowed to settle for a time. After the heavier and coarser fractions have gone to the bottom the suspended portion can be gently pumped off without disturbing the bottom layer.

Although water is usually a rather inexpensive commodity, it may prove economical in some cases to recycle it for your milling operations. Nothing more than a sump bucket to catch the overflow from your last unit and a pump and tubing to return it to the head end are required. Normally no settling period is needed before recycling since "dirty" water seems to work just about as well as sparkling clean water does.

Mixing, Blending and Sampling

The need for carrying a fairly large inventory of ceramic material that you have obtained in the field has already been discussed. Let us now consider how this finely ground material is to be handled so that you can use identical batches from it from time to time in the future. The practice of mixing, blending and sampling of ores has a long history and most of the problems have been resolved.

The terms mixing, blending and sampling need, perhaps, to be defined.

Mixing is the thorough intermingling of material having the same approximate composition.

Blending is the bringing together of two or more carefully weighed components, as in a glaze formulation, and intermingling them so thoroughly that complete uniformity of composition is achieved.

Sampling is taking a small quantity of material that is truly representative of the original mass. A chunk of ore taken from a vein is not a sample of the vein; it is only a specimen.

There are any number of mechanical devices available for performing the tasks of mixing, blending and sampling, but here we will confine our remarks to simple equipment and hand methods that are easily mastered.

MIXING

The objective here is to achieve as complete a mixing as possible of a single-mineral ore or concentrate so that it will have a uniform composition. Very few ores or concentrates are ever perfectly pure. Most contain impurities which will affect, in one way or another, their chemical or physical activity when used in a glaze formulation. Some impurities, such as iron, produce adverse results even when present in very small quantities; others, such as quartz or feldspar, may have little impact other than to dilute the overall purity of the concentrate.

Mixing will not upgrade an ore or concentrate, but it will evenly distribute its impurities throughout your finely ground material.

If you have merely dumped your ceramic glaze material into a container after fine grinding it is a safe bet that no two samples taken from the material will be anywhere near identical. Careful mixing is required, followed by equally careful taking of the sample.

One of the simplest, and yet sufficiently accurate procedures for mixing finely

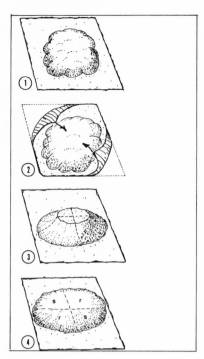

Figure 3.20 *Steps required to obtain a small representative sample from a larger quantity.*

ground ores involves nothing more than a square of heavy plastic, rubberized cloth, or finely woven canvas. The size of the sheet needed will depend upon the amount of material to be handled. Several factors are important here: (1) *All* of the material in your container must be mixed at the same time, or if very large amounts are on hand you can divide it into two piles, mixing each individually and then combining small samples from each pile and mixing them; (2) when placed on the sheet, the pile of material should be small enough to permit all of it to be rolled readily; (3) sheet size should not exceed about three feet square and the diameter of the heap should not be more than about one-half the width of the sheet. As the sample is reduced in size you can use smaller sheets to speed the work.

We are now ready to begin mixing. Pile the material in the center of the sheet, Figure 3.20 (1), grasp one corner and pull it toward the opposite one, rolling the pile over, Figure 3.20 (2). Now reverse the action by grasping the opposite corner. Repeat this several times and then roll the pile back and forth with the other two corners. When this has been done, grasp each corner in turn and roll the material into a pile. Great care must be taken when mixing a material which may have a fairly wide range of particle sizes. The larger particles are more apt to roll down the slope of a pile than smaller ones, thus causing a possible un-mixing of the mass. If the rolling action on the cloth is performed properly there should be no sliding or cascading which tends to separate materials of different particle sizes.

Now flatten the cone you have made, Figure 3.20 (3), and divide it into quarters Figure 3.20(4). This can be done in several ways and the size of the cone and the potter's ingenuity will determine the best method. One simple device consists of two thin boards, such as quarter-inch thick plywood notched half way at their centers so that when they are fitted together they form a cross. Figure 3.21 illustrates the gadget. This device can be used as either a slip-fit and take-apart model or, if storage space is no problem and frequent use is to be anticipated, then the two pieces can be permanently joined together with small metal angle braces. In the drawing no dimensions have been shown since the size will depend upon the amount of material to be quartered. Perhaps two or more crosses might be constructed, a large one for the first size reductions, the second one smaller for the final quarterings.

Opposite quarters are now scraped away. These are called "rejects", even though they are every bit as good as the material in the other two quarters, See Figure 3.20 (4). The rejects are returned to the original container. The remaining quarters are then rolled and mixed again as described above, and coned and quartered. This process is repeated until two quarters give you approximately the quantity of material you need.

If you anticipate needing a number of batches of identical material you can prepare them all at the same time by using two quarters for stock and rolling the pile after each batch has been removed. Any material left over after making up the batches can then be returned to the original supply.

Since one batch of finely powdered ceramic material looks very much like any other, even though they may have widely differing chemical and ceramic properties, the need for careful labelling is apparent. Notations made on containers with pen, pencil, felt tip pen, or grease pencil tend to become illegible after handling a few times. Numbered metal or plastic discs are available but are expensive. Perhaps the household model labelmaker which embosses a high quality, self-stick plastic tape with either numbers or letters is the answer. The raised characters are highly legible and even if coated with dried clay can be read easily after being wiped. Many professional samplers affix a label to the outside of the container and then place an identical one inside, just to be on the safe side.

All of this seems like a lot of work but once you get the hang of it the job of mixing, rolling and quartering goes very quickly. If you follow this procedure

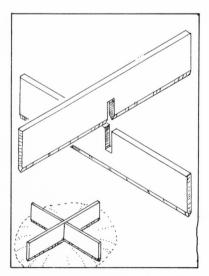

Figure 3.21 *Knock-down device for quartering samples.*

you can add small amounts of new material to your stock at any time and it will get thoroughly mixed in with the much larger mass before you quarter-out your work batch.

CALCULATING WEIGHTED AVERAGES

The following computations illustrate what happens when small amounts of material having a slightly different composition are added to larger quantities and thoroughly mixed together. Values for both composition and weight of the "new" material that is to be added and of the "old" stock can, of course, be changed to suit your own situation. In the three examples which follow, batches of new material weighing 1, 10 and 20 pounds and containing 37.5 percent SiO_2 are to be added to 100 pounds of material containing 38.0 percent SiO_2.

	Weight		SiO_2% Analysis		Weighting	
New	1	×	37.5	=	37.5	
Old	100	×	38.0	=	3800.0	
Total	101				3837.5	÷ 101 = 37.99% SiO_2
New	10	×	37.5	=	375.0	
Old	100	×	38.0	=	3800.0	
Total	110				4175.0	÷ 110 = 37.95% SiO_2
New	20	×	37.5	=	750.0	
Old	100	×	38.0	=	3800.00	
Total	120				4550.0	÷ 120 = 37.92% SiO_2

From the above examples it can be readily seen that if the chemical difference of the material to be added is small the addition of up to about 20 percent by weight has relatively little effect on the total mixture. Depending upon the ceramic material that is being added to existing stocks the tolerance levels for variation will be different and will have to be taken into consideration before the actual mixing is done.

By following the calculation model shown above the amount of new material that may be added safely can be quickly determined. It should be noted that these calculations are in no way related to standard glaze formulas, and are intended only to provide a method for determining how much new material may be added to your inventory without exceeding the variation from the norm that you have established, or alternatively, what the effect on your reserve supply will be if the new material is added to it. Once again, though, the success of this entire operation depends almost entirely upon the complete and thorough mixing by rolling and quartering of the entire mass.

BLENDING

Although the mechanical operations of blending two or more ceramic materials are almost identical to those followed in mixing as discussed above, there are some very real differences in the approach to the problem. Rather than merely mixing two almost identical materials, you will be attempting to get components of different densities; different shapes and sizes of grains; different susceptibilities to picking up moisture from the air; and perhaps significant differences in their ability to generate static charges to bind together. All these factors have a negative impact on the ease with which they may be successfully blended into a homogeneous mass. It can be done, but vigilance is the watchword.

After carefully weighing out the required amounts of each of the ingredients they should be screened at least twice through a screen slightly coarser than the largest particles in the batch. Screening is an excellent mixing operation and one that is totally unrelated in principle to rolling and quartering which should be done next.

After piling your ceramic material on a sampling cloth it should be rolled back and forth repeatedly, using alternate corners after two or three rolls, until the entire mass has the same appearance. Make sure when you are rolling that the entire pile is turned over each time. Failure to do this will almost certainly result in a certain amount of un-mixing, with the heavy fractions wending their way to the bottom of the pile. When quartering, be careful to remove every bit of the opposing quarters, sweeping the quarter areas of cloth clean with a paint brush before continuing.

Careful labelling of blended materials is, of course, a must. It is totally impossible to unravel the composition of a properly blended mass of ceramic material. Far too much effort and expense have been put forth on the batch to risk getting it confused with something else.

Blending two clays having somewhat different characteristics may produce some rather surprising results. In one instance a brick and tile clay which had drying and shrinkage problems was greatly improved by blending it with a more plastic clay, since less water had to be added for proper workability. The second clay had a rather high firing temperature but when mixed with the first clay this was lowered considerably, much more than a simple arithmetical average would indicate. There seems to be no simple formula for arriving at the "best" combination of two clays and only a series of tests, using various proportions of the two materials, will reveal what happens.

SAMPLING

The object of sampling is to obtain a small, often the smallest possible, amount of material that is truly representative of the original mass. Methods for obtaining samples are commonly controlled by the nature of the material itself, the uses to which it will be put, and the latitude permissible in variations from the norm. Sampling often takes place at two different stages in the search for, and preparation of, ceramic materials.

In the field samples are commonly taken in the form of chunks or lumps of clay or ore, collected from a variety of points scattered over the available surface, from channels cut across the deposit or even from drill holes penetrating the ore body. Properly taken, these samples should give a fairly close representation of that portion of the mass that was sampled. All too often the samples are representative only of the material lying on the exposed plane of the ore body and lack any third dimensional characteristic.

Figure 3.22 illustrates the point. Five surface samples have been taken, but they represent only the top few inches of the deposit. In 'b', holes have been drilled through the deposit at the same five points and a three-dimensional, representative sample of the entire block has been obtained. The spacing of the sample points will vary from deposit to deposit, depending on the nature of the material, the configuration of the deposit, and the use to which the material is to be put.

In the shop, sampling is often conducted on crushed or ground ceramic materials. It is entirely feasible and practicable to combine mixing and sampling operations, since the final quarters will indeed be truly representative of the entire mass. If the material to be sampled has already been mixed it is a simple matter to obtain suitable samples by using small diameter, thin-walled tubes which are inserted vertically into the container or pile at numerous points. The number of sampling points is determined by the nature of the material and the uses to which it is to be put. A five-gallon bucket of material might require a total of five or six samples, while a large dump truck load of ore could easily require thirty or forty sampling points.

The column of material collected inside the tube represents a true cross-section

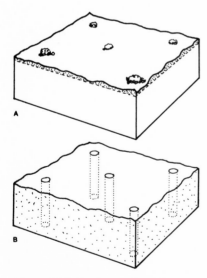

Figure 3.22 *Grab samples (A) sample surface of deposit only; drill holes (B) sample entire thickness of deposit and provide a representative sample.*

of the mass at that point (assuming that the tube penetrated all the way to the bottom of the mass). After all of the individual samples have been taken they are rolled and quartered in the normal manner.

Grindability

Fine grinding requires a lot of energy, particularly if the ore to be ground is quartz or other minerals of the same or greater hardness. Figure 3.23 illustrates the problem. Every time you halve the edge dimension of a cube the surface is doubled. A one inch cube has a surface area of six square inches. Dividing the cube up into half-inch cubes increases the surface to twelve square inches, and if you grind those cubes down to pass through a 270 mesh screen the surface is over twenty square feet, or 480 times the surface that you started out with. Also there are over 100 million particles.

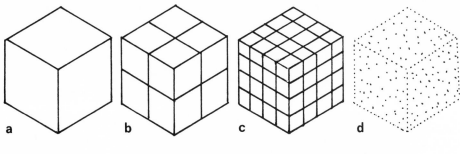

Edge Length	Number of Pieces	Surface Area
(a) 1″	1	6 sq. in.
(b) .5″	8	12 sq. in.
(c) .25″	64	24 sq. in.
(d) .0021″*	100,000,000	20 sq. ft.
*270 mesh		

Figure 3.23 *Particle size compared to surface area and number of particles per unit of volume.*

Rick's Law tackles the problem slightly differently: the force required to break a particle by impact (crushing) is proportional to the volume of the particle. In other words, the smaller the piece, the less energy required to break it. The only catch is that every time you reduce the volume of the individual particle you generate a lot more particles that have to be broken.

The trick is to start off with coarse ore and comparatively few large grinding media, grind for an hour or so and then screen off an intermediate-sized fraction and grind it with smaller and more numerous balls, pebbles, or whatever. This speeds the work, saves time and energy and is precisely what industry does in large mineral treatment mills. It is called stage grinding.

NATURAL GLAZE MATERIALS

INTRODUCTION

There are numerous opportunities for potters to obtain raw, natural glaze minerals in the field. The wide variety of these commonly used glaze substances, which include salines, sulphides, oxides, and sulphates, makes impossible any generalization as to their mineralogy, geology, and geographic distribution.

Since the craft potter is more interested in the usable oxides that can be obtained from a mineral than he is in a particular mineral, the material that follows has been arranged on that basis. If information is needed for a particular mineral, it can be found by consulting the index.

Only very general locations are given for most of the minerals since the list of occurrences would be inordinately large otherwise. State and provincial departments of geology can provide you with specific information on local occurrences.

Natural glaze materials have few similarities with the clays to which they will ultimately be joined. Glaze materials should be as fresh and unweathered as possible, in sharp contrast to clays which should be deeply weathered. Many glaze minerals are hard and brittle, occur in veins or stringers, and only occasionally will be found in transported deposits. Only deposits of glaze minerals which occur in surface outcrops will be of any interest to the prospector-potter, since searching for hidden ore bodies usally entails a great deal of effort and an adverse success-to-failure ratio. Fortunately the location of nearly all surface deposits of economic minerals is well documented, and detailed information is available from various state, provincial and government agencies.

In some cases just plain common sense may dictate against going out and digging your own glaze materials. Either the nearest known deposits are too far away, the amount that you need is too small to justify the effort, or the difficulty in mining, beneficiating and grinding is too great.

On the other hand, many minerals that you need are readily available, require little effort to mine, and can be up-graded and powdered with comparative ease. Many potters will develop an overriding and sometimes compelling interest in using only materials that they have acquired in the field. This is a wonderful incentive to mine your own materials, and if done intelligently, can yield a personal satisfaction that is hard to beat. Mining just might save you some money, but this latter consideration should not be given too much weight.

Detailed information on how to process and beneficiate raw ceramic materials appears in the section at the end of this chapter. A selected, but by no means all-inclusive, list of references on glazes appears in the Bibliography.

Since some potters may have difficulty in the identification of the various minerals, several excellent books on the subject have been listed.

Purity and Particle Size of Glaze Materials

The end-product in a glazing operation is a very thin "skin" which must adhere tightly to the ware, and have a coefficient of expansion compatible with the clay to which it is fused. The glaze must also possess a texture, color, and either transparency or opacity that was sought and which can be duplicated repeatedly. To achieve these objectives, which are accomplished pyrochemically, great care must be exercised in the preparation of the glaze materials.

If there is one word that best describes all of the steps used in the preparation of glaze materials, it is UNIFORMITY. Chemical uniformity of the various materials in the glaze recipe is important but should not overshadow the need for carefully sized material.

Except in very unusual circumstances, it is almost impossible for an individual potter to prepare perfectly pure glaze materials. There will always be some impurities, even though they may be present in amounts far less than one percent. It is important that the impurities must not only be evenly distributed all through the mass, but that this distribution remains constant during the continued use of the product.

Uniformity of particle size in glaze recipes is particularly important since it has a direct impact on the rate of sintering, fusion, the liquid state and possible volatilization of the mineral grains. Because the various components of a glaze formula react with each other and the surface of the ware as the temperature of the kiln increases and then decreases, any appreciable disparity in grain size could effect the completion of the necessary chemical reactions.

Fluxes

The preparation of fluxes presents some special problems to the prospector-potter. Fluxes occupy a special niche in a glaze formula and their behavior during firing is crucial to the success of the operation. Fluxes perform a variety of tasks in glazing. Although silica is of paramount importance in ceramic bodies it cannot be used without a flux since its melting point (1713° C, 3115° F) is much too high for the average craft potter. A single flux can be used in a glaze recipe but the presence of two or more fluxes usually results in the further lowering of the melting point due to the formation of several eutectics.

Fluxes can improve the viscosity and stability of a glaze and increase the firing range. Fluxes are often necessary to assure that opaque glazes develop sufficient crystal growth upon cooling. Pigment colors in or under a glaze are often enhanced, transparency improved, and craze resistance altered by fluxes.

A flux interacts not only with other glaze components and fluxes but with the surface of the fired ware and the kiln atmosphere. These complex reactions must take place within a fairly narrow range of temperatures, and in a rather short period of time.

To be both useful and dependable, flux materials must not only be uniform in composition and grain size but must not contain impurities which would diminish or destroy the effect sought. Some fluxes, such as calcium oxide, act as a refractory at low temperatures but above 1100° C become increasingly active. Lead oxide can only be used in low temperature firing, while the oxides of barium, zinc and magnesium will flux only at high temperatures.

Since particle size is directly related to chemical activity, the fineness of flux materials is of great importance. Too coarse a material may inhibit proper pyrochemical activity, and fluxes ground too finely may react prematurely or too aggressively.

The foregoing comments apply to glazes and fluxes that are to be used in the standard mode, and where reproducibility is important. When developing your own glaze materials, you have an opportunity to experiment not only with new materials and combinations of materials but also with variations in particle size. By selecting certain, specific size fractions, you may discover that unusual texture or color patterns are developed in a glaze. By using, for instance, a small percentage of a rather coarse screen fraction, such as –16 +40, of a mineral which will not be dissolved or only partly dissolved during your glaze firing, you create a surface with a "feel" that enhances your ware. It goes without saying that the variations in particle size, percentage used, and the choice of mineral are almost endless and much experimentation is suggested.

Variations in color patterns, using screen sizes for control, are based on the mass-action effect which occurs during firing. Smaller particles are more readily assimilated into the melt than larger ones, and the varying degrees of this interaction can result in a glaze having greater "depth" than the typically "flat" surfaces developed with glazes composed of mineral grains which are all of the same, or nearly the same, size. See the section on "Screening" in the "Beneficiation and Processing" chapter for a discussion of screening and screen-size fractions.

Testing Glaze Materials

Two distinct types of testing are required when you start to use a new glaze material. The first is the positive identification of the metallic elements in the glaze minerals. The second is the behavior, when fired, of the new material that you are using in a glaze formula.

TESTS FOR METALLIC ELEMENTS

When dealing with untried, raw glaze materials it is helpful to determine what metallic elements might be present. This can be accomplished quickly and easily for some minerals with the borax bead test or the flame test.

For the borax bead test a two and a half inch length of No. 28 platinum wire is inserted into the end of a glass rod about four inches long which has been softened by heating to redness. The other end of the wire is formed into a small loop by coiling it around the lead of a pencil. To make a test, heat the loop in a Bunsen burner flame and then dip it into some powdered borax. Reheat the loop, melt the borax and repeat until enough has been accumulated to fill the loop. At this point the bead should be absolutely colorless. If not, reheat the bead, shake it off when molten and then build up another one.

When a clear bead has been formed, heat it once again until molten and quickly touch it to a tiny speck of the material to be tested. Reheat the bead in an oxidizing flame until all action ceases and observe its color both while hot and when cold. The same bead is then heated in a reducing flame and the hot and cold color is again noted. The oxidizing part of a Bunsen burner flame is near the tip and the reducing portion is the blue center. Some metals will show decided differences in the color of the beads heated in the oxidizing and reducing flames, and also between hot and cold, while others will show no change. If too much mineral is picked up in the bead the color may be too dark for proper diagnosis. If this happens merely shake the bead off when molten, add more borax, and try again. Sulphide and arsenic minerals must be first powdered and heated with an oxidizing flame until all odor disappears. Before testing a second sample be sure that all traces of the previous test have been removed by fusing some borax until a perfectly clear bead is formed. It is suggested that before starting to use the borax bead method on your ceramic materials that you obtain samples of the various minerals and make up a set of reference beads. Although the borax bead test is an excellent method to use, it is extremely sensitive and misinterpretations are possible. Variations in technique, too much sample, and carelessness in proper heating in the correct portion of the flame all contribute to inaccuracies.

Bead colors for six common metallic elements are given in Figure 4.1.

Element	Oxidizing flame		Reducing flame	
	hot	cold	hot	cold
Chromium	yellow-red	yellow-green	emerald green	
Cobalt	blue	blue	blue	blue
Copper	green	blue-green	green	blue-green
Iron	pale yellow to brownish red	colorless to yellow	bottle green	
Manganese	violet	red	colorless or faint rose	
Nickel	violet	red-brown	gray — turbid	

Figure 4.1 *Bead colors for six common metallic elements.*

The flame test is extremely simple. Heat a small, preferably thin, sliver of mineral in the flame of a Bunsen burner or, better yet, in the flame produced by a blowpipe in conjunction with the burner, and observe the color of the flame. The specimen should be held in the outer, oxidizing portion of the burner flame. If any sulfides or arsenides are present the typical sulfur or garlic odor will be given off during the heating. Figure 4.2 lists color of flames for most of the common elements. The test for calcium is best done with the application of dilute hydrochloric acid to the specimen.

Element	Color of Flame
Antimony	greenish-blue
Arsenic	whitish-blue
Barium	yellowish-green
Boron	siskine-green
Calcium	orange-red
Copper chloride	azure-blue
Copper oxide	emerald-green
Lead	blue
Lithium	carmine-red
Phosphate	bluish-green
Potassium	violet
Selenium	azure-blue
Sodium	yellow
Strontium	purple-red
Zinc	bluish-green (streaks)

Figure 4.2 *Flame colors for selected elements.*

FIRING TESTS

The degree of testing by firing will depend on the nature of the material being substituted and the use to which it will be put. No matter how simple or how involved your testing is, do keep careful and detailed records. There is no point in doing a lot of testing and then finding that you can't quite remember just where that new material came from, what it is, or how you prepared it.

When testing for color, use horizontal surfaces of test tiles, and compare with a standard color tile under artificial light. The unfired test tiles should all be made from the same clay. To check for other physical characteristics of a glaze when fired, both vertical and horizontal sections are needed since the effects on the two surfaces may differ. Sections cut from pots serve nicely for these tests.

The American Society for Testing Materials is an organization which tests and devises tests for a bewildering variety of substances, and which also acts, through it published Standards, as the final arbiter on correct testing procedures. The A.S.T.M. has published numerous Standards for ceramic materials. The Standards are revised from time to time and the identification number, particularly the final digits, may change. The Standards may either be purchased from the Society or inspected at the larger libraries.

SOURCES OF GLAZE MATERIALS

In this section are listed the chemical, mineralogical and geological properties of materials used to supply the dozen most commonly used elements in ceramic glazes. Some of the more noteworthy localities for the various minerals are also given. Neither the suggested list of minerals containing glaze elements nor the compilation of deposits should be regarded as being exhaustive. The opportunities for experimentation with source materials is practically limitless and all too little work has been done in exploring the possibilities available from local deposits. Volcanic rocks are plentiful in the Pacific West and offer the potter a bountiful source of high temperature glaze material. Basalt is the commonest of these. It has been used for dark-colored glazes by some art potters. Other volcanic rocks, including volcanic ash, also contain useful glaze elements.

Here, in alphabetical order, are the twelve most important elements used in glaze formulations, together with the minerals in which these elements occur, their chemical composition, notes on the physical properties of some of the minerals, and suggestions as to where to find them in the field. The list of minerals containing elements useful in glaze formulations is very long. Many of these minerals are either rare, difficult to obtain or resist reduction to a form useful to a ceramist. If further inquiry in this direction is desired a college-level textbook on mineralogy is suggested. Mineralogy books commonly include appendices which contain lists of minerals arranged by their principal elements with detailed descriptions of the mineral, its properties and important localities in the text. More specific information may be obtained from state, provincial and federal geological surveys.

A word or two of explanation as to why in the discussion of possible glaze minerals the oxide form is first given followed by examples of minerals which are sulphides, sulphates, carbonates or silicates. Glaze formulae are based on the presence of the element in an oxide form. This standardization makes it easy to compare one glaze with another, to effect substitutions, and to calculate the requirements for new glaze formulas. However, many minerals occur as sulphides, sulphates, carbonates and silicates. When dealing with these minerals as a source for elements in your glazes you will have to recalculate them as oxides.

The oxide content of a mineral is determined in the following manner: Step 1. Using the values shown in Appendix 4 add up the total molecular weight of the formula for the mineral. Step 2. Divide the molecular weight of the oxide portion of the mineral formula by the total molecular weight of the formula for the mineral. This quotient is the conversion factor which is useful in determining the amount of raw mineral required to produce a sufficient amount of the oxide wanted for a glaze formula. The chemical composition of some selected glaze materials, together with their formulas, molecular weights, the molecular weight of the contained oxide and the conversion factor are given in Appendix 4.

Here is an example of how the molecular weight and the conversion factor of an oxide contained in a glaze material are determined.

Oxide Sought	Mineral	Formula	Molecular Weight	Mol. Wt. of Oxide	Conversion Factor
Al_2O_3	Orthoclase	$K_2O \cdot Al_2O_3 \cdot 6SiO_2$	556*	102*	.183
		94 + 102 + 360 =	556	$\dfrac{102}{556}$ =	.183

*Values have been rounded from the more precise figures appearing in Appendix 4.

The conversion factor is used to calculate the amount of raw mineral required in the following manner. Assume that 6 pounds of aluminum oxide, Al_2O_3, are required for a glaze formula and that orthoclase is to be used as a source. By dividing the 6 pounds of oxide that is required by the conversion factor (.183), it is found that 32.787 pounds of orthoclase is needed. The conversion factor can also be used to determine the yield of an oxide from any mineral whose chemical formula is known. The relative "efficiency" of various mineral sources for oxides can be determined readily by comparing their conversion factors. For example: quartz is more than twice as "efficient" as a source of SiO_2 as china clay which contains only 46.6 percent as much.

In order to familiarize yourself with the minerals that you will be looking for I recommend that you either visit a mineral museum and examine carefully their specimens, or better yet, acquire small typical specimens to study and to use for comparison when in the field.

Availability of Glaze Materials

Figure 4.3 lists 30 minerals, together with their chemical compositions which might provide elements for glazes. Those minerals that have been flagged with an "f" generally require fritting before they can be used in a glaze recipe. Minerals that are soluble in aqueous glaze mixes are indicated with an "s", and those that should be calcined before use are indicated with a "c".

Before attempting to work up any of these potential glaze minerals take a look at their hardness, which is shown in the column over at the right. Any mineral having a hardness greater than about 5.5 is going to require considerable effort to reduce it to the required fineness. Quartz and flint with a hardness of 7 and corundum with 9 are definitely difficult to grind, particularly in an iron-free state. However, see the section on "Iron-free Grinding" in the chapter on "Beneficiation and Processing" before abandoning all hope.

At this point it might be well to say a word or two about minerals that may save you some headaches later on. Although a crystal of a mineral is supposed to be perfectly pure, and all crystals of that same mineral should have the same precise chemical makeup — they don't. Trace amounts of contaminants may be present, either incorporated into the crystal lattice, as coatings on the exterior surface, or lining the walls of microscopic fractures in the crystal.

Crystals of the heavy metals such as iron, lead, copper, zinc, etc., are often diluted with other metals and cannot be purified short of treatment in a commercial smelter. The saline minerals are all too prone to diluents in the form of other closely similar but still different minerals which may affect the glaze formula adversely. Feldspars are excellent crystallizers, but the albite-anorthite series of six minerals have molecules that are completely miscible and range from the pure soda feldspar albite to the pure lime feldspar anorthite, with oligoclase, andesine, labradorite and bytownite arranged in-between. Figure 4.4 shows this relationship in graphic form. The feldspar group is far too important to be ignored. However, much caution, and the collection and processing of rather large quantities, is needed to insure uniformity of product once you have established that the material is suitable.

In summary, it is entirely possible that you can procure some of your own glaze minerals, the choice depending on where you live. Raw minerals may or may not be pure, and only studio testing will determine their quality. Some minerals may be just too hard to grind efficiently and others much too mixed up to use. Let your common sense dictate whether to use commercial glazes or to develop your own from raw minerals.

ALUMINA

Aluminum oxide Al_2O_3. Mineral sources for aluminum oxide: Corundum, bauxite, gibbsite, feldspar. If pure material is required the use of the commercially prepared oxide is suggested. Although the element alumina is the second most

Rock or Mineral	Composition	Elements													
		Al	Ba	B	Ca	Pb	Li	Mg	K	Si	Na	Sr	Zn	H	Sp Gr
Albite	$Na_2O \cdot Al_2O_3 \cdot 6SiO_2$	x								x	x			6.0	2.5
Anorthite	$CaO \cdot Al_2O_3 \cdot 2SiO_2$	x			x					x				6.0	2.5
Barite	$BaSO_4$ (f)		x											2.5	4.4
Bauxite	$Al_2O_3 \cdot 3H_2O$	x												2.5	—
Borax	$Na_2O \cdot 2B_2O_3 \cdot 10H_2O$			x							x			2.0	1.7
Calcite	$CaCO_3$				x									3.0	2.7
Colemanite	$2CaO \cdot 3B_2O_3 \cdot 5H_2O$			x	x									4.0	2.4
Corundum	Al_2O_3	x												9.0	4.0
Diaspore	$Al_2O_3 \cdot H_2O$	x												6.5	3.4
Dolomite	$CaCO_3 \cdot MgCO_3$				x			x						3.5	2.8
Flint	SiO_2									x				7.0	2.7
Galena	PbS (f)					x								2.5	7.5
Gibbsite	$Al_2O_3 \cdot 3H_2O$	x												2.5	2.3
Halite	$NaCl$										x			2.5	2.1
Lepidolite	$Li_2O \cdot Al_2O_3 \cdot K_2O \cdot SiO_2$	x					x		x	x				2.5	2.8
Leucite	$K_2O \cdot Al_2O_3 \cdot 4SiO_2$	x							x					5.5	2.5
Magnesite	$MgCO_3$							x						3.5	3.0
Microcline	$K_2O \cdot Al_2O_3 \cdot 6SiO_2$	x							x	x				6.0	2.5
Nepheline syenite	(rock)	x							x	x	x			—	—
Orthoclase	$K_2O \cdot Al_2O_3 \cdot 6SiO_2$	x							x	x				6.0	2.5
Perthite	(mixed feldspars)	x			x				x	x				6.0	2.5
Petalite	$Li_2O \cdot Al_2O_3 \cdot 8SiO_2$	x					x			x				6.0	2.4
Quartz	SiO_2									x				7.0	2.6
Smithsonite	$ZnCO_3$ (f)												x	5.5	4.3
Sodium carbonate	Na_2CO_3 (s)										x			—	—
Spodumene	$Li_2O \cdot Al_2O_3 \cdot 4SiO_2$	x					x			x				6.5	3.1
Steatite	$3MgO \cdot 4SiO_2 \cdot H_2O$							x		x				1.0	2.7
Ulexite	$NaCaB_5O_9 \cdot 8H_2O$ (f)			x	x						x			1.0	1.6
Witherite	$BaCO_3$		x											3.0	4.3
Zincite	ZnO (c)												x	4.0	5.4
Most sulphide and sulphate minerals		(c)			x	x		x	x		x	x	x		

f = fritting required
s = soluble
c = must be calcined

Figure 4.3 *Principal elements used in ceramic glazes.*

abundant in the world it is one of the most difficult of the common elements for the craft potter to obtain in a pure, natural form that is useful to him. Pure aluminum oxide minerals are almost all hard and occur only in limited quantities. Bauxite, when chemically pure, consists of aluminum oxide plus water. In the Pacific West deposits of pure, iron-free bauxite are unknown.

All three types of feldspars, potash, soda, and lime are excellent sources of alumina (but inextricably mixed with silica and a flux). Feldspars are discussed at some length a bit farther on.

Corundum, Al_2O_3, is a very hard mineral (H 9) and would be extremely difficult to reduce to a powder.

China clay, when iron-free, is often used as a source of aluminum.

Alumina is exceeded only by silica in importance in glaze formulas. Alumina helps to make fluxes more viscous and stable, prevents devitrification, and adds to the durability and craze resistance.

BARIUM

Barium oxide BaO. Mineral sources for barium oxide: witherite, barite, Witherite, a barium carbonate, $BaCO_3$, is not a common mineral. Barite, a barium sulphate, is rather more common. The element barium is sometimes used in glaze formulas where it serves as a high temperature flux in the temperature range above 1130° C. Although the commercial source of barium is usually barium carbonate which has been refined and precipitated chemically, both natural barium carbonate in the form of the mineral witherite, and barium sulphate found in the mineral barite, sometimes called heavy spar, are used in frits.

Barite is a very heavy, generally light-colored mineral with shades of yellow, gray, blue, red, or brown common. The mineral often has a pearly or resinous lustre, and may be transparent, translucent or opaque. Barite is soft, (H 2.5 to 3.5). Although barite occurs in a variety of crystal forms, much of it will be found in massive formations, often associated with metalliferous veins. Barite, when pure, is composed of barium sulphate, $BaSO_4$, with a molecular weight of 329. The mineral is quite easily identified by its great weight, insolubility in acid, and a green color when heated in a flame. Some barite also gives off a fetid odor when rubbed.

Deposits of barite are widespread in both the United States and Canada. In the U.S. large deposits are found in Missouri, Georgia, Nevada and Arkansas, with lesser amounts in California, Tennessee and Alaska. Barite deposits are also known in 20 other states. In Canada there is a large deposit near Walton, Nova Scotia, and large deposits occur in British Columbia near Golden. Western Canadian concentrating plants annually produce large quantities of mill tailings containing barite which is associated with the metalliferous ores.

Barium oxide is used as a high temperature flux (above 1130 C) to produce satiny, matte glazes.

BORON

Boric Acid, B_2O_3. Mineral sources of boric oxide: borax, colemanite, ulexite. These minerals are found typically in desert playas. Borax is composed of sodium, boron and water, and colemanite contains calcium, boron and water. Ulexite is a hydrous borate of sodium and calcium. Borax forms rather large, white crystals and has a fairly sweetish taste. Colemanite tends to form in massive or granular lumps and irregular pieces, is white to colorless and may be transparent or even translucent. Ulexite has no taste and commonly occurs in white, fibrous, silky masses. Identification of these three minerals may be difficult due to the presence of other similar appearing evaporation products on the playa surface. Boron compounds color a flame an intense yellowish-green.

When found as individual crystals or masses of crystals the mineral should be quite chemically pure.

At the present time California is the only state producing boron minerals. Deposits of borax at Boron in the Upper Mojave Desert, and at Furnace Creek Wash on the east side of Death Valley, and brines from the Searles Lake area which is located between Boron and Death Valley are being worked.

Boron-containing minerals are formed when waters in closed basins in arid regions evaporate and deposit their salts. Small encrustations of these minerals can be found in many playas in the basin-and-range country of southwestern United States.

Boric oxide is a good low temperature flux having good craze resistance when used up to 15 percent. Boric oxide is soluble and either frits or the mineral colemanite must be used.

CALCIUM

Calcium oxide CaO. Mineral sources of calcium oxide: calcite, dolomite, anorthite. Calcite, calcium carbonate, $CaCO_3$, is a common rock-forming mineral and is the principal component of limestone, marble, travertine and dolomite. Calcite is an excellent crystallizer and cavities and crevices in rock formations are often lined with beautiful crystals, some of which may be water-clear. Calcite is identified easily by its hardness (H 3). It can be scratched with a copper penny, and a drop of weak hydrochloric acid (1:1 HCl) will make it bubble furiously.

Deposits of high grade limestone and marble are scattered widely in the United States and Canada.

Calcium oxide is one of the principal fluxes used in medium to high temperature glazes for stoneware and porcelains. The oxide actually acts as a refractory at low temperatures but above 1100° C it becomes an increasingly active flux. At high temperature calcium increases the viscosity of a glaze when used in concentrations over 15 percent.

Anorthite, one of the plagioclase feldspars, is a possible source of calcium and is discussed more fully in the Feldspar section. Specific information on anorthosite deposits (anorthosite is a rock composed largely of the calcium-rich plagioclase feldspars, principally anorthite) is very sparse since there has been relatively little ceramic interest in the commodity.

FELDSPAR

The various aluminum-silicate minerals that have been grouped together as feldspars play such an important role in supplying ceramic materials, particularly glazes, that more space should be devoted to them.

There are two main types of these minerals: (1) the potash feldspars; and (2) the soda-lime, or plagioclase group. In the first group there are two principal minerals:

Mineral	Potash Feldspars Composition	Oxides Si%	Al%	K%
Orthoclase	$KAlSi_3O_8$	64.7	18.4	16.9
Microcline	$KAlSi_3O_8$	64.7	18.4	16.9

In the second group there are six minerals which grade imperceptibly from albite to anorthite, as shown in Figure 4.4. The two "end minerals" are:

			Oxides	
Albite	$NaAlSi_3O_8$	68.7% Si	19.5% Al	11.8% Na (soda feldspar)
Anorthite	$CaAl_2Si_2O_8$	43.2% Si	36.7% Al	20.1% Ca (lime feldspar)

Soda-lime or Plagioclase Feldspars

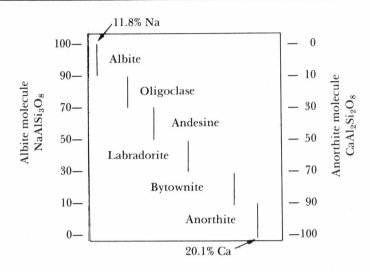

Figure 4.4 *Diagram of the soda-lime feldspars.*

Unfortunately few feldspars ever conform strictly to the theoretical analyses shown. It is common for the potash feldspars to contain some sodium and the plagioclase minerals to have some potash.

As a group feldspars constitute almost complete glazes in themselves since they contain a flux, alumina and silica. For this reason feldspar is often the dominant constituent in stoneware and porcelain glazes and commonly used as a flux for pottery bodies. Feldspars are important rock-forming minerals and are found in the majority of rocks. Often the crystals are quite small and somewhat difficult to separate from other minerals.

In some deposits there are intimate inter-growths of either orthoclase or microcline and albite, which form perthite. Perthite is lower in potassium than either orthoclase or microcline and higher in potassium than albite, but the presence of both alumina and silica remains unchanged.

Coarse-grained granites and even coarser-grained pegmatites may have large, even huge, feldspar crystals that are easy to identify, simple to separate from the rock mass, and are usually pure. Pegmatites are rocks much like granites, except that most of their crystals are very large. It is this feature that makes them of special interest to potters, since it is possible to mine lumps of feldspar which do not have to be beneficiated before they are ground and used in a glaze mix. Old mine dumps in pegmatite areas may have chunks of feldspar which were discarded because they contained no metals.

The identification of feldspar is not difficult, once a basic familiarity with the more common varieties has been developed. Inspection of some known occurrences in the field is most helpful. Feldspar crystals come in many colors, even for the same specific mineral, but all of them have a distinctive internal pattern which, once seen, is easily remembered.

Feldspars have a hardness of 6 to 6.5, which means that any grinding of raw material down to fines will require a considerable effort. On the other hand you may come upon some feldspar that neatly fits your glaze requirements without a lot of doctoring.

As a group, feldspars constitute one of the most important of the rock-forming minerals. As a consequence feldspars of one type or another, in deposits of widely varying sizes, are to be found in a great many places. Since the prospector-potter will probably be interested only in deposits containing rather large, easily identified masses or crystals of a particular feldspar, his attention should be directed to outcrops of pegmatite. In the United States the principal pegmatite areas are: Southwestern Maine, New Hampshire, Massachusetts, Connecticut, Virginia, the Carolinas, Georgia, Alabama, the Black Hills of South Dakota, and the Rocky Mountain states, especially Colorado and New Mexico. Minor deposits also occur in California, Arizona, Idaho, Texas, and Wyoming. Any metal mining district having its ores associated with either granite or pegmatite is a possible source for feldspar.

It has been noted above that not all feldspar deposits are composed of a single, pure mineral. In most cases it will not pay to attempt to beneficiate these rocks or to try and use them. Occasionally it may prove, after studio testing, that some material, even though considerably mixed-up, does fit your needs. If this is the case and you can obtain a rather large amount, grind and mix it thoroughly to insure uniformity, and use it without any problems.

LEAD

Lead oxide, PbO. Mineral sources of lead oxide: galena. Galena is a very heavy lead sulphide, PbS, which characteristically forms perfect, silvery cubes. Galena is often found in mineralized veins associated with other sulphide minerals. Galena may also contain a wide variety of other elements, including gold, silver, copper, zinc, antimony and others. It is easily crushed, having a hardness of 2.5. Galena is one of the most common of the sulphide minerals and as such is found in nearly all metal-mining districts. Galena's great weight, silvery color, and tendency to form perfect cubes when shattered, make identification easy.

Although galena has a very long history of use in ceramic glazes the health hazard involved in handling the finely powdered mineral in the pottery and the subsequent toxic threat from using lead-glazed ware to store consumptible liquids and food has resulted in the practice of fritting. By converting the lead into a silicate form in a special furnace this problem is circumvented without destroying the properties sought originally, with the exception that the firing range is markedly reduced.

Fritting is not really suggested for the individual potter. It can be done, provided you have facilities for heating a crucible to almost 2100° F., and holding it there for half an hour or so. The fritting process includes weighing out the ingredients for the glaze recipe (but withholding any clay for addition during later grinding and heating in a clay crucible which will withstand the required temperatures. Since much gas is evolved during the melting phase the furnace should be located outdoors. After the melting has permitted the dissolving of water-soluble materials into the glaze solution the crucible is carefully removed and the contents poured into a container of water. Extreme care must be exercised in this step since the very hot molten contents of the crucible react most spectacularly upon entering the water. Protective clothing and goggles are a must. The frit must then be ground to –200 mesh, at which time any clay in the glaze formula is added. It should be remembered that galena likes to associate with many other metals and these often are disseminated through a seemingly pure mass of the mineral. The presence of these metallic impurities may have unexpected results in your glaze.

Alternative commercial products include litharge, red lead, white lead, lead monosilicate, lead bisilicate and lead sesquisilicate. These, like the natural galena, should be fritted before being used as glaze materials.

LITHIUM

Lithium oxide, LiO_2. Mineral sources of lithium oxide: petalite, lepidolite, spodumene, plus brines containing small amounts of lithium. Spodumene is mined in pegmatites in the tin-spodumene belt of North Carolina, and brines containing a few hundredths of a percent of lithium oxide are recovered at Searles Lake, California, and at Silver Peak, Nevada. In Canada lithium minerals occur in pegmatites at the Preissac-Lacorne district in Western Quebec and at the Bernic Lake area of Manitoba.

Lithium is used in ceramics to impart high mechanical strength, thermal shock resistance, and good chemical resistance. Inexpensive Japanese ovenware uses large quantities of petalite to minimize thermal expansion in the ware and glaze. Both petalite and lepidolite can be used without refining, but spodumene must be processed to remove excess iron. Lithium carbonate, an industrial product, is normally employed as a secondary flux to provide a source of lithium oxide for high temperature porcelain and stoneware glazes. Another lithium chemical, lithium fluoride, is used as a flux in glazes, and also in porcelains.

MAGNESIA

Magnesium oxide, MgO. Mineral sources of magnesium oxide: magnesite, dolomite, steatite. Magnesite is a magnesium carbonate, $MgCO_3$, with a hardness of 3.5. Dolomite is a calcium-magnesium carbonate, $CaCO_3.MgCO_3$, with a hardness of 3.5. Dolomite and magnesite contain 21.7 percent and 47.6 percent magnesia respectively.

Both dolomite and magnesite effervesce when finely powdered in warm hydrochloric acid but have only slight reaction to cold acid. Both minerals are about the same hardness, but magnesite is somewhat heavier. Dolomite often resembles marble, while magnesite is commonly massive, granular, or earthy.

Dolomite is not as refractory as either calcium or magnesium when used separately.

Large quantities of magnesite, associated with dolomite, occur near Chewelah, Washington, and near Gabbs, Nevada. In Canada the mineral is found near Kilmar, Quebec, and in northern Ontario. In British Columbia crystalline magnesite outcrops in the East Kootenays, and massive pods are common in the serpentine formations of the Clinton and Bridge River areas in the central part of the Province, while veins of white magnesite occur along the Yalakom River and Pinchi Mountain areas.

Dolomite is a cheap and convenient mineral to use whenever both magnesia and lime are needed in a glaze. Magnesite is also used as a source of magnesia, but the raw mineral often contains small amounts of iron oxide. Much of the magnesia sold commercially is obtained from sea water or subsurface brines.

Steatite, or talc, as it is more commonly called, is magnesium silicate, $Mg_3(OH)_2Si_4O_{10}$. It is very soft (H 1). When mixed with a minor amount of impurities in nature, talc is called soapstone. Talc is often found with serpentine and dolomite in regions of high magnesian rocks or with sedimentary rocks which have been altered by magnesium-bearing solutions at depth. Pure steatite contains 31.7 percent magnesia.

Talc is useful in ceramics, not only as a source of magnesia but also because it imparts a constant rate of shrinkage upon firing, makes lower firing temperatures possible, helps develop a high compression glaze which reduces possible crazing, improves the appearance of white-fired bodies, and in some applications permits faster firing schedules.

Talc is mined in the following states: Alabama, California, Georgia, Maryland, Montana, New York, North Carolina, Oregon, Texas and Vermont. Additional reserves are known to occur in: Arkansas, Massachusetts, Michigan, Nevada, New Hampshire, New Jersey, New Mexico, Pennsylvania, Rhode Island, Virginia, Washington, and Wisconsin.

Alternative sources of magnesium are dolomite chunks sold as building stone, or possibly ground dolomitic limestone sold for soil amendment in garden supply stores.

POTASSIUM

Potassium oxide, K_2O. Mineral sources of potassium oxide: orthoclase, leucite, nepheline syenite. Orthoclase is one of the potash feldspars, along with microcline. (For a discussion of all of the feldspars, see the section on feldspar.)

Leucite, although not a true feldspar, is closely similar in several respects. Chemical composition is $KAl(SiO_3)_2$. Hardness is 5.5. Although quite rare, deposits of leucite occur in the Bearpaw Mountains of north central Montana and as drift boulders along the shores of Vancouver Island, British Columbia.

Nepheline syenite is an igneous rock that has no quartz and is composed of the feldspars albite and microcline, and the feldspathoid mineral nepheline $(Na_3KAl_4Si_4O_{16})$, together with varying amounts of hornblende, pyroxene and biotite. Minor amounts of magnetite, ilmenite, calcite, garnet, zircon and corundum may also be included.

Commercially refined nepheline syenite contains at least 60 percent feldspar, 20 percent nepheline and seldom more than 5 percent accessory minerals. A typical analysis is: Al_2O_3 23%; SiO_2 60%; Na_2O 10%; K_2O 4.5%; Fe_2O_3 .07%. Nepheline syenite meeting these specifications is used as a substitute for feldspar since it serves as a vitrifying agent. Nepheline syenite reduces the need for body fluxes and lowers firing temperatures or permits faster firing schedules.

Nepheline syenite is produced in the vicinity of Blue Mountain, in Methuen Township, in the province of Ontario, Canada. Other Canadian deposits occur in British Columbia at Ice River and at Kruger Mountain. In the United States nepheline syenite is produced at several points near Little Rock, Arkansas, but the ore contains over 4 percent Fe_2O_3, and is not suitable for ceramic applications. Only the Blue Mountain deposit, which contains roughly 1.5 percent Fe_2O_3 is used ceramically.

SILICON

Silicon dioxide, SiO_2. Mineral sources of silicon dioxide: flint, quartz, china clay. Both flint and quartz, when pure, contain nothing but silicon dioxide and have a hardness of 7. Flint is associated with chalk deposits where lumps of it are found distributed throughout the formation. Flint and quartz are extremely refractory, with a melting point of over 3000° F. Quartz is one of the most abundant minerals in the earth's crust, where it forms the important constituent of many rocks and sands of the rivers, deserts, and coastal sand dunes. Veins and masses of quartz, often quite pure, are found in mineralized areas. Some quartz veins are intimately mixed with metalliferous minerals, such as gold, silver, copper, lead, and zinc, plus many others. Barren quartz with no contained metallic minerals is discarded during mining operations, and many mine dumps have quantities of pure, or nearly pure, quartz. The great hardness of both quartz and flint, together with quartzite, a metamorphic rock composed entirely of quartz grains, makes grinding rather difficult and expensive since quartz will scratch mild steel with ease.

Quartz is an abundant mineral, widely distributed. There are literally thousands of high quality quartz deposits scattered over the countryside which are too small to be of economic interest but which would handily serve the needs of all the craft potters.

China clay, kaolin, Cornwall or Cornish stone is the commercial alternate for supplying silica for a glaze mixture.

SODIUM

Sodium oxide, Na_2O. Mineral sources of sodium oxide: albite, nepheline syenite, sodium carbonate, Cornish stone, and borax. Albite is a soda feldspar and is discussed under "Feldspar" above. Although the chemical formula for albite is appealing as a raw source of sodium for a glaze formula, it unfortunately is almost always found intimately associated with other feldspars. This could be a problem since the percentages of the various feldspars making up the ore may vary. If the material is tested and found to be satisfactory, a rather large amount should be collected, ground and mixed thoroughly to assure uniformity of feed-stock.

For information on nepheline syenite see the section on "Potassium" in this chapter.

There are vast deposits of salines in the basin-and-range areas of the West that contain large quantities of sodium carbonate. The difficulty in using this material as a source of sodium lies in the complex nature of the various chemicals that compose the solid salts and liquid brines. Without rather expensive chemical analyses it is impossible to determine the chemical composition closely enough for glaze formulas. Sodium compounds obtained from saline environments are soluble in water and must be fritted before they can be introduced into a glaze formula.

STRONTIUM

Strontium oxide, SrO. Mineral sources of strontium oxide: There are relatively few strontium minerals and all of them are rather rare. Commercially prepared strontium carbonate, $SrCO_3$, which is insoluble, is the normal source for this element in glazes.

ZINC

Zinc oxide, ZnO. Mineral sources of zinc oxide: zincite and smithsonite. Although zincite, ZnO, occurs in large masses at such places as Franklin Furnace, New Jersey, it is uncommon elsewhere. Smithsonite, $ZnCO_3$, is also rather difficult to find locally, although deposits occur in the Tintic district of Utah. Industrial zinc oxide, which is insoluble, is used to supply the element in glazes.

OTHER MATERIALS USEFUL TO POTTERS

This completes the list of the twelve most commonly used glaze elements. There are three other glaze materials that are of interest to potters. The first is simplicity itself to apply, but as with so many "easy" things, there are strings attached. The second requires a great deal of preliminary preparation but once used it exacts no further tribute. The third may save you money.

Rock Salt

Sodium chloride, NaCl. Mineral sources of sodium chloride: halite. Halite is the technical name for the common rock salt you use in the winter to de-ice your driveway. It contains no additives, is cheap, readily available and non-toxic. It is entirely possible to prepare your own salt by boiling either sea water or brines from some local salt spring. However, this procedure does not make good economic sense, and in the case of sea water you are apt to end up with a potpourri of many other elements in addition to sodium and chlorine, which is not good.

Halite, like most other salines found naturally, may be contaminated with other closely similar minerals which were deposited from slowly evaporating bodies of water. This mixing may cause no problems, but care should be used to test the material thoroughly and then to obtain a rather large amount of the mineral to crush and mix.

Deposits of halite are distributed widely across the United States and Canada. Unfortunately for the prospector-potter, many of them are deeply buried and are mined with hard-rock methods. Any surface exposures are almost entirely limited to arid regions since the rainfall in humid areas would quickly dissolve the salt.

Wood Ash

Wood ash glazes were undoubtedly discovered by observant potters using wood-fired kilns. The ash fallout from the fuel tended to light upon horizontal surfaces of the ware during firing. From this simple awareness the use of ash glazes has been developed.

While most potters know that hardwood ashes can be used for glazing and are particularly effective when somewhat softer tones and more subtle color changes are sought, few realize that ash glazes vary from location to location from the same species of tree. Trees remove various elements from the soil in which they grow. Different types of soils supply different assortments of minerals which are introduced into the woody tissues of the tree and eventually show up in the wood ash. A fruit tree growing in deeply weathered transported soil may produce a different glaze than the same variety growing in relatively unweathered *in situ* formations of rock and soil which have had relatively little soluble matter removed.

In some areas hardwoods are a bit difficult to come by and hardwood ash even more so. A mill using large quantities of hardwood for furniture manufacture might burn scraps for heat and thus produce a good ash. Almost certainly there are other manufacturers using various hardwoods, and a bit of sleuthing may be productive.

While ash glazes actually contain no elements which are not readily obtainable commercially, such as feldspar and frits, they have a distinctive quality and appearance that is unmatched. Once a batch of ash glaze is used up it is practically impossible to duplicate it. In addition to hardwood, some potters have resorted to burning corn cobs or even fruit pits.

Of the hardwoods, hickory, apple, pear and beech are best, giving good color. Oak ashes yield a bland tone. Neither pine for fir are considered good ash sources. Acting on the "elephant theory" (you look for elephants in Africa rather than in Alaska), potters looking for ashes from apple and pear trees should check out the fruit-growing areas. Fruit orchards produce tons of prunings annually when the trees are trimmed during the dormant season. Alder, which is dispensed widely over North America, is extensively used in furniture manufacturing so furniture factories have considerable quantities of scrap wood. Canneries processing stone fruits such as peaches, plums and prunes are good sources for fruit pits, but the problem of sorting them out from other cannery wastes might be burdensome.

If the above comments have not been too discouraging, and you still want to work up your own ash glaze, here's how you do it. Take a large amount of ash, screen it through a 60 mesh screen (common fly screen is usually only about 16 mesh), mix it with a quantity of water, allow to settle and decant the water, using rubber gloves and safety glasses or a face mask, since you are essentially working with lye. Dry the sludge, and you have an ash glazing material. This forms the base of a glaze mix consisting of about 30 percent ash (by weight), 30 percent feldspar and 40 percent clay. Another formulation favored by some potters is: ash

40 percent, ball clay 40 percent, and feldspar 20 percent. Straight ash glazes tend to give coarse, matte surfaces. The mix is then added to water until a thick, creamy consistency is reached. Varying the amount of water will alter the physical property of the glaze when added to the ware. Ash glazes often act as fluxing agents and much experimentation is needed. Reduction firing produces a warm color when using ash glazes. One final caution: It takes a *lot* of raw ash to make a *little* glaze material.

Volcanic glasses

To the geologist the term volcanic glass includes those extrusive igneous rocks which welled up from deep in the earth in an incandescent mass and then were chilled so rapidly that crystal growth was severely restricted. Obsidian is the most readily recognizable of the volcanic glasses but pumice, volcanic ash, perlite and basalt, to name a few of the more commonly found rocks, are also glasses. These same glasses, if permitted to cool very slowly for a long period of time, will normally develop a crystal structure, even to the point of becoming granitic in texture.

Investigation has revealed that various volcanic glasses can serve as satisfactory substitutes for feldspar in glazes applied to ware other than whiteware. The presence of small amounts of iron oxide in the glasses precludes their use on whiteware since a slight coloring results. The great abundance and wide distribution of volcanic glasses throughout the Pacific West make it easy-to-obtain material for testing. There is also a large amount of published and unpublished information on volcanic rocks, including detailed chemical and mineralogical analyses. If you are interested in pursuing this matter further, one of the best places to start is the nearest university offering courses in earth science. They should have information on studies made by staff and students. Bibliographies attached to these studies are usually quite comprehensive and can lead you to additional sources.

Results of a series of tests run using volcanic glasses as a substitute for feldspar or nepheline syenite are given in one of the references for glazes in the Bibliography. Here is a typical glaze formula using washed perlite in place of feldspar:

washed perlite	34	parts
dolomite	6	parts
colemanite	4	parts
flint	6	parts

When fired to Cone 3-4, the glaze produces a fair-to-good semi-matte glaze with minor bubbling and good opacity, a definite yellow color (due to iron content of the perlite), and a minor pin-holing and crazing.

Huge quantities of volcanic ash were erupted by Mount St. Helens during its May 1980 eruption with measurable thicknesses deposited over parts of Oregon, Washington, Idaho, and Montana. The particle size of the airborne ash was quite fine and was roughly related to the distance travelled. A sample collected in central Washington gave the following sieve analysis (in microns): more than 250 — .2%; 250-150 — 18%; 150-75 — 52%; 75-35 — 23%; less than 35 — 5%. A spectrographic analysis of the same sample showed: Si 60.5%; Al 16.6%; Fe 6.0%; Na 4.2%; Zn 4.1%; Ca 4.0%; Mg 2.6%; Phos 1.2%; Sr .06%. It was also determined that the sample contained discrete crystals of the magnetic iron oxide mineral magnetite which could be removed readily with a simple hand-held magnet. This would lower the iron content of the ash significantly.

The wide variety of candidate raw glasses, their relatively easy accessibility throughout the Pacific West and their ease of preparation should make volcanic glasses of interest to the potter. One word of caution, if you select obsidian to experiment with don't forget that it is already a glass and has some extremely sharp edges. After all, remember that the Indians made knives and arrowheads from raw obsidian.

Minerals for Coloring Glazes

Oxides of various metals provide most of the colorants used in ceramic glazes. Oxides of chromium, cobalt, copper, iron, manganese, nickel and vanadium are most commonly used, with antimony and the minerals rutile and ilmenite utilized to a lesser extent.

The iron oxide, hematite, is the only mineral that can supply one of the above oxides on a common basis. All of the others are either limited in occurrence or have chemical problems that make them unsuitable for glaze applications.

Cuprite, a copper oxide, stibnite, an antimony sulfide, and pyrolusite, a manganese oxide, are fairly common but only in mineralized areas. Stibnite, being a sulfide, would have to be roasted to remove the sulfur. The chromium oxide mineral, chromite, is found at scattered localities in Oregon, Montana, and California, but its usefulness is impaired by the presence of variable amounts of iron in the chemical formula.

The two principal titanium minerals are ilmenite and rutile. Ilmenite, FeO, TiO_2, is far more common that rutile, TiO_2. In certain beach placers the two minerals are found together, but in solid rock formations rutile is rare. Compared to practically all of the other glaze and pigment minerals, ilmenite and rutile are scarce, and, with the exception of a few beach placers on the West Coast, their concentration is too low to be considered by individuals as a practical source of titanium oxide.

Titaniferous iron ores containing ilmenite, hematite, magnetite and rarely rutile, are mined commercially in the state of New York and New Jersey. The ilmenite crystals in the ore are sufficiently large to permit their separation by milling. Sands containing both ilmenite and rutile are mined and concentrated at several mines in Florida, but only one mine is reported to ship rutile and ilmenite separately. Presently most of the rutile used in the U.S. is imported from the east coast of Australia.

Craft potters wishing to use either ilmenite or rutile in sand-grain-sized particles have three possibilities for acquiring a supply that might be worth exploring. First, you might obtain a list of domestic ilmenite and rutile producers from the U.S. Bureau of Mines and the Canadian Department of Energy, Mines and Resources (see Appendix 7) and try to buy directly at their mills. The second way would be to attempt to purchase from some domestic consumer who buys in large quantities. (Again, the federal agencies can provide a list of plants). In either case, it is suggested that you pool your purchasing and buy in quantities rather than small amounts. If your needs are limited, there is a third option. Nearly every large city has at least one industrial mineral wholesaler, and he may either have supplies on hand or can arrange to get some for you.

Just so you will know what you are buying, here are the physical properties of ilmenite and rutile:

Property	Ilmenite	Rutile
Color	iron-black	reddish-brown, but red, yellowish, violet, and black at times
H.	5-6	6-6.5
Sp. Gr.	4.5-5.0	4.2-5.2
Streak	submetallic; powder black to brownish red	pale brown
Fracture	conchoidal	sub-conchoidal to uneven
Lustre	sub-metallic	metallic, sub-adamantine
Crystals	thick, tabular	commonly prismatic

Figure 4.5 *Physical properties of rutile and ilmenite.*

Both of these minerals are quite hard, so if you plan on fine-grinding them, you had better use mechanical equipment if you need more than a pound or two.

Mineral	Composition	H	Sp Gr	Streak	Color	Availability
Cuprite	Cu_2O	4	6	brownish-red	red	common in mineralized areas
Chromite	$Cr_2O_3 \cdot FeO$	5.5	4.5	brown	iron-black	not common
Hematite	Fe_2O_3	5.5	5	red-brown	iron-black	common
Pyrolusite	MnO_2	2.5	4.7	black	iron-black	common in mineralized areas
Rutile	TiO_2	6	4	pale brown	reddish-brown	common but in low concentrations
Ilmenite	$FeO \cdot TiO_2$	5.5	4.5	brown-red	iron-black	common but in low concentrations

Figure 4.6 *Minerals supplying metal oxides for colored glazes.*

BENEFICIATION AND PROCESSING OF GLAZE MATERIALS

Extreme care must be exercized in the selection, beneficiation and processing of glaze minerals since they form the exterior, highly visible outer surface of the finished ceramic product. Any impurities or digressions from the norm will report either in the firing behavior or the final appearance of the ware, or both.

If the original glaze material is a mineral that has formed in rather large crystals the task of selecting only that mineral is greatly simplified. Disseminated ores will require careful separation from the gangue, probably by panning or some other washing technique.

Before attempting to separate two or more minerals by panning, however, take a look at the specific gravities of the minerals making up your ore. If they are all quite close together you will have a most difficult time effecting the singling out of unwanted material. For instance, do not attempt to separate quartz and feldspar since their specific gravities (2.65 and 2.56) are almost identical. The two black minerals, magnetite and galena, can be easily panned since the difference is quite large (5.1 and 7.5). In this latter case the separation would most likely be made with a magnet rather than by gravitational methods.

Ores that have been stained by weathering may be hard to identify, and if the discoloration has come from some other adjacent mineral, then serious consideration should be given to rejecting it since the surface impurity might be inimical to the objective sought. Make sure that the mineral is what you think it is and make doubly sure that no other matter gets into your feed-stock.

Before starting to crush and grind your glaze minerals do this: (1) clean all of your equipment thoroughly; (2) run a small quantity of your ore through the entire flow-sheet and throw it away (this scours out any left-over material from the previous run). See the chapter on "Beneficiation and Processing" for suggestions on treating your ore.

Generally speaking, iron in any form is not wanted in the normal glaze formula due to its potential for discoloring. The magnetic form of iron, the mineral magnetite, is easy to remove with a powerful hand magnet, provided the individual magnetite crystals are freed from the other minerals that may be present. The removal of non-magnetic iron oxide minerals is more involved and subject to some uncertainties. After being finely ground, ores suspected of harboring such material can be heated in a reducing atmosphere (and allowed to cool there). With luck the iron will have been reduced to a magnetic form. The addition of charcoal will help to create a reducing condition while the ore is being heated. The uncertainty arises in part from the difficulty in exposing all of the ore to the reducing atmosphere and maintaining this condition during the cooling phase. The presence of other minerals may also inhibit the transformation to the magnetic oxide form.

The preparation of minerals to be used in coloring glazes is almost identical to that for the standard glaze materials. The emphasis here, however, is to produce as high a concentration of the various metal oxides as possible. This not only makes the finished product more effective, but by increasing the concentration of the oxide, the impurities are thereby decreased.

BIBLIOGRAPHIES

TECHNICAL PUBLICATIONS

The technical literature that is available on every phase of the geology, mineralization, mining, beneficiation and processing of ceramic materials is far too extensive to be included in any one bibliography. Modern library data retrieval systems have greatly simplified and expanded the search for reference materials and any potter seeking specific information should have little difficulty in finding it.

It is helpful, however, to have some points of entry into a subject, and the following references to standard works have been included to acquaint one with the subject matter, to suggest avenues for further inquiry, and in many cases to provide specific information.

SELECTED TECHNICAL REFERENCES, ANNOTATED

Anon., 1977, Anatomy of a mine from prospect to production, U.S. Dept. of Agriculture, Forest Service, Intermountain Forest and Range Experiment Station, Ogden, Utah, Gen. Tech. Rpt., Int.-35, 69 pp. An excellent overview of most of the factors involved in setting up a mining operation. Numerous line drawings, but no bibliography.

Dana, E.S., (revised by Ford, W.E.), A textbook of mineralogy, 4th edition, John Wiley & Sons, 851 pp. The "Bible" for information on minerals. The first edition was issued in 1898 and the book has been the standard reference ever since. Appendix contains various keys to mineral identification.

Holmes, Arthur, 1965, Principles of physical geology, The Ronald Press Co., New York, 1288 pp. Very probably the best over-all text on the processes and products that go to make up physical geology. Many photos and diagrams.

Klinefelter, T.A., and Hamlin, H.P., 1957, Syllabus of clay testing, U.S. Bur. of Mines, Bull. 565, 67 pp, plus bibliography with 209 entries. Discusses classification, description, testing and marketing requirements for clays.

Lang, A.H., 1970, Prospecting in Canada, 4th ed., Geol. Survey of Canada, Econ. Geol. Rpt., no. 7, 308 pp. A complete manual on all phases of prospecting, particularly in the far north.

Lefond, Stanley J., editor, 1975, Industrial minerals and rocks, 4th edit., American Inst. Mining, Metallurgical and Petroleum Engrs., New York, 1360 pp. Individual chapters deal with the uses for ceramic raw materials, mineral pigments, and refractories. Other chapters discuss each of the industrial minerals in considerable detail. Comprehensive bibliographies for each mineral. A 5th edition of this work, which is updated every five years, was due off the press in 1981. Earlier editions also contain additional related information.

Maley, T.S., 1977, Handbook of mineral law, MMRC Publications, Boise, Idaho, 293 pp. This volume attempts to explain the more important aspects of the mining law in terms understandable by the layman. Good treatment of legal descriptions, legal citations, location of mining claims and many other subjects related to mining and mining claims.

Parmelee, C.W., and Schroyer, C.R., 1922, Classification of clays, in Clay, U.S. Bur. of Mines Inf. Circ. 6155, pp 12-15.

Pearl, Richard, 1955, How to know the minerals and rocks, McGraw-Hill. One of the good, popular books on the identification of rocks and minerals.

——,——, 1973, Handbook for prospectors and operators of small mines, 5th edition, McGraw-Hill, 472 pp. A most practical book for the prospector and small miner. This text was originally edited by Von Berne-witz for many years and has been considered one of the most informative books on this subject.

Peele, Robert, 1941, Mining engineer's handbook, John Wiley & Sons, 2505 pp., in two volumes. An abundance of detailed information on just about every kind of mining that has ever been attempted. Much detailed cost compari-sons and discussions on relative merits of various mining techniques and equipment.

Smith, Orsino, 1940, Mineral identification simplified, a handbook of the min-erals, Wetzel Publishing Co., 271 pp. A less detailed work than Smith's 1953 publication described next. Good for work with the more common miner-als.

_____,_____, 1953, Identification and qualitative chemical analysis of minerals, 2nd edition, Van Nostrand, 385 pp. Much of the text is comprised of tables and charts useful in the identification of minerals. Color plates show the characteristic appearance of beads and fusions conducted on charcoal and plaster tablets. Good information on how to test and the equipment required.

Taggart, A.V., 1945, Handbook of mineral dressing, John Wiley & Sons, 1915 pp. The term "mineral dressing" includes all of the steps required to change raw ore to a usable, finished concentrate. This text discusses all of the myriad ways that ores are beneficiated, and the equipment used.

Thrush, P.A., 1968, A dictionary of mining, mineral and related terms, U.S. Bur. of Mines Special Pub., 1269 pp. About 55,000 terms and 150,000 definitions.

Trask, Parker, D., editor, 1950, Applied Sedimentation, John Wiley & Sons, 707 pp. Excellent discussion of clay formation and deposits, including chapter by Grim, Ralph, E., Application of studies of the composition of clays in the field of ceramics, pp 464-474.

Tyler, Paul, M., 1929, Clay, U.S. Bur. of Mines Inf. Circ. 6155, 63 pp. Summarizes information on clay deposits, mining and preparation of raw clays.

SELECTED REFERENCES TO CERAMIC MATERIALS

Allen, J.B., and Charsley, T.J., 1968, Nepheline syenite and phonolite, Inst. of Geol. Sci., Minerals Resources Div., London, England, 169 pp.

Anon., 1967, Mining and milling nepheline syenite, Canadian Clay and Ceram-ics, Vol. 40, No. 5, p 12.

Castle, J.E., and Gillson, J.L., 1960, Feldspar, nepheline syenite and aplite, in Industrial Min. and Rocks, 3rd edit. Chap. 16, pp 339-362, American Inst. Mng. and Metall. Engrs, New York.

Cleveland, George B., editor, 1956, Basic studies in the clay industry, California Div. of Mines, California Jour. of Mines and Geology, vol. 52, No. 2, 227 pp. Ten authors discuss exploration, winning, testing, mineralogy, prop-erties, preparation and firing of clays.

Clews, F.H., 1969, Heavy clay technology, 2nd edit., Academic Press, N.Y., 481 pp.

Cooper, J.D., 1970, Clays, in Mineral Facts and Problems, U.S. Bur. of Mines Bull. 650, pp 923-938.

Fraser, Harry, 1974. Glazes for the craft potter: Watson-Guptill Publications, N.Y., 146 pp.

Fryklund, V.C., Jr., 1951. A reconnaissance of some Idaho feldspar deposits, with a note on the occurrence of columbite and samarskite: Idaho Bur. of Mines and Geology, Pamphlet 91, 30 pp.

Grim, Ralph E., 1968, Clay mineralogy, 2nd edit., McGraw-Hill, New York, 596 pp.

Grimshaw, R.W., 1972, The chemistry and physics of clays and other ceramic raw materials, 4th edit. rev., Wiley-Interscience, N.Y., 1024 pp.

Hewitt, D.F., 1960, Nepheline syenite deposits of Southern Ontario, Ontario Dept. of Mines, Vol. 69, Pt. 8, 194 pp.

Hodge, E.T., 1938, Northwest clays, *in* Market for Columbia River Hydro-electric power, using northwest minerals, Sec. 4, War Dept. Corps of Eng., U.S. Army, Office of Div. Engr., North Pac. Div., Portland, Oregon, 1079 pp.

Kelly, H.J., 1956, Ceramic industry development and raw material resources of Oregon, Washington, Idaho and Montana; Inf. Circ. 7752, U.S. Bur. of Mines, 77 pp.

Klinefelter, T.A., et al, 1943, Syllabus of clay testing, pt. 1, U.S. Bur. of Mines, Bull. 451., 35 pp.

Klinefelter, T.A., and Hamlin, H.P., 1957, Syllabus of clay testing, pt. 2, U.S. Bur. of Mines, Bull. 565, 67 pp. Discusses classification, description, marketing and testing of clays. Bibliography has 209 entries.

Lang, W.B., et al, 1940, Clay investigations in the southern states, 1934-5, U.S. Geol. Survey, Bull. 901, 346 pp.

Lohman, L.H., 1956, Testing of clays, California Journal of Mines and Geology, vol. 52, no. 2, pp. 151-154.

Millot, G., 1964, Geologie des argiles, (translated by Farrand, W.R., and Paquet, H.), published as Geology of Clays, Springer-Verlag, N.Y., 1970, 425 pp.

Murdoch, Joseph, and Webb, R.W., 1956, Minerals of California, California Div. of Mines, Bull. 173, 452 pp. Essentially a catalog of mineral species. Nearly 100 pages of references.

Murray, H.H., 1960, Clay, *in* Industrial Minerals and Rocks, 3rd edit., J.L. Gillson ed., American Inst. Mining and Metall. Engrs., pp. 259-284.

Pask, JA., and Turner, M.D., 1961, Clays and clay technology, California Div. of Mines, Bull. 169, 2nd edit., 326 pp.

Patterson, S.H., and Murray, H.H., 1975, Clays, *in* Industrial Minerals and Rocks, 3rd edit., American Inst. Mng. and Metall. Engrs., pp 577-585. A comprehensive discussion of clays worldwide, with a total of 325 titles listed in the Bibliography.

Rhodes, Daniel, 1959, Stoneware and porcelain — the art of high-fired pottery, Chilton Co.

——, ——, 1973, Clay and glazes for the potter: 2nd rev. edit, Pittman, 350 pp.

Ries, H., and Keele, J., 1912, Preliminary report on the clay and shale deposits of the Western Provinces, (Part I), Memoir 24-E, Geol. Survey of Canada. Series also contains: Part II, Memoir 25; Part III, Memoir 47; and Part IV, Memoir 65, issued subsequently.

Skinner, K.G., and Kelly, Hal J., 1949, Preliminary ceramic tests of clays from seven Pacific Northwest deposits, U.S. Bur. of Mines Rpt. of Inv. 4449, 59 pp, 47 figs. Describes tests to determine suitability of seven Pacific Northwest clay deposits for producing refractories.

Sohn, I.G., 1952, Industrial clays, other than potential sources of alumina of the Columbia Basin, U.S. Geol. Survey, Circ. 158, 18 pp.

Tyler, Paul M., 1935, Clay, U.S. Bur. of Mines, Inf. Circ. 6155 rev., 66 pp. Discusses varieties of clays at some length. Bibliography contains 40 references.

Wild, Alfred, and Key, W.W., 1963, Methods and practices in clay mining, processing and utilization, Kraftile Co., Fremont, California, U.S. Bur. of

Mines, Inf. Circ. 8194, 44 pp., 19 figs. Presents technical information on processing raw clay to finished product. Describes prospecting, exploration and test methods for raw clays.

Wilson, Hewitt, 1934, Kaolin and china clay in the Pacific Northwest, Washington University Exper. Sta., Bull. 76, 188 pp.

SELECTED REFERENCES TO GLAZE MATERIALS

Allen, J.B. and Charsley, T.J., 1968, Nepheline syenite and phonolite, Inst. of Geol. Sci., Minerals Resources Div., London, England, 169 pp.

Anon., 1967, Mining and milling nepheline syenite, Canadian Clay and Ceramics, vol. 40, no. 5, 12 pp.

Asher, R.R., 1965, Volcanic construction materials in Idaho, Idaho Bur. of Mines and Geol., Pamph. 135, 150 pp.

Campbell, Ian, editor, 1966, The mineral industry of California, compiled by U.S. Geol. Survey and California Div. of Mines and Geol., issued by California Div. of Mines as Bull. 191, 450 pp.

Castle, J.E., and Gillson, J.L., 1960, Feldspar, nepheline syenite, and aplite, *in* Industrial Minerals and Rocks, 3rd edit., Chap 16, pp. 339-362, American Inst. Mng. and Metall. Engrs., New York.

Fraser, Harry, 1974, Glazes for the craft potter, Watson-Guptill Publications, New York, 146 pp.

Fryklund, V.C., Jr., 1951, A reconnaissance of some Idaho feldspar deposits, with a note on the occurrence of columbite and samarskite, Idaho Bur. of Mines and Geol., Pamph. 91, 30 pp.

Hewitt, D.F., 1960, Nepheline syenite deposits of Southern Ontario, Ontario Dept. of Mines, vol. 69, pt. 8, 194 pp.

Jacobs, Charles, W.F., 1950, Glazes from Oregon volcanic glass, Oregon Dept. of Geol. and Mineral Indust., GMI Short Paper no. 20, 16 pp.

Koch, W.J., Harman, C.G., and O'Bannon, L.S., 1950, Some physical and chemical properties of experimental glazes for vitrified institutional whiteware, *in* Journ. of the Amer. Cer. Soc., 33 (1) 1-8, (1950).

Rhodes, Daniel, 1959, Stoneware and porcelain — the art of high-fired pottery, Chilton Co.

_____, _____, 1973, Clay and glazes for the potter, 2nd rev. edit., Pittman, 350 pp.

Wilson, Hewitt, 1934, Kaolin and china clay in the Pacific Northwest, Washington Univ. Exper. Sta. Bull. 76, 188 pp.

Wright, Lauren A., 1957, Talc and soapstone, *in* Mineral Commodities of California, California Div. of Mines, Bull. 176, pp. 623-634.

See also lists of state and provincial publications, pages 131 through 141 in the Appendix.

APPENDICES

APPENDIX 1

WATER OF PLASTICITY FOR SOME CLAY MINERALS

Attapulgite	92%
Halloysite	33-50
Illite	17-38
Kaolinite	9-56
Montmorillonite	83-250

Water of plasticity is the percent of water, based on water loss at 110 deg. C., required to develop a workable plastic state.

APPENDIX 2

CLASSIFICATION OF CLAYS

Clays can be classified in many ways. Some of the more important are shown in outline form here. The selection has been made to assist the reader in unravelling some of the confusing terminology used to describe clays and to help him in arriving at a better understanding of the relationships of one clay or clay mineral to another and its composition, properties, and end-uses. One potter's ball clay may be a dense-burning, non-refractory, medium-shrink, light-colored clay to a second; and called either kaolin or china clay by a third.

By Geological Origin

Most scientific geological terms are really a form of shorthand. One word stands for a paragraph or two. See the Glossary for fuller descriptions.
1. Residual, or primary
2. Transported, or secondary
    a. alluvial (by streams on flood-plains, river banks)
    b. lacustrine (in lakes)
    c. estuarine (in bays, submerged river mouths)
    d. marine (near or off-shore)
    e. glacial (by glaciers, often sorted or un-sorted by water)
    f. eolian (by wind, dunes, loess deposits)
    g. colluvial (by gravity)

By Mineral Composition

Most clays are composed of one or more clay minerals. Many descriptions of clays are based upon their mineral content and the behavior of a clay during forming, drying and firing is determined largely by its mineral makeup. The minerals listed below have been arranged into three groups; the minerals in each having roughly similar characteristics.

Kaolin Group	Montmorillonite Group	Hydrous Mica Group
kaolinite	montmorillonite	bravasite
dickite	beidellite	Ordovician bentonites
nacrite	nontronite	illite
anauxite	saponite	
halloysite	sauconite	
allophane	hectorite	

By Chemical Description

The following descriptive terms are rather imprecise. The values following each term may vary somewhat with different authors but in general the limits are typical.

High alumina	(clays with at least 38% Al_2O_3)
Bauxitic	(intermediate between kaolin and bauxite)
Siliceous	(clays with high silica content)
Ferruginous	(clays with 8-10% FeO or more)
Calcareous	(clays with 2% or more lime)
Carbonaceous	(clays with high carbon, shales commonly are high carbon)

By Physical Properties

Plasticity	plastic, fat, semiplastic, short, flint, semi-flint
Particle size	colloidal, fine- or coarse-grained
Refractoriness	refractory, fire clay
Color	colors in raw and fired state

By Geographic Nomenclature

By countries:	domestic, English, German, etc.
By localities:	Dorset, Georgia, Ione, etc.

By Statistical Nomenclature

All statistical data on clays reported by the U.S. Bureau of Mines in its various publications is tabulated under these six classifications.

1. kaolin or china clay
2. ball clay
3. fire clay, including stoneware
4. bentonite
5. fuller's earth
6. common clay and shale

By Laboratory Testing*

I. Clays burning white or cream, not calcareous.
  A. Open-burning clays (i.e. still distinctly porous) at cone 15 (2,606° F., 1430° C.)
    Uses: If of good color or of good strength — pottery. If of good or high degree of refractoriness — refractories.
  B. Dense-burning (i.e. become nearly or completely non-porous between cones 10 and 15 (2,426-2,606° F., 1330-1430° C.). Medium to high strength, medium shrinkage.
    a. Non-refractory clays:
      1. Good color. Uses: pottery, certain whiteware, porcelains, stoneware.
      2. Poor color. Uses: stoneware, terra cotta, face brick, saggers.
    b. Refractory clays:
      1. Good color. Uses: refractories, pottery, whiteware, porcelain, stoneware.
  C. Dense-burning between cones 5 and 10 (2,246-2,426° F., 1230-1330° C.), and

---

*Parmelee, C. Ward, and Schroyer, C.R.; 1922, Further investigations of Illinois fireclays, Illinois Geol. Survey Bull. 38, pp 278-279.

do not overburn seriously at 5 cones (about 180° F., 82° C.) higher than the temperature at which minimum porosity is reached.

   a. Non-refractory clays, medium to high strength, medium shrinkage:

      1. Good color; usually reach minimum porosity between cones 5 and 8 (2,246-2,354° F., 1230-1290° C.). Type: Ball clays. Uses: pottery, whiteware, porcelain and stoneware.

      2. Poor color. Uses: stoneware, terra cotta, face brick, saggers.

   b. Refractory clays:

      1. Dense-burning at cone 5 (2,246° F., 1230° C); do not seriously overburn for 12 cones (about 432° F., 222° C.) higher; highly refractory; softening point at cone 31 (3,182° F., 1750° C.) or higher.

      2. Dense-burning at cone 8 (2,354° F., 1290° C.); not overfiring at cones 13 or 14 (2,550° F., 1399° C.). Strength and softening point as in (1) above.

      3. Dense-burning at cone 8 (2,354° F., 1290° C.); not overfiring at cone 15 (2,606° F., 1430° C.). Softening point, cone 29 or higher.

II. Buff-burning clay.

   A. Refractory clays.

      a. Open-burning (5 percent porosity or more) at cone 15 (2,606° F., 1430° C.) or above. Indurated. Non-plastic, or slightly plastic (unless weathered). Type: flint clays.

         1. Alumina 40 percent or less. Use: refractories.

         2. High-alumina (over 40 percent). Type: diaspore clays. Uses: refractories.

      b. Open-burning (5 percent porosity or more) at cone 15 (2,606° F., 1430° C.) but plastic.

         3. Silica 65 percent or less. Uses: firebrick and other refractories, terra cotta, glazed brick.

         4. High/silica (over 65 percent). Uses: firebrick and other refractories.

      c. Dense-burning (porosity under 5 percent) between cones 10 and 15 (2,426-2,606° F., 1330-1430° C.).

         5. Medium to high strength, not overburning for 5 cones (about 180° F., 82° C.) higher than point of minimum porosity. Uses: saggers and other refractories; architectural terra cotta, enameled and face brick.

      d. Dense-burning (porosity under 5 percent) at cone 10 (2,426° F., 1330° C.) or lower.

         6. Dense-burning at cone 5 (see I b 1. above).

         7. Dense-burning at cone 8 (see I b 2. above).

         8. Dense-burning at cone 8 (see I b 3. above).

         Uses: firebrick, saggers, miscellaneous refractories, architectural terra cotta, enameled and face bricks.

   B. Non-refractory clays.

      a. Open-burning (5 percent porosity or more) at cones lower than 10 (2,426° F., 1330° C.).

         1. High or medium strength. Uses: architectural terra cotta, stoneware, yellow ware, face brick.

         2. Low strength. Use: brick.

      b. Dense-burning (porosity under 5 percent) at cones lower than 10 (2,426° F., 1330° C.).

         3. High or medium strength. Uses: architectural terra cotta, stoneware, face brick.

III. Clays burning red, brown, or other dark colors.

   A. Open-burning (do not attain low porosity at any temperature short of actual fusion).

      1. Medium or high strength. Uses: brick, flower pots.

2. Low strength. Use: brick.
B. Dense-burning clays.
  a. Having a long vitrification range (5 cones or about 180° F., 82° C.).
    3. High or medium strength. Uses: art ware, face brick, architectural terra cotta.
    4. Low strength. Uses: floor tile.
  b. Having a short vitrification range:
    5. High or medium strength. Uses: building brick, face brick, flower pots.
  c. Highly fusible, forming a glass at about cone 5 (2,246° F., 1230° C.).
    6. Slip clays
IV. Clays burning light gray or light cream.
  A. Containing calcium or magnesium carbonate or both. Never attain low porosity. Very short heat range. Use: common brick.

By Usage

Although only the fired portion of the classification will probably interest most potters, a few of the uses for un-fired clays are included to round out the general clay utilization picture.

A. **Fired**
1. **Whiteware clays**
  Kaolins
  Ball clay
  China clay
2. **Refractory**
  Plastic fire-clay
  Flint clay
  Refractory shale
3. **Expansible clays and shales**
  Bloating clays and shales

4. **Vitrifying clays**
  Paving brick clay and shale
  Sewer pipe clay and shale
  Roofing tile clay and shale
5. **Brick clays**
  Common brick clay and shale
  Terra cotta clay and shale
  Drain tile clay and shale
6. **Gumbo clays**
7. **Slip clays**
8. **Miscellaneous clays**
  Portland cement clays
  Pigment clays
  Taconite pelletizing clays

B. **Un-Fired**
9. **Miscellaneous clays**
  Filler, extender, carrier clays
  Adobe brick clay
  Oil well drilling mud clays
  Slurry wall mud clays
  Oil and grease adsorbent clays
  Decolorizing clays

APPENDIX 3

MOHS SCALE OF HARDNESS MINERALS AND HARDNESS OF SELECTED CERAMIC MINERALS

1. Talc					have greasy feel
2. Gypsum	Borax Galena	Barite			easily scratched with finger-nail
3. Calcite	Gibbsite Witherite	Dolomite	Magnesite		readily cut with knife
4. Fluorite	Colemanite				cut rather easily with knife
5. Apatite	Limonite	Goethite			scratched with some difficulty with knife
6. Orthoclase	Hematite Diaspore	Anorthite	Leucite	Albite	barely scratched with knife
7. Quartz					scratch glass easily
8. Tourmaline					
9. Corundum					
10. Diamond					

The Mohs scale of hardness for minerals is based on nine common minerals, plus diamond, which are arranged in an ascending order of hardness. There is no quantitative mathematical relationship between the hardness of one mineral and another. A mineral with a hardness of 4 will scratch minerals with smaller numbers, and in turn be scratched by those with higher ones. Minerals having smooth crystal faces should be used for hardness testing whenever possible since specimens with rough or sugary surfaces will powder and appear to have been scratched even when they are too hard. A common pocket-knife blade, with a little practice will help in determining the hardness for minerals ranging from 1 to 7. The minerals having a hardness of 8 or more are usually classed as gemstones.

APPENDIX 4

CHEMICAL COMPOSITION OF SELECTED GLAZE MATERIALS

Oxide Sought	Mineral	Formula	Molecular Weight	Molecular Wt. of Oxide	Conversion Factor (3)
Al_2O_3	Orthoclase	$K_2O \cdot Al_2O_3 \cdot 6SiO_2$	556.50	101.94	.183
BaO	barite	$BaSO_4$	233.42	153.36	.657
	witherite	$BaCO_3$	197.36	153.36	.777
B_2O_3	borax	$Na_2O \cdot 2B_2O_3 \cdot 10H_2O$	381.28	69.64	.365
	colemanite	$2CaO \cdot 3B_2O_3 \cdot 5H_2O$	401.08	69.64	.521
	ulexite	$NaCaB_5O_9 \cdot 8H_2O$	405.18	69.64	.489
CaO	calcite	$CaCO_3$	100.08	56.08	.560
	dolomite	$CaCO_3 \cdot MgCO_3$	184.40	56.08	.304
	anorthite	$CaO \cdot Al_2O_3 \cdot 2SiO_2$	278.14	56.08	.202
PbO	galena	PbS (2)			
Li_2O	petalite	$Li_2O \cdot Al_2O_3 \cdot 8SiO_2$	612.30	29.88	.049
	lepidolite	$Li_2O \cdot Al_2O_3 \cdot K_2O \cdot SiO_2$	406.20	29.88	.074
	spodumene	$Li_2O \cdot Al_2O_3 \cdot 4SiO_2$	372.06	29.88	.080
MgO	magnesite	$MgCO_3$	84.32	40.32	.478
	steatite	$3MgO \cdot 4SiO_2 \cdot H_2O$	379.20	40.32	.319
K_2O	orthoclase	$K_2O \cdot Al_2O_3 \cdot 6SiO_2$	556.50	94.20	.169
	leucite	$K_2O \cdot Al_2O_3 \cdot 4SiO_2$	436.38	94.20	.216
SiO_2	flint	SiO_2	60.06	60.06	1.000
	quartz	SiO_2	60.06	60.06	1.000
	china clay	$Al_2O_3 \cdot 2SiO_2 \cdot 2H_2O$	258.06	60.06	.466
Na_2O	albite	$Na_2O \cdot Al_2O_3 \cdot 6SiO_2$	524.30	62.00	.118
SrO (1)	strontianite	$SrCO_3$	147.63	103.63	.702
ZnO	zincite	ZnO	81.38	81.38	1.000
	smithsonite	$ZnCO_3$	125.38	81.38	.649

(1) No readily available minerals. Commercial chemicals suggested.
(2) See text for health hazards when using raw mineral.
(3) Molecular weight of oxide divided by weight of mineral.

APPENDIX 5

GEOLOGIC TIME CHART

STRATIGRAPHIC DIVISIONS			TIME	DOMINANT LIFE	
ERA	SYSTEM OR PERIOD	SERIES OR EPOCH	Estimated ages of time boundaries in millions of years	ANIMALS	PLANTS
CENOZOIC	QUATERNARY	Holocene Pleistocene ——— 2-3 ———		Man	
	TERTIARY	Pliocene ——— 12 ——— Miocene ——— 26 ——— Oligocene ——— 37-38 ——— Eocene ——— 53-54 ——— Paleocene		Mammals, birds, bony fish, mollusks, arthropods and insects	Flowering trees and shrubs
			——— 65 ———		
MESOZOIC	CRETACEOUS	Upper (Late) Lower (Early)		Dinosaurs and Flying and swimming reptiles	Conifers, Cycads, Ginkgos and Ferns
			——— 136 ———		
	JURASSIC	Upper (Late) Middle (Middle) Lower (Early)			
			——— 190-195 ———		
	TRIASSIC	Upper (Late) Middle (Middle) Lower (Early)		Ammonites	
			——— 225 ———		
PALEOZOIC	PERMIAN	Upper (Late) Lower (Early)		Giant insects, Primitive reptiles & Amphibians	Scale trees, Cordaites, Calamites, and Tree ferns
			——— 280 ———		
	Carboniferous PENNSYLVANIAN	Upper (Late) Middle (Middle) Lower (Early)			
	Carboniferous MISSISSIPPIAN	Upper (Late) Lower (Early)		Crinoids and Blastoids	Primitive scale trees and tree ferns
			——— 345 ———		
	DEVONIAN	Upper (Late) Middle (Middle) Lower (Early)		Sharks & Lungfish	
			——— 395 ———		
	SILURIAN	Upper (Late) Middle (Middle) Lower (Early)		Corals,	Lycopods and Psilophytes
			——— 430-440 ———		
	ORDOVICIAN	Upper (Late) Middle (Middle) Lower (Early)		Brachiopods, and	Algae and Fungi
			——— 500 ———		
	CAMBRIAN	Upper (Late) Middle (Middle) Lower (Early)		Trilobites	
			——— 570 ———		
PRECAMBRIAN (More than 80% of earth's estimated 4.5 billion years falls within this era)	Z - base of Cambrian to 800 m.y. Y - 800 to 1,600 m.y. X - 1,600 to 2,500 m.y. W - older than 2,500 m.y. (U.S.G.S. Bull. 1394-A, 1974)			Beginning of primitive plant and animal life	

APPENDIX 6

TABLE OF ELEMENTS COMMONLY USED IN CERAMIC GLAZES

Element	Symbol	Atomic Wt	Chemical Formula of oxide	Molecular Weight
Aluminum	Al	27	Al_2O_3	102
Boron	B	11	B_2O_3	70
Calcium	Ca	40	CaO	56
Cobalt	Co	59	Co_2O_3	166
Lead	Pb	207	PbO	223
Lithium	Li	7	Li_2O	30
Magnesium	Mg	24	MgO	40
Potassium	K	39	K_2O	94
Silicon	Si	28	SiO_2	60
Sodium	Na	23	Na_2O	62
Strontium	Sr	88	SrO	104
Zinc	Zn	65	ZnO	81
Oxygen	O	16		
Hydrogen	H	1		
Nitrogen	N	14		
Iron	Fe	56	Fe_2O_3	160
Manganese	Mn	55	MnO_2	87
Nickel	Ni	59	Ni_2O_3	165
Copper	Cu	64	CuO	80
Sulphur	S	32	SO_2	64
Phosphorus	P	31	P_2O_5	142

APPENDIX 7

PUBLIC AGENCIES OF INTEREST TO THE PROSPECTOR-POTTER

Government agencies in both Canada and the United States have published a great many bulletins, reports and maps useful to the craft potter. Many of these are sold through agency sales offices and nearly all of them have been placed in repository libraries in numerous cities. State and provincial geology departments have also published much material, some of which is available at nominal cost, or has been placed in a limited number of libraries. Selected references published by some of the state geology departments are listed.

Many states have published, in cooperation with the U.S. Geological Survey, a report "Mineral and Water Resources of - - -". These publications contain a great deal of basic information of interest to the craft potter, including sections on various types of clays, natural pigments, glaze minerals, and other ceramic materials. The reports are distributed through individual state agencies.

Both national and state agencies have publication lists which give both in-print and out-of-print titles. Reading lists may sometimes be obtained from state libraries. These lists may include unpublished thesis submitted by degree candidates at the state universities.

Members of national engineering societies can also call upon the services of the Engineering Societies Library in New York. The library contains one of the most complete collections of engineering and technologic data in the world. The library assesses a charge for its many and varied services. The individual societies also produce a variety of information, either through their monthly house organs or by means of separates of single papers and bound volumes containing a collection of related articles. The societies usually have printed lists of publications or can provide a list of titles on the subject in question.

A. State Departments of Geology

State departments of geology tend to be relatively low key, small, and almost unknown to all but the professional community. For this reason pertinent information about each agency has been assembled in the following section, together with, in some cases, a brief comment on clays that might be of interest to the craft potter.

ALABAMA   Numerous publications are available on the state's extensive ceramic clays. Clays suitable for craft potters are found in many parts of the state. Research data on the state's clays and shales may be obtained from the Alabama Geological Survey, P.O. Drawer O, University, Alabama, 35486; Tel.: (205) 349-2852.

ALASKA   Clays, including the infamous Bootlegger Cove clay, have been studied by the Alaska Division of Geological and Geophysical Surveys. The Division is located at 3001 Porcupine Drive, Anchorage, Alaska, 99501; Tel.:

(907) 279-1433. The Division also has an office in Fairbanks, P.O. Box 80007, College, Alaska; Tel.: (907) 479-6123.

ARIZONA   Limited published information on clay. Inquiries may be directed to the Bureau of Geology and Mineral Technology, Geological Survey Branch, 845 N. Park Ave., Tucson, Arizona, 85719; Tel.: (602) 626-2733.

ARKANSAS   The state has large deposits of kaolin. Inquiries should be sent to Arkansas Geólogical Commission, Vardelle Parham Geology Center, 3815 West Roosevelt Road, Little Rock, Arkansas, 72204; Tel.: (501) 371-1646.

CALIFORNIA   Common pottery clays widely scattered throughout the state. Numerous publications and maps available by mail from California Division of Mines and Geology, P.O. Box 2980, Sacramento, California, 98512, and over-the-counter from district offices in Sacramento, San Francisco, and Los Angeles. Inquiries may be directed to district offices: Sacramento, 2814 "O" Street; Tel.: (916) 445-5716; San Francisco, Ferry Building, Room 2022; Tel.: (916) 557-0633; Los Angeles, Junipero Serra Building, Room 1065, 107 South Broadway at First Street; Tel.: (213) 620-3560.

COLORADO   A total of twenty publications have been issued by various organizations on the clay resources of the state. The Colorado Geological Survey is located at 715 State Centennial Building, 1313 Sherman Street, Denver, Colorado, 80203; Tel.: (303) 839-2611.

CONNECTICUT   The Department has no current publications on clays, and no staff ceramist. Direct inquiries to Connecticut Geological and Natural History Survey, Department of Environmental Protection, State Office Building, Room 561, Hartford, Connecticut, 06115; Tel.: (203) 566-3540.

DELAWARE   Clays gathered from forty-eight localities in the state have been tested. The Delaware Geological Survey is located in 101 Penny Hall on the University of Delaware campus, Newark, Delaware, 19711; Tel.: (302) 738-2833.

FLORIDA   Several publications of interest to the potter are available. The Florida Bureau of Geology is located at 903 West Tennessee Street, Tallahassee, Florida, 32304; Tel.: (904) 488-4191.

GEORGIA   Numerous excellent publications on the clays of the state. Inquiries may be directed to the Georgia Geologic Survey, 4th Floor, Agriculture Building, 19 Martin Luther King, Jr. Dr., S.W., Atlanta, Georgia, 30334; Tel.: (404) 656-3214.

IDAHO   Craft potters work clays of many different qualities from widely scattered locations in the state. Numerous publications have been issued by the Idaho Bureau of Mines and Geology, Moscow, Idaho, 83843; Tel.: (208) 885-6785.

ILLINOIS   The state Geological Survey has issued nearly two hundred reports on clay resources, technology and mineralogy. Circular 233 "Pottery clay resources of Illinois" gives general locations of the state's clays. The Illinois Geological Survey is located in the Natural Resources Building, Urbana, Illinois, 61801; Tel.: (217) 344-1481. The Survey has a clay mineralogist on its staff who can assist craft potters in many ways.

INDIANA   Several publications and open file reports on local clays. The Department has tested many clays and any inquiries should be sent to the Department of Natural Resources, Geological Survey, 611 North Walnut Grove, Bloomington, Indiana, 47405; Tel.: (812) 337-2862. Order publications from the same address; Tel.: (812) 337-7636.

IOWA   Six publications provide data on the properties of the state's clays. Clays associated with coal deposits are considered superior to the more recent Pleistocene deposits. Direct inquiries to the Iowa Geological Survey, 123 North Capitol Street, Iowa City, Iowa, 52242; Tel.: (319) 338-1173.

KANSAS   Half a dozen reports have been published by the Kansas Geological Survey which has two staff members who can answer inquiries concerning pottery clays. Technical problems should be addressed to the Mineral Resources Section which has two staff ceramists. The Section telephone is (913) 864-4991. The Kansas Geological Survey is located at 1930 Avenue "A", Campus West, Lawrence, Kansas, 66044; Tel.: (913) 864-3965.

KENTUCKY   Numerous publications on clay. Clay analyses published in the Reports of Investigation series. Requests for publications and information should be directed to Kentucky Geological Survey, University of Kentucky, 311 Breckenridge Hall, Lexington, Kentucky, 40506; Tel.: (606) 258-5863.

LOUISIANA   No studies or reports on clay or shale have been made. The Louisiana Geological Survey is housed in the Louisiana State University Geology building in Baton Rouge. Mail address is P.O. Box G, Baton Rouge, Louisiana, 70893; Tel.: (504) 342-6754.

MAINE   Several publications, including the Surficial Geologic maps and the Surficial Geology handbook for coastal Maine are available. Address: Maine Geological Survey, Ray Building, State House Station #22, Augusta, Maine, 04333; Tel.: (207) 289-2801.

MARYLAND   The address of the Maryland Geological Survey is Merryman Hall, Johns Hopkins University, Baltimore, Maryland, 21218; Tel.: (301) 235-0771.

MASSACHUSETTS   Little published information on clays. Inquiries should be directed to Department of Environmental Quality Engineering, Division of Waterways, Room 532, 100 Nashau Street, Boston, Massachusetts, 02144; Tel.: (617) 727-4793.

MICHIGAN   Common clays widespread. Various publications available. Direct inquiries to Michigan Department of Natural Resources, Geological Survey Division, P.O. Box 30028, Lansing, Michigan, 48909; Tel.: (517) 373-1256.

MINNESOTA   Four reports on the geology of the state's kaolin clays have been published. The Minnesota Geological Survey is located at 1633 Eustis Street, St. Paul, Minnesota, 55108; Tel.: (612) 373-3372.

MISSISSIPPI   A total of twenty-nine publications contain data on clay. Inquiries and orders for publications should be addressed to the Mississippi Geological Economic and Topographical Survey, P.O. Box 4915, Jackson, Mississippi, 39216; Tel.: (601) 354-6228.

MISSOURI   Various publications, some out-of-print, have been issued on the state's clay minerals and clay deposits. Inquiries should be sent to the Missouri Department of Natural Resources, Division of Geology and Land Survey, P.O. Box 250, Rolla, Missouri, 65401; Tel.: (314) 364-1752.

MONTANA   A series of publications gives test results on many clay samples. Copies of the reports may be obtained by writing the Montana Bureau of Mines and Geology, Butte, Montana, 59701; Tel.: (406) 792-8321. The Bureau is located in Room 206, Main Hall, Montana College of Mineral Science and Technology, Butte.

NEBRASKA   The state has published no reports on clays or shales that are helpful to the craft potter. Cretaceous age clays have been used by the art department of the University of Nebraska at Lincoln. The Nebraska Conservation and Survey Division is located at 113 Nebraska Hall, 901 North 17th Street, Lincoln, Nebraska, 68588; Tel.: (402) 472-3471.

NEVADA   One of the few states currently having a staff specialist on clay minerals and their occurrence. Information on montmorillonite, bentonite, fuller's earth, clays, and other ceramic materials has been published. Inquiries should be directed to the Nevada Bureau of Mines and Geology, University of Nevada, Reno, Nevada, 89557; Tel.; (702) 784-6691.

NEW HAMPSHIRE   The office of the New Hampshire State Geologist is in

James Hall, University of New Hampshire, Durham, New Hampshire, 03824; Tel.: (603) 862-1216.

NEW JERSEY   Numerous localities have clays of interest to the craft potter. The New Jersey Bureau of Geology and Topography is located on the 4th floor at 88 East State Street, Trenton, New Jersey, 08625; Tel.: (609) 292-2576. Order publications from Publication Sales Office, Bureau of Geology, P.O. Box 1390, Trenton, New Jersey, 08625.

NEW MEXICO   Published information on clays is available. Address inquiries to New Mexico Bureau of Mines and Mineral Resources, Campus Station, Socorro, New Mexico, 87801; Tel.: (505) 835-5420.

NEW YORK   The New York State Geological Survey is located in the State Education Building, Albany, New York, 12234; Tel.: (518) 474-5816.

NORTH CAROLINA   Several helpful publications on clays have been issued. Address of the agency is North Carolina Geological Survey, P.O. Box 27687, Raleigh, North Carolina, 27611; Tel.: (919) 733-2423.

NORTH DAKOTA   Various publications on clays and shales, including an overview of clays in the state, together with extensive selected references. Direct inquiries to North Dakota Geological Survey at either the University Station, Grand Forks, North Dakota, 58202; Tel.: (701) 777-2231; or 900 East Boulevard, State Office Building, Bismarck, North Dakota, 58505; Tel.: (701) 224-2969; or 311 Main Street, P.O. Box 997, Williston, North Dakota, 58801; Tel.: (701) 572-7707.

OHIO   The state has published nine reports on clays. Some of the early publications are out-of-print but available at many libraries throughout the state. The Department maintains a staff clay mineralogist. Inquiries should be directed to the Ohio Division of Geological Survey, Fountain Square, Columbus, Ohio, 43224; Tel.: (614) 466-5344.

OKLAHOMA   Several publications on clay materials. Facilities and staff for testing and identifying clay minerals. Analytical work provided free to Oklahoma residents. The Oklahoma Geological Survey is located at the University of Oklahoma, 830 Van Vleet Oval, Room 163, Norman, Oklahoma, 73019; Tel.: (405) 325-3031.

OREGON   Several publications issued by the Department are of interest to the craft potter. The Oregon Department of Geology and Mineral Industries is located in the State Office Building, 1400 Southwest 5th Avenue, Portland, 97201; Tel.: (503) 229-5580. Field offices are located at 2033 First Street, Baker, Oregon, 97814; Tel.: (503) 523-3133; and at 312 Southeast "H" Street, Grants Pass, Oregon, 97526; Tel.: (503) 476-2496.

PENNSYLVANIA   Many published reports on various clays of interest largely to industrial producers. No individual analyses, but results of field tests on clays available. Additional technical information may be obtained by visiting Room 805, Executive House, 2nd and Chestnut Streets, Harrisburg, Pennsylvania, 17120; Tel.: (717) 787-5897. Write the Pennsylvania Geological Survey, Department of Environmental Resources, P.O. Box 2357, Harrisburg, Pennsylvania, 17120 for publication price list.

SOUTH CAROLINA   The northwestern terminus of the Georgia-South Carolina kaolin belt is located near the southwestern border of the state. The South Carolina Geological Survey is located on Harbison Forest Road, Columbia, South Carolina, 29210; Tel.: (803) 758-6431.

SOUTH DAKOTA   No reports have been published on the clay resources of the state. Some pottery clay is mined near Hermosa in Custer County and on the Pine Ridge Indian Reservation in neighboring Shannon County in the southwestern corner of the state. The South Dakota Geological Survey is located on the campus of the University of South Dakota in the Science Center, Vermillion, South Dakota, 57069; Tel.: (605) 624-4471.

TENNESSEE   The address of the Tennessee Division of Geology is G-5, State Office Building, Nashville, Tennessee, 37219; Tel.: (615) 741-2726.

TEXAS   Various publications on clays. Address inquiries and publication orders to Bureau of Economic Geology, the University of Texas at Austin, University Station, Box X, Austin, Texas, 78712; Tel.: (512) 471-1534. The Bureau is located on the 5th floor of the Geology building on the University campus.

UTAH   The refractory clays of the state are described in one Bulletin. Direct inquiries to Utah Geological and Mineral Survey, 606 Black Hawk Way, Salt Lake City, Utah, 84108; Tel.: (801) 581-6831.

VERMONT   The first discovery of kaolin in the United States was made in Vermont in the late eighteenth century. The state has published sixteen reports on clays. Inquiries should be addressed to the Division of Geology and Earth Resources, 5 Court Street, Montpelier, Vermont, 05602; Tel.: (802) 828-3357.

VIRGINIA   Nearly fifty publications have been issued that deal with clay. Inquiries and orders for publications should be sent to the Commonwealth of Virginia Division of Mineral Resources, Natural Resources Building, McCormick Road, Box 3667, Charlottsville, Virginia, 22903; Tel.: (804) 293-5121.

WASHINGTON   More than one hundred references to clays are included in the "Annotated Bibliography of Washington Clays" which is available from the Washington Division of Geology and Earth Resources, 4224 6th Avenue, S.E., Building 1, Rowe-Six, Lacey, Washington, 98503; Tel.: (206) 753-6183. Over the years the Division has conducted extensive studies on the state's clays and numerous test results have been published.

WEST VIRGINIA   A wealth of information on the clays of the state has been published by the Survey. Inquiries should be sent to West Virginia Geological and Economic Survey, P.O. Box 879, Morgantown, West Virginia, 26505; Tel.: (304) 292-6331. Offices are located at Mont Chateau, Mont Chateau Road, Exit 10 off U.S. Hwy. 48.

WISCONSIN   A great deal of information has been published on clays that is of interest to the potter. The Wisconsin Geological and Natural History Survey is located at 1815 University Avenue, Madison, Wisconsin, 53706; Tel.: (608) 262-1705.

WYOMING   No specific publications on pottery clays. Direct inquiries to Geological Survey of Wyoming, University of Wyoming, Box 3008, University Station, Laramie, Wyoming, 82071; Tel.: (307) 742-2054.

State Publications of Interest to the Prospector-Potter

Numerous excellent publications of interest to the prospector-potter have been produced by the various geology departments. Press runs are typically short and their publications tend to go out of print in a few years. For this reason it is strongly suggested that before ordering, you write for a list of publications which will show both availability and price. Some departments require minimum orders and most make a charge for postage. Many departments have an exchange agreement with neighboring state's libraries and copies of out-of-print publications can often be examined there.

Agency publication lists may sometimes contain titles of pertinent U.S.G.S. publications and maps. These should, however, be ordered from the appropriate federal agency and *not* the state.

In addition to state geologic maps there are soil maps which can be helpful in the search for native clays. Ordinarily soil maps are published by the U.S. Department of agriculture in cooperation with local governments. Information concerning the availability and coverage of these maps can often be obtained from the state geological departments, however.

One of the most useful state publications is "Mineral and Water Resources of (State)" which were issued by the various state geology departments in cooperation with the U.S. Geological Survey and other organizations. These publications discuss each mineral resource briefly, have an individual map for each mineral commodity and usually an excellent bibliography.

Immediately following is a list, in alphabetical order by state, of some selected references to clays and shales that have been either issued by that state's geology department or in cooperation with the federal government.

Arkansas — Smothers, W.J., et al, 1952, Ceramic evaluation of Arkansas nepheline syenite, Arkansas Resources and Devel. Comm., Research Ser. no 24, 21 pp.

California — Cleveland, G.B. 1957, Clay, *in* Mineral commodities of California, California Div. of Mines, Bull. 176, pp 131-152.

Dietrich, W.F., 1928, The clay resources and the ceramic industry of California, California Div. of Mines and Mining, Bull. 99, 383 pp.

Colorado — Van Sant, J.N., 1959, Refractory clay deposits of Colorado, U.S. Bur. of Mines Rept. of Investigations 5553, 156 pp.

Connecticut — Loughlin, G.F., 1905, The clays and clay industries of Connecticut, Connecticut Geological Survey, Bull. 4, 121 pp.

Delaware — Pickett, T.E., 1970, Delaware Clay Resources, Delaware Geological Survey, Rept. of Inv. No. 14, 70 pp.

Florida — Calver, J.L., 1949, Florida kaolins and clays, Florida Dept. of Natural Resources, Inf. Circ. 2, 59 pp.

Georgia — Smith, R.W., 1966, Sedimentary kaolins of the coastal plain of Georgia, Georgia Geologic Survey, Bull. 44, 2nd edition, 482 pp.

Idaho — Skeels, F.H., 1920, A preliminary report on the clays of Idaho, Idaho Bur. of Mines and Geology, Bull. 2, 74 pp.

— Hubbard, C.R., 1956, Clay deposits of north Idaho, Idaho Bur. of Mines and Geol., Pamph. no. 109, 26 pp.

Illinois — Parmelee, C.W., and Schroyer, C.R., 1922, Further investigations of Illinois Fireclays, Illinois Geol. Survey, Bull. 38, pp 278-9.

Indiana — Harrison, Jack, L., and Murray, H.H., 1964, Clays and shales of Indiana, Indiana Geological Survey, Bull. 31, 40 pp. The mineralogic and chemical composition of clays, tests, and uses are discussed, as well as descriptions of the principal geologic clay-bearing formations in the state.

Austin, G.S., 1975, Clay and shale resources of Indiana, Indiana Geological Survey, Bull. 42-L, 40 pp. plus colored geologic map of the state. Essentially an up-date of the 1964 publication cited above.

Iowa — Rudesill, R., 1978, Some aspects of the use of native materials for art ceramics, unpub. M.S. thesis, Univ. of Iowa, 107 pp.

Gwynne, C.S., 1941, Ceramic shales and clays of Iowa, Iowa Geol. Survey, Ann. Rpt., vol. 38, pp 263-378.

Marston, A., 1903, Tests of clay products, Iowa Geol. Survey, Ann. Rpt. vol. 14, pp 556-620.

Kansas — Grisafe, D.A., and Bauleke, M., 1977, Kansas clays for the ceramic hobbyist, Kansas Geological Survey, Educational Ser. 3, 35 pp.

Plummer, N., and Romary, J.F., 1947, Kansas clay, Dakota formation, Kansas Geological Survey, Bull. 67, 241 pp.

Kentucky — McGrain, P., 1966, Some sources of ceramic materials in Kentucky, Kentucky Geological Survey, Reprint 21.

McGrain, P., et al., Miscellaneous clay and shale analyses for the period 1951-1970, (consisting of five separate publications, in the Rpts. of Investigation series IX,) Kentucky Geological Survey.

Michigan — Sorensen, H.O., 1970, Michigan's clay deposits and industry, Michigan Geological Survey, reprint from Miscellany 1, paper presented at 6th Forum on Geology of Industrial Minerals, Ann Arbor, April 2-3, 1970, 12 pp.

Brown, G.G., 1926, Clay and shale of Michigan and their uses, Michigan Geological Survey, Ser. 30, 444 pp.

Minnesota — Parham, W.E. and Austin, G.S., 1969, Clay mineralogy, fabric, and industrial uses of the shale of the Decorah Formation, southeastern Minnesota, Minnesota Geological Survey, Rpt. of Investigation 10, 32 pp.

————, ————, 1970, Clay mineralogy and geology of Minnesota's kaolin clays, Minnesota Geological Survey Special Pub. 10, 142 pp.

Mississippi — Logan, W.N., 1907, Clays of Mississippi: Part I, Brick clays and clay industry of northern Mississippi, Mississippi Geological Survey, Bull. 2, 225 pp.

————, ————, 1908, Clays of Mississippi: Part II, Brick clays and clay industry of Southern Mississippi, Mississippi Geological Survey, Bull. 4, 72 pp.

————, ————, 1914, The pottery clays of Mississippi, Mississippi Geological Survey, Bull. 6, 228 pp.

Missouri — Davis, W.E., et al, 1941, Further investigations of southeastern Missouri clays, *in* Bien. Rpt. of the State Geologist to the 61st Gen. Assembly, Missouri Division of Geology, 48 pp.

McQueen, H.S., 1943, Geology of the fire clay districts of East central Missouri, Missouri Div. of Geology, vol. 28, 250 pp. + 39 pls., 6 figs., 31 tables.

Tennissen, A.C., 1967, Clay mineralogy and ceramic properties of Lower Cabiniss under clays in western Missouri, Missouri Div. of Geology, Rpt. of Inv. 36. 56 pp. - 21 figs., 11 tables.

Montana — Sahinen, U.M., and others, Progress report on clays of Montana, Montana Bur. of Mines and Geology. A series of reports including Inf. Circ. 23, Bulls. 13, 27, 45, 55, 70, 80, and 99 give test results on 777 clay samples.

New Mexico — Hawks, W.L., 1970, Test data for New Mexico clay materials, Part I, Central New Mexico, New Mexico Bur. of Mines and Mineral Resources, Circular 110, 37 pp.

New York — Anon., 1951, Clays and shales of New York State, New York Dept. Commerce, 347 pp. A detailed and comprehensive study of the state's clays, together with test results.

North Carolina — Anon., 1925, The kaolins of North Carolina, North Carolina Geological Survey.

Ohio — Lamborn, R.E., et al, 1938, Shales and surface clays of Ohio, Ohio Geological Survey, Bull. 39, 281 pp., 2 maps.

Oregon — Wilson, H., and Treasher, R.C., 1938, Preliminary report of some of the refractory clays of western Oregon, Oregon Dept. of Geology and Mineral Industries, Bull. No. 6, 93 pp.

Pennsylvania — Leighton, H., 1941, Clay and shale resources in Pennsylvania, Pennsylvania Topographic and Geologic Survey, Min. Res. Rpt. 23, 245 pp.

— O'Neill, B.J., Jr., 1965, Properties and uses of Pennsylavania shales and clays, Pennsylvania Topographic and Geologic Survey, Min. Res. Rpt. 51, 448 pp.

Hoover, K.V., et al, 1971, Properties and uses of Pennsylavania shales and clays, southeastern Pennsylvania, Pennsylvania Geol. Survey, Mineral Res. Rpt. M 63, 329 pp., Results from testing 159 clay localities in southeastern Pennsylvania.

South Carolina — Robinson, G.C., et al., 1961, Common clays of the coastal plain of South Carolina and their use in structural clay products, South Carolina Div. Geology, Bull. 21, 71 pp.

Tennessee and Kentucky — Phelps, G.W., 1972, The ball clays of Tennessee and Kentucky Amer. Inst. Mining and Metall. Engrs. SME Preprint No. 72-H-305, SME Fall meeting, Birmingham, Ala, Oct., 11 pp.

Texas — Fisher, W.L., and others, 1965, Rock and mineral resources of East Texas, Univ. of Texas, Austin, Bur. of Econ. Geology, Rpt. of Inv. 54, 439 pp.

Utah — Van Sant, J.N., 1964, Refractory clay deposits of Utah, U.S. Bur. of Mines, Inf. Circ. 8213, 176 pp.,

Vermont — Jacobs, E.C., 1940, Clay, *in* Vermont Agency of Environmental Cons., Rpt. of the State Geologist 1939-1940, 9 pp.

Virginia — Sweet, P.C., 1976, Clay-material resources in Virginia, Virginia Div. of Mineral Resources, Min. Res. Rpt. 13, 56 pp.

Washington — Shedd, S., 1910, The clays of the state of Washington; their geology, mineralogy, and technology; Pullman Wash., State Coll. of Washington, 341 pp. An old but comprehensive report on the clays of the state.

West Virginia — Lessing, P., and others, 1973, Clays of West Virginia, West Virginia Geological and Economic Survey, Min. Res. Ser. No. 3, Part I, 190 pp.: Part II, 1977, 109 pp.

Wisconsin — Buckley, E.R., 1901, The clays and clay industry of Wisconsin, Wisconsin Geological Survey, Bull. 7, 304 pp.

Wyoming — Van Sant, J.N., 1961, Refractory clay deposits of Wyoming, U.S. Bur. of Mines, Rpt. of Inv. 5652, 195 pp., 31 figs.

B. Canadian Provincial Departments of Mines

Much the same type of service as that provided by the various state departments of geology in the United States is available from the corresponding provincial agencies. The Canadian agencies issue a prodigous quantity of excellent geologic maps and reports which are available from the addresses given below.

Ministry of Energy, Mines, & Petroleum Resources
Parliament Buildings
Victoria, B.C.
V8V 1X4

Dept. of Energy and Natural Resources
Petroleum Plaza
South Tower
9915-108 St.
Edmonton, Alberta
T5K 2C9

Dept. of Mineral Resources
Toronto-Dominion Building
1914 Hamilton St.
Regina, Sask.
S4P 4V4

Dept. of Energy and Mines
933 Century St.
Winnipeg, Man.
R3H OW4

Mineral Resources Group
Ministry of Natural Resources
6341 Whitney Block
Queen's Park
Toronto, Ont.
M7A 1W3

Dept. of Energy and Resources
200 Chemin Ste-Foy
Quebec, Quebec
G1R 4X7

Mines Division
Dept. of Natural Resources
Centennial Building
Fredericton, N.B.
E3B 5H1

Dept. of Mines
1690 Hollis St.
P.O. Box 1087
Halifax, N.S.
B3J 2X1

Dept. of Tourism, Industry, and Energy
P.O. Box 2000
Charlottetown, P.E.I.
C1A 7N8

Dept. of Mines and Energy
Eastern Canada Building
95 Bonaventure Ave.
St. John's, Nfld.
A1C 5T7

Publication lists are available from the above agencies, and bibliographies of some of the provinces may be shelved at your local library.

Unfortunately many of the early provincial publications on clay and shale are now out-of-print, but larger libraries often have copies. Listed below are some selected references on ceramic materials that have been published by Canadian provinces. Additional publications, issued by the Canadian national government are also listed.

Canadian Clays and Shales*

COMMON CLAY AND SHALE

Common clays and shales are the principal raw materials available from Canadian deposits for the manufacture of clay products. These materials are usually higher in alkalis, alkaline materials, and ironbearing minerals and much lower in alumina than the high-quality kaolins, fireclays, ball clays, and stoneware clays.

Common clays and shales are found in all parts of Canada, but deposits having

---

*Adapted from an article by G.O. Vagt, Canadian Mineral Policy Sector, Dept. Energy, Mines and Resources, 1979.

excellent drying and firing properties are generally scarce. Most of the surface deposits of common clays in Canada are the result of continental glaciation and subsequent stream transport. Such Pleistocene deposits are of interest to the ceramist, and include stoneless marine and lake sediments, reworked glacial till, interglacial clays and floodplain clays. These deposits are characterized by low melting temperatures.

The common shales provide the best sources of raw material for making brick. In particular, those found in Cambrian, Ordovician, and Carboniferous rocks in eastern Canada, and Jurassic, Cretaceous and tertiary rocks in western Canada, are utilized by the ceramic industry. In many instances these shales are more refractory than the Pleistocene clays.

CHINA CLAY (KAOLIN)

In southern Saskatchewan, deposits of sandy kaolin occur near Wood Mountain, Fir Mountain, Knollys, Flintoft and other localities. A deposit or refractory clay which is very plastic to very sandy, and is similar to a secondary china clay, occurs along the Fraser River near Prince George, British Columbia. The deposit has been investigated as a source of kaolin, as a fire clay and as a raw material for facing brick.

Various kaolinitic-rock deposits have been investigated in Manitoba. The reported deposits are principally in the northwest at Cross Lake and Pine River, on Deer Island (Punk Island) and Black Island in Lake Winnipeg, and at Arborg.

Kaolin-bearing rock occurs at St.-Remi-d'Amherst, Papineau County; Brebeuf, Terrebonne County; Point Comfort, on Thirty-one Mile Lake, Gatineau County; and Chateau-Richer, Montmorency County. Extensive deposits of kaolin-silica sand mixtures occur in northern Ontario along the Missinaibi and Mattagami rivers.

BALL CLAY

Ball clays are known to occur in the Whitemud Formation of southern Saskatchewan. Good-quality deposits are present at Willows, Readlyn, Big Muddy Valley, Blue Hills, Willow Bunch, Flintoft and in other areas. Clay from the Willows area has been used for many years in the potteries at Medicine Hat and Vancouver. Some ball clays from the Flintoft area are used for white-to-buff facing brick and for household pottery and crocks.

FIRE CLAY

Various grades of good-quality fire clay occur in the Whitemud Formation in southern Saskatchewan. Good-quality clays are found on Sumas Mountain in British Columbia. Fire clay, associated with lignite as well as with kaolin-silica sand mixtures, occurs in the James Bay watershed of northern Ontario along the Missinaibi, Abitibi, Moose and Mattagami rivers.

At Shubenacadie, Nova Scotia, some seams of clay are sufficiently refractory for medium-duty refractories. Ontario and Quebec have no producing sources of fire clay.

STONEWARE CLAY

The principal source of stoneware clay in Canada is the Whitemud Formation in southern Saskatchewan and southeastern Alberta. The Eastend area in Saskatchewan was formerly the source of much of the clay used at Medicine Hat. Stoneware clay pits are located in the Alberta Cypress Hills, southeast of Medicine Hat, and at Avonlea, Saskatchewan. Stoneware clays have been found on Sumas Mountain, near Abbotsford, British Columbia.

In Nova Scotia, stoneware clays occur at Shubenacadie and Musquodoboit. Other similar deposits occur at Swan River, Manitoba, Kergwenan, Manitoba, and in British Columbia at Chimney Creek Bridge, Williams Lake, Quesnel, and near the Alaska Highway at Coal River.

More detailed information may be obtained from the various provincial agencies listed.

Selected Provincial Publications

ALBERTA

Ells, S.C., 1915, Notes on clay deposits near McMurray, Alberta, Can. Dept. Mines, Rpt. no. 336, 15 pp.

Maiklem, W.R., and Campbell, F.A., 1965, A study of the clays from the upper Cretaceous bentonites and shales in Alberta, Can. Mineralogist, vol. 8, pt. 3, pp. 354-371.

Ries, H., 1915, Clays of British Columbia and Alberta, Can. Dept. Mines, Geol. Sur. Branch, Summary Rpt. 1913, pp. 284-287.

Worcester, W.G., 1932, The clay and shale resources of Turner Valley (Alberta), and nearby districts, Can. Dept. Mines, Mines Branch Rpt. no. 729, 126 pp.

BRITISH COLUMBIA

Brady, J.G., and Dean, R.S., 1964, Ceramic clays and shales of British Columbia, Can. Dept. Mines and Tech. Surveys, Mines Branch, Tech. Bull. 54, reprinted from Jour. Can. Cer. Soc., vol. 32, 1963, pp. 46-71.

Cummings, J.M., and McCammon, J.W., 1952, Clay and shale deposits of British Columbia, British Columbia Dept. Mines, Victoria, Bull. no. 30.

Keele, J., 1918, Clay and shale resources of British Columbia and of eastern and northern Ontario, in Can. Dept. Mines, Mines Branch Rpt. 509, Summary Rpt. of the Mining Branch of the Dept. of Mines for calendar year ending Dec. 31, 1918, 225 pp.

Ries, H., 1915, Clays of British Columbia and Alberta, Can. Dept. Mines, Geol. Survey Branch, Summary Rpt., 1913, pp. 284-287.

MANITOBA

Brady, J.G., and Stone, W.J.D., 1958, Investigation of a clay from Arborg, Manitoba, Can. Dept. Mines and Tech. Surveys, Mines Branch, Ottawa, Investigation Rpt. IR 58-214.

Cole, L.H., and McMahon, J.F., 1928, Kaolin and associated clays of Punk Island (Manitoba), Can. Dept. Mines, Mines Branch, Rpt. no. 690, pp. 25-35.

Wells, J.W., 1905, Preliminary report on the industrial value of the clays and shales of Manitoba, Can. Dept. Mines, Mines Branch Rpt. no. 8, 41 pp.

NEW BRUNSWICK

Barnett, D.E., and Abbot, D., 1966, The evaluation of possible ceramic materials from New Brunswick, New Brunswick Research and Productivity Council, Fredericton, Research Note 6.

Keele, J., 1914, Clay and shale deposits of New Brunswick, Can. Dept. Mines, Geol. Survey Branch, Ottawa, Memoir 44.

———, ———, 1916, Notes on the industrial values of the clay and shale deposits in the Moncton map area, New Brunswick, Can. Dept. Mines, Mines Branch, Summary Rpt. no. 421 for 1915, pp. 131-141.

NEWFOUNDLAND

Carr, G.F., 1958, The industrial minerals of Newfoundland, Can. Dept. Mines and Tech. Surveys, Mines Branch, Rpt. no. 855.

Gillespie, C.R., 1960, Preliminary report, brick shales and clays, Random Island area (Newfoundland), Newfoundland Dept. Mines, Agric. and Resources, Mineral Res. Div., unpublished report, 20 pp., 1 map.

McKillop, J.H., 1961, Brick shale investigation, Manuels River area (Newfoundland), Newfoundland Dept. Mines, Agric. and Resources, Min. Res. Div., unpublished report, 13 pp., 2 maps.

NOVA SCOTIA

Cameron, E.L., 1951, White clay in Middleton District (Nova Scotia), Nova Scotia Dept. Mines, Halifax, Ann. Rpt. on Mines 1950, pp. 119-130.

Flynn, A.E., 1924, Report on china clay (kaolin) deposit at Middleton, Annapolis County, Nova Scotia, Nova Scotia Mines Rpt.

Ries, Heinrich, and Kelle, Joseph, 1911, The clay and shale deposits of Nova Scotia and portions of New Brunswick, Can. Dept. Mines, Geol. Survey Branch, Ottawa, Memoir 16-E.

ONTARIO

Brady, J.G., and Dean, R.S., 1966, Ceramic clays and shales of Ontario, Can. Dept. Mines and Tech. Surveys, Mines Branch, Research Rpt. R 175, 125 pp. plus map.

Guillet, G.R., 1964, Clay and shale in Ontario, a review, Ontario Dept. Mines, Toronto, PR 1964-2.

Keele, J., 1918, Clay and shale resources of British Columbia and of eastern and northern Ontario, in Can. Dept. Mines, Mines Branch Rpt. 509, Summary Rpt. of the Mining Branch of the Dept. of Mines for calendar year ending Dec. 31, 1918, 225 pp.

——, ——, 1924, Preliminary report on the clay and shale deposits of Ontario, Can. Dept. Mines, Geol. Survey Branch, Ottawa, Memoir 142.

Vos, M.A., 1975, Potcuhal clay and shale resources of central Ontario, Ontario Dept. Mines OFR 5133.

PRINCE EDWARD ISLAND

Brady, J.G., 1958, Clay products from Prince Edward Island clays and shales, Can. Dept. Mines and Tech. Surveys, Mines Branch, Ottawa, Investigation Report IR 58-195.

MacPherson, A.R., 1946, Clays and shales of Prince Edward Island, Can. Dept. Mines and Resources, Mines Branch, Memorandum Ser. no. 91, 17 pp.

Prest, V.K., and Brady, J.G., 1964, The geology and ceramic properties of shale from Bacon Point, Prince Edward Island, Can. Dept. Mines and Tech Surveys, Geol. Survey of Can., Paper 63035.

QUEBEC

Bell, K.E., 1960, Investigation into some possible ceramic uses of a kaolinized feldspar from Chateau Richer, Province of Quebec, Can. Dept. Mines and Tech. Surveys, Mines Branch, Ottawa, Inv. Rpt. IR 60-113.

Brady, J.G., and Dean, R.S., 1967, Composition and properties of ceramic clays and shales of Quebec, Can. Dept. Mines and Tech. Surveys, Mines Branch Research Rpt. R 187, 107 pp.

Keele, J., 1915, Preliminary report on the clay and shale deposits of the Province of Quebec, Can. Dept. Mines, Geol. Survey Branch, Ottawa, Memoir 64.

___, ___, 1920, Kaolin in the Gatineau Valley, Quebec, Can. Dept. Mines, Mines Branch, Summary Rpt. 542 for 1919, pp. 108-109.

SASKATCHEWAN
MacPherson, A.R., and Cole, L.H., 1948, Preliminary report on kaolin and silica sand from Knollys and Wood Mountain areas, Saskatchewan, Can. Bur. of Mines, Mineral Dressing and Metallurgy Laboratories, Ottawa, Investigation no. 2396.
Peterson, D.I., and Tomkins, R.V., 1950, Light-burning Saskatchewan clays of high strength, Jour. Can. Ceram. Soc., 19, 33-37.
Worcester, W.G., 1950, Clay resources of Saskatchewan, Dept. Nat. Resources, Regina, Tech. and Econ. Series Rpt. no. 2.

C. Government Agencies with Publications of Interest to the Craft Potter

United States Government
U.S. Geological Survey
Branch of Distribution
P.O. Box 25286 Federal Center
Denver, Colorado, 80225

U.S.G.S. topographic maps and indexes for maps of areas west of the Mississippi River. (Indexes list private sales outlets for maps in Western states.)

U.S. Geological Survey
Branch of Distribution
1200 South Eads Street
Arlington Virginia, 22202

U.S.G.S. topographic maps and indexes for maps of areas east of the Mississippi River, including Minnesota.

In addition to the above outlets maps may be purchased over-the-counter at Geological Survey Sales Offices in the following cities: Los Angeles, San Francisco, Menlo Park, Washington, D.C., Reston, Va. and Spokane.

Reference map files are maintained at many libraries in the larger cities and universities.

Superintendent of Documents
U.S. Government Printing
    Office
Washington, D.C. 20402

Sales publications, other than topographic maps, issued by either the Geological Survey or the Bureau of Mines.

U.S. Bureau of Mines
Publications Distribution
    Branch
4800 Forbes Street
Pittsburgh, Pennsylvania 15213

Publications issued free-of-charge are available at this outlet only. Charge publications sold by Superintendent of Documents, (which see).

Publications issued by either the Survey or the Bureau that are of special interest to the potter are listed in the Bibliography.

D. Canadian Department of Energy, Mines and Resources

Mines Branch
555 Booth Street
Ottawa, Canada, K1A 0G1

Geological Survey of Canada
601 Booth Street
Ottawa, Canada, K1A 0E8

Surveys and Mapping Branch
Canada Map Office
615 Booth Street
Ottawa, Canada, K1A 0E9

Regional Offices
Geological Survey of Canada Library
6th Floor, Sun Building
100 West Pender Street
Vancouver, British Columbia, V6B 1R8

Institute of Sedimentary and Petroleum Geology
3303 33rd Street NW
Calgary, Alberta, T2L 2A7

Bibliography of Selected Canadian National Publications on Ceramics

Anon., 1975, Ceramic plants in Canada, Canadian Dept. of Energy, Mines and Resources, Mineral Policy Sector, Operator's List Rpt. no. 6, 59 pp.

Bell, K.E., Brady, J.G., and Zemgals, L.K., 1978, Ceramic clays and shales of the Atlantic Provinces, Can. Dept. Mines and Tech. Surveys, Center for Mineral and Energy Technology, CANMET Rpt. 78-21.

Brady, J.G., 1961, Nature and properties of some western Canada clays, Canadian Min. Res. Div., Mines Branch Tech. Bull. 21, 33 pp.

de Schmid, H.S., 1916, Feldspar in Canada, Canada Dept. of Mines, Mines Branch Pub. no. 401, Ottawa, 125 pp.

Douglas, R.J.W., 1970, Geology and economic minerals of Canada, 1970, Geol. Survey of Canada, Econ. Geol., Rpt. no. 7, 838 pp. plus separate volume of maps.

Frechette, Howells, Annual reports on Canadian clays *in* Canadian Mines Branch Reports; R 610, R 619, R 645, R 672, R 690, R 697, R 722, R 726. Contains reports on clays from various Provinces. See also the Annual Reports by Keele, J.

——,——, 1930. The clays of Canada, Canadian Dept. of Mines, Memorandum Series no. MS41, 3 pp.

Keele, J., Annual reports on Canadian clays in Canadian Mines Branch Reports, R 421, R 454, R 493, R 509, R 542, R 578, R 591.

——,——, 1922, Pottery clays in Canada, Canadian Mineral Resources Div., Mines Branch, 8 pp.

Lang, A.H., 1970, Prospecting in Canada, 4th ed., Geol. Sur. of Canada, Econ. Geol. Rpt. no. 7, 308 pp. A complete manual on all phases of prospecting.

McMahon, J.F., 1932, Refractory clays in Canada, Can. Dept. Mines, Mines Branch, Memorandum Ser. no. 57. 26 pp.

Pearse, G.H.K., 1978, Talc, soapstone and pyrophyllite, Candaian Dept. of Energy, Mines and Resources, Mineral Policy Sector, Ann. Mineral Review Series no. 79-398, 1977, 58 pp.

——,——, 1977, Nepheline syenite and feldspar, Canadian Dept. of Energy, Mines and Resources, Mineral Policy Sector, Ann. Mineral Rev. Ser. no. 79-379, 1978, 6 pp.

Phillips, J.G., 1956, Clays and shales of Eastern Canada, Canadian Dept. of Mines and Technical Services, Mines Branch Inf. Circ. no. IM 3, 13 pp.

Ries, H., 1911, Clay and shale deposits of Western Canada, Geol. Sur. of Canada, Summary Rpt., 1910, pp. 174-180.

———,———, 1913, Report on the clay and shale deposits of the western Provinces, Pt. II, Geol. Sur. of Canada, Memoir 25.

———,———, 1914a, Clay investigations in Western Canada, Geol. Sur. of Canada, Summary Rpt., 1912, pp. 229-233.

———,———, 1914b, Clay and shale deposits of the western Provinces, Pt. III, Geol. Sur. of Canada, Memoir 47.

———,———, 1915, Clay and shale deposits of the western Provinces, Pt. IV, Geol. Sur. of Canada, Memoir 65.

———,———, and Keele, J., 1912, Preliminary report on the clay and shale deposits of the western Provinces, Geol. Sur. of Canada, Memoir 24-E.

Rose, E.R., 1969, Geology of titanium and titaniferous deposits of Canada, Geol. Sur. of Canada, Econ. Geol. Rpt. no. 25, 177 pp. plus maps.

Sabina, Ann, P., 1964, Rock and mineral collecting in Canada, Geol. Sur. of Canada, vol. 1, 147 pp. plus maps. Describes localities in Yukon, Northwest Territories, British Columbia, Alberta, Saskatchewan and Manitoba.

Spence, H.S., 1932, Feldspar, Canada Dept. of Mines, Mines Branch Pub. no. 731, Ottawa, 145 pp.

———,———, 1940, Talc, steatite, soapstone and pyrophyllite, Canada Bur. of Mines Rpt. no. 803, 146 pp.

Vagt, G.O., 1979, Clays and clay products, Can. Dept. Energy, Mines Resources, Min. Policy Sector, Ann. Review, 12 pp.

E. Professional Geologic and Mining Societies in the United States

The American Society for Testing Materials, a non-profit organization which not only tests but devises tests and standards for a wide variety of substances, publishes the results of their findings in a series of Standards. The individual Standards, which include tests and standards for clays, pigments, and glazes, may be purchased from the Society or examined at the larger libraries. The Society is commonly referred to as ASTM.

Nearly all of the professional groups listed below publish technical reports. Many of their publications are available in public and university libraries or may be ordered from the societies directly.

Mining & Geological Associations, Societies, and Institutes

American Geological Institute, 2201 M St., N.W., Washington, D.C. 20037.

American Institute of Professional Geologists, 345 S. Union Blvd., Denver, Colo. 80228.

American Mining Congress, Suite 1100, 1200 18th St., N.W., Washington, D.C. 20036.

Association of American State Geologists, Wyoming Geological Survey, P.O. Box 3008, Laramie, Wyo. 82071.

The Geological Society of America, Inc., 3300 Penrose Place, Boulder, Colo. 80301.

Society of Economic Geologists, Inc., Box 1549, Knoxville, Tenn. 37901.

Society of Mining Engineers of AIME, 540 Arapeen Dr., Research Park, Salt Lake City, Utah 84108.

F. Professional Geologic and Mining Societies in Canada

The Canadian Institute of Mining & Metallurgy, 906-1117 Ste. Catherine St. W., Montreal 2, Que.

In affiliation — The Mining Society of Nova Scotia, Halifax.
Geological Association of Canada, 111 St. Clair Ave. W., Toronto, Ont.

G. United States Colleges and Schools of Mines

Many of the colleges and schools of mines that appear in the list below have repository libraries for government, state and provincial publications. Some of these institutions also generate post-graduate theses on mining and geological subjects which can be examined in their libraries.

Dept. of Civil and Mineral Engineering, University of Alabama, University 35486.
Dept. of Mining & Metallurgy, College of Earth Sciences & Mineral Industry, University of Alaska, College 99735.
College of Mines, University of Arizona, Tucson 85721.
Dept. of Mineral Technology, University of California, Berkeley 94720.
School of Earth Sciences, Stanford University, Stanford, Calif. 94305.
Mining Engrg. Dept., Colorado School of Mines, Golden 80401.
Dept. of Earth Science, Dartmouth College, Hanover, N.H. 03755.
Mineral Engrg. Br., Georgia Institute of Technology, Atlanta 30332.
Dept. of Mining Engrg. and Metallurgy, University of Idaho, Moscow 83843.
Dept. of Metallurgy, University of Illinois, Urbana 61801.
Mining Engrg., Civil Engrg. Dept., University of Kentucky, Lexington 40506.
Dept. of Mining Engrg., Michigan Technological University, Houghton 49931.
Dept. of Civil & Mineral Engrg., University of Minnesota, Minneapolis 55455.
School of Mines & Metallurgy, University of Missouri, Rolla 65401.
Montana College of Mineral Science & Technology, Butte 59701.
Dept. of Metallurgical and Materials Engineering, University of Nevada-Reno, Reno 89507.
Mackay School of Mines, University of Nevada, Reno 89507.
Dept. of Petroleum & Mining Engineering, New Mexico Institute of Mining & Technology, Socorro 87801.
Henry Krumb School of Mines, Columbia University, Seeley W. Mudd Bldg., New York 10027.
Dept. of Mineral Engineering, College of Earth and Mineral Sciences, Pennsylvania State University, University Park 16802.
Dept. of Mining Engrg., South Dakota School of Mines & Technology, Rapid City 57701.
Dept. of Mining & Metallurgy, Texas Western College, El Paso 79902.
College of Mines and Mineral Industries, University of Utah, Salt Lake City 84112.
Div. of Minerals Engineering, Virginia Polytechnic Institute & State University, Blacksburg 24061.
Dept. of Mining, Metallurgical and Ceramic Engineering, University of Washington, Seattle, Wash. 98195.
Dept. of Mining, Washington State University, Pullman 99163.
College of Mineral & Energy Resources, West Virginia University, Morgantown 26506.
Dept. of Metallurgical & Mineral Engineering, University of Wisconsin, Madison 53706.
Dept. of Mining Engrg., University of Wisconsin-Platteville, Platteville 53818.

H. Canadian Colleges and Schools of Mines

University of Alberta, F. of Engrg., Edmonton, Alta.
University of British Columbia, F. of Applied Science, Vancouver, B.C.

Dept. of Mining Engrg., Nova Scotia Technical College, P.O. Box 1000, Halifax, N.S.

Queen's University, F. of Applied Science, Kingston, Ont.

Ecole Polytechnique. 2500 Ave. Marie-Guyard, Montreal 26, Que.

Laval University, F. of Science, Quebec City, Que.

Dept. of Mining Engrg. & Applied Science, McGill University, Montreal 2, Que.

I. United States Professional Geology and Mining Periodicals

The following list of publications consists of both professional society house organs and commercial magazines devoted to a specific segment of the mineral industry. Many of these are available for inspection in the larger libraries and at most college and schools of mining libraries. The society publications often contain articles on the search for, and extraction of, various minerals. The trade papers tend to feature the use of equipment used in the various stages of mineral exploration and production. The latter type of publication has numerous advertisements for all types of laboratory and field equipment.

E/MJ Engineering & Mining Journal, 1221 Ave. of the Americas, New York, N.Y. 10020.

The Mines Magazine, Guggenheim Hall, Golden, Colo. 80401.

Mining Congress Journal, American Mining Congress, 1100 Ring Bldg., Washington, D.C. 20036.

Mining Engineering, Society of Mining Engineers of AIME, 540 Arapeen Dr., Research Park, Salt Lake City, Utah 84108.

Pit and Quarry, 105 W. Adams St., Chicago, Ill. 60603.

Rock Products, 300 W. Adams St., Chicago, Ill. 60606.

World Mining, 500 Howard St., San Francisco, Calif. 94105.

J. Canadian Professional Geology and Mining Periodicals

CIM Bulletin, The Canadian Institute of Mining & Metallurgy, 906-1117 Ste. Catherine St. W., Montreal 2, Que.

Canadian Mining Journal, Gardenvale, Que.

Canadian Pit and Quarry, Don Mills, Ont.

APPENDIX 8

HOW TO PAN

Panning is the simple process of shaking heavy particles to the bottom of a gold pan and washing the lighter particles off at the top. It is as simple as that. The separation that is achieved by panning is the result of two separate processes: (1) sizing, and (2) gravity concentration. You can put some dry sand and gravel into a fruit jar, gently shake it back and forth, and in a minute or two you will see that the mixture has sorted itself, with the fine sand on the bottom and the coarse gravel on top. In other words you have sized the material. Now, if you scrape off the gravel, take the sand alone and continue the gentle shaking, you will gradually settle the heavy grains of mineral to the bottom of the jar, and the lighter grains will rise to the top. You have now concentrated the heavy minerals.

Water speeds up the operation by acting as a lubricant and as an agent that increases the relative difference in specific gravity of the various minerals. For example, the ratio of specific gravity of quartz (2.7) to magnetite (5.1) in air is 1:1.89, while the ratio for the two minerals in water is 1:2.41. Water also flushes away unwanted dust and fines and any water-soluble impurities.

So much for the theory of panning. Here is how the actual panning is done. Fill your pan with material and gently submerge it in water, kneading it gently with your hands to break up lumps of clay or clumps of mineral. Now agitate the pan (still under water) with a brisk back-and forth rotary motion to cause the coarser gravel to rise to the top where you can rake it off with your fingers. Repeat the process several times to get rid of as much coarse material as possible. Now agitate the pan in the water as before but with a little more gentleness. Tilt the pan forward slowly, keeping the lip under water. This causes the heavy minerals on the bottom to congregate in the sharp bend made by the side and bottom. With the pan in this position, and with the lip just below the surface, use a gentle forward-upward-and-backward-down motion so that little waves rush into the pan and carry away the lighter grains as they recede. You can speed the process by sweeping obviously unwanted material away with your fingers. Alternate the rotary motion, with pan only slightly tilted, with the washing motion, with the pan tilted more sharply upward, until only the heavier fraction remains. In the final step add clear water and give your pan a light, quick swirl to cause the concentrates to "tail" out. This will reveal the presence of any unwanted grains.

It does take practice and skill to be able to pan quickly and accurately but there is nothing secret about it. Not any more, anyway.

APPENDIX 9

TYLER STANDARD SCREEN SIEVE OPENINGS

Sieve Designation Standard mm. (New U.S. Nos.)	Alternate (Old U.S. Series) inches	Sieve Oppening inches	Tyler Screen Scale Equivalent Designation
9.5	⅜	0.375	.371 Mesh
8.00	5/16	0.312	2½
6.7	.265	0.265	3
6.3	¼† No.	0.250	—
5.6	3½	0.223	3½
4.75	4	0.187	4
4.00	5	0.157	5
3.35	6	0.132	6
2.80	7	0.111	7
2.36	8	0.0937	8
2.00	10	0.0787	9
1.70	12	0.0661	10
1.40	14	0.0555	12
1.18	16	0.0469	14
1.00	18	0.0394	16
Micrometers			
850	20	0.0331	20
710	25	0.0278	24
600	30	0.0234	28
500	35	0.0197	32
425	40	0.0165	35
355	45	0.0139	42
300	50	0.0117	48
250	60	0.0098	60
212	70	0.0083	65
180	80	0.0070	80
150	100	0.0059	100
125	120	0.0049	115
106	140	0.0041	150
90	170	0.0035	170
75	200	0.0029	200
63	230	0.0025	250
53	270	0.0021	270
45	325	0.0017	325
38	400	0.0015	400

APPENDIX 10

TYPICAL CHEMICAL ANALYSES OF KAOLINITE AND ILLITE

	Kaolinite			Illite		
	1	2	3	4	5	6
SiO_2	44.81	45.20	48.80	52.23	48.66	49.40
Al_2O_3	37.82	37.02	35.18	25.85	8.46	10.20
Fe_2O_3	0.92	0.27	1.24	4.04	18.80	18.00
FeO	—	0.06	—	—	3.98	3.10
MgO	0.35	0.47	—	2.69	3.56	3.50
CaO	0.43	0.52	0.22	0.60	0.62	0.60
K_2O	—	0.49	0.40	6.56	8.31	5.10
Na_2O	—	0.36	0.25	0.33	0.00	1.40
TiO_2	0.37	1.20	0.61	0.37	—	—
H_2O-	1.10	1.55	1.16	—	—	—
H_2O+	14.27	13.27	12.81	7.88	6.56	8.30
Total	99.92	100.47	100.67	100.55	98.95	99.60

1. Texas   2. Georgia   3. Ione, California   4. Illinois   5. Missouri   6. Wisconsin
(Grim: Clay Mineralogy, 1953, pp. 370, 372)

APPENDIX 11

DRILLER'S LOG

Location _____

Owner _____ County _____ Sec. _____ Twp. _____ Rge. _____

Sampled by _____ Drilled by _____

Hole No. _____ Total depth _____ Bottomed in _____ Date _____

Sample No.	From	To	Feet	Description

Hole No. _____ Total depth _____ Bottomed in _____ Date _____

Hole No. _____ Total depth _____ Bottomed in _____ Date _____

Hole No. _____ Total depth _____ Bottomed in _____ Date _____

APPENDIX 12

HISTORIC HAND-GRINDING DEVICES

Here are four grinding devices (Figure 5.1) that depend entirely on your own muscles to operate them, require only simple, natural materials for construction and have been around for a long time. All of them can doubtless be improved upon if desired, and all of them take a lot of energy to operate. They are, however, real conversation pieces and the Tom Sawyer-and-the-painted-fence principle could be made to apply here, with some free crushing as a result.

The first device is the forerunner to the modern rolling mill. It consists of two stones, one rather large and flat, the other as round as possible. The size of the stones will have to depend on your particular situation. The rounded stone must be large enough, or the material to be crushed small enough, to provide the minimum nip angle discussed previously. One suggested improvement would be to drill a hole about three-quarters of an inch in diameter and several inches deep in the round stone and insert a short handle with a knob about two inches in diameter attached at the end. To operate, grasp the handle in one hand, hold the handle horizontally and with the other hand propel the stone back and forth over the ore. After the entire surface has been rolled, tilt the handle into a vertical position and rock the stone back and forth in all directions with a circular motion of the handle, as shown in the illustration. An alternative improvement would be to pierce the rolling stone with a hole and thread a handle through it to form an axle. This could then be grasped with both hands and the operator's weight from the waist up could be brought to bear.

If the original surface of the lower stone is somewhat uneven it can be dressed by selecting a smaller stone which can be readily handled and which has a fairly smooth surface, and grinding crushed quartz between them. The abrasive action will wear down any high spots. Be sure to slide the upper stone over the lower stone in many different directions to prevent grooving and to help in developing a truly flat surface. The same procedure should be employed from time to time to keep the grinding surface smooth. This technique can be employed for the other grinding devices described below.

The second hand-grinding system is over 4000 years old and comes from Egypt where even today a smooth, flat stone measuring about a foot wide and two feet long is placed so that its long dimension slants gently toward one of the ends. A second, flat-bottomed stone, small enough to be slid over the surface of the lower stone, but large enough to be gripped by both hands, completes the grinder which is known as a saddle-stone and muller. In practice the ore is placed on the saddle-stone about the center and the muller stone is slid over it with the leading edge slightly raised. This produces a very thin wedge between the two stone surfaces. As the stone moves forward the ever-narrowing confines of the wedge grinds the ore to fineness. On the back stroke the stone is tipped slightly the other way and a second grinding action takes place. The slight slope of the saddle-

Figure 5.1 *Ancient devices for hand-grinding ore. (1) roller and anvil; (2) saddle stone and muller; (3) quern; (4) mano and metate.*

stone causes the finely powdered material to work its way toward the lower edge where it is caught eventually in a container placed just below the edge of the stone.

This grinding system has its modern counterpart in the buck board and muller made of iron. With some ingenuity and the use of epoxy-type adhesive it should be possible to affix a handle to the stone muller and improve its efficiency.

The third hand-grinder comes out of ancient Mesopotamia, the cultural center for ceramic art. The Quern is a grinding mechanism somewhat similar to the Egyptian saddle-stone. In practice the upper stone, which may or may not have a central vertical hole drilled in it, is slid in various directions over the surface of the lower stone. The central hole is filled with unground material which slowly works its way down between the two stones as grinding proceeds. The finished product is ejected over the edge of the lower stone on all sides.

A fourth grinding device, age-old but still in use today, is the mano and metate. Indian potters of the Southwest grind their ceramic materials with two stones, one of which has a hollowed-out upper surface, the other is rather long, roughly cylindrical and of a diameter that will easily fit into the hollow of the other stone. In use the mano is thrust forcibly down into the metate repeatedly until the material is powdered.

To keep the iron content of the ceramic material low select cobbles of quartzite or some other tough, low-iron stone. In contrast to the other three methods described this is a percussion type operation rather than a more gentle sliding one. It will take some research, trial and error and quite a bit of searching to find just the right shape for the two stones. The depression in the metate need not be large to start with since the grinding action will enlarge it. The use of some hard mineral pieces to begin with will help to shape both the hole and the lower end of the mano. The mano must be comfortable to grasp and not too heavy, since many up-and-down motions will be needed. Working with a mano and metate does wonders for firming up tummy and pectoral muscles. An inexpensive two-inch wide paintbrush works fine for sweeping the ground-up material into the sieve.

Since these four rather primitive grinding methods depend heavily upon raw muscle power and individual technique, the variation in size of the ground material is rather wide. Depending on circumstances these devices could be used simply to reduce primary crushed ore to a size suitable for fine-grinding, or, with a bit of screening and recycling — and quite a bit of extra effort, the entire charge could be ground to a finished size. Quite probably the former, rather than the latter, objective is the more realistic.

Some thought should be given to the type of material that will be ground in any of these devices. If possible, use stones with the lowest possible iron content. If this is done then you can, depending on the hardness of the ore, grind much of your iron-free and low-iron and all of your high-iron ceramic material.

GLOSSARIES

GLOSSARY I

Terms used to describe types of clay, clay-forming processes and clay deposits

Argillite   A thick-bedded clayey rock.

Bauxite   Deeply weathered rock from which most of the original silica and iron has been leached, leaving aluminum oxide. An ore of aluminum. Colors range from off-white to brick red, depending on degree of weathering and iron content.

Bentonite   The alteration product of volcanic rocks and related ash, composed essentially of smectite minerals. Many bentonites have a high drying shrinkage.

China clay   Another term for kaolin.

Clay   A naturally occurring, earthy, fine-grained material composed largely of a group of crystalline minerals known as clay minerals. They are hydrous silicates composed mainly of silica, alumina, and water.

Colluvium   Material that has been transported by gravity. Avalanches, rock falls, landslides and soil creep are the principal transporting agents.

Clay loam   Essentially a clay-rich soil also containing sand and silt.

Detritus   Mechanical debris produced by the weathering and erosion of rock. Grit, sand, silt, clay are common forms.

Eolian   The process involving the work of the wind and the effects and deposits generated by it. Loess (which see) is an eolian deposit.

Fault gouge   Finely crushed rocks and minerals formed by the movement along a fault. Often mistaken for clay. Gray, blue are common colors.

Fire-clay   Clay often found under coal seams. It may or may not be fire-clay in the strict ceramic sense. Also called underclay.

Flint-clay   A hard, dense, massive, unslakable, non-plastic clay with flint-like characteristics.

Glacial   The process involving the collection and movement of large masses of ice, either across the countryside as continental ice sheets, or down mountain valleys in narrow ice streams called glaciers.

Hydrothermal   The alteration of surface or near-surface rocks by the action of chemically charged hot water rising from deep underground.

Illite   A clay mineral of the mica-type with substantially no expanding-lattice characteristics.

In situ clay   Clay that has formed in place. Deposits that have been weathered, or hydrothermally altered, in place are said to be *in situ* deposits.

Laminae   Thin layers or beds of sediments.

Laterite   A brick-red, deeply weathered rock formed in humid climates.

Loam   A soil, usually transported, containing sand, silt, and clay.

Loess   Fine, uniformly sized soil derived from rocks ground by glacial activity and transported as dust to its present resting place by wind.

Oölites   Rounded, fish-egg sized lumps in a rock matrix. Oölites of magnetite are commonly found in Western bauxites having a high iron content.

Montmorillonite   The most common clay mineral in the smectite group occurring in bentonite. A hydrous aluminum silicate, soft, unctuous, white, gray, to rose-red in color.

Primary clay   Another term for *in situ* or residual clay.

Pisolites   Similar to oölites but somewhat larger lumps.

Pyroclastics   Volcanic rocks that have been fragmented by heat, such as volcanic ash and tuff.

Quartzite   A metamorphic rock consisting of nearly pure quartz grains that have been deformed by pressure to form a solid, coherent rock.

Residual Material remaining at the site after extensive weathering and erosion. See *in situ* and primary clay.

Secondary clay Equivalent to transported clay.

Shale A sedimentary rock consisting of consolidated fine mud. Some shales contain fossil shells and detritus.

Silt loam A soil containing a large proportion of silt, together with sand and clay.

Silt The fine-grained sediment, commonly muddy, laid down by running water in quiet bodies of water.

Smectite A group name for the most common clay minerals in bentonite.

Transported clay Clay that has been moved from where it was originally formed to its present location by running water, wind, glaciation or gravity. Also called secondary clay.

Tuff A volcanic rock composed essentially of volcanic ash that has been laid down, after air-lofting from a volcano, either on land or in quiet bodies of water. Fine-grained, often colorfully banded.

Volcanic ash Fine-grained rock and mineral particles discharged from volcanos. Weathering of the ash may produce bentonite.

GLOSSARY II

List of terms used in the mining, beneficiation and processing of minerals

Ball Mill A mill using either steel, porcelain or glass balls for grinding media.

Battery A series of mills, operating either in parallel or tandem, to stage-grind ore.

Beneficiation The various processes applied to raw ore to separate the valuable minerals from the gangue materials.

Batch grinding Fine-grinding ore in a closed mill until the desired fineness is reached.

Buckboard A hardened iron plate on which ore is ground with the aid of a hand-operated muller.

Calcining Heating ore in an oxidizing atmosphere to burn off impurities such as sulfur, arsenic, antimony and hydrocarbons.

Cascading The tumbling action of ore and grinding media in a mill that is revolving at proper speed.

Cataracting The free-falling of ore and grinding media in a mill that is revolving too rapidly for efficient grinding.

Charge A measured quantity of material introduced into a mill, furnace, or other device for treatment.

Concentrate Ore that has been upgraded by beneficiation to a product as free from waste or gangue as feasible.

Critical speed The rate of rotation of a mill which forces the ore and grinding media to cling to the lining by centrifugal force. See also cascading and cataracting. No grinding action is possible when a mill revolves at critical speed.

Disseminated ore Rock in which small, individual grains or crystals of ore minerals are scattered throughout the matrix.

Double jack A sledge with a long handle and weighing about 8 pounds.

Dressing The concentration of the valuable minerals in raw ore. Ore dressing and beneficiation are roughly equivalent terms.

Gangue The unwanted or waste portion of an ore being beneficiated.

Grinding media Rods, tubes, cylinders, balls or lumps of hard, tough, material introduced into a mill to assist in grinding the ore. Grinding media should not contain any material deleterious to the charge being ground.

Hand cobbing   Rough sorting of ore from country rock at the mine prior to crushing and beneficiation.

Heads   Ore used as feed for a mill. Untreated ore ready for beneficiation.

High-grade (n)   Very pure ore requiring only crushing and grinding before use.

High-grade (v)   To mine only the richest ore in a deposit.

Hybrid   Grains of ore containing two or more mineral crystals.

Jigging   A concentration process accomplished by the rapid up-and-down motions, in water, of a sieve containing ore.

Lawn   Fine cloth used in screening.

Low-grade   Disseminated ore, or ore containing much waste that must be removed by beneficiation.

Metallurgical balance   An accounting system for tracing the distribution of the ore and waste minerals in a given amount of raw ore as it passes through the various stages of beneficiation in a flowsheet. The amount of ore minerals present in the heads must equal that eventually reported in the concentrates, middlings and tails. It is a metallurgical audit of every step of the beneficiation and processing operation.

Middlings, mids   Partly beneficiated ore that is intermediate in grade between concentrates and tailings. Middlings that are hybrids are recycled through a mill to separate them into concentrates and tailings.

Mill   A device for fine-grinding ore, usually with a rotary motion, consisting of a container made of glass, stoneware, porcelain, or metal when used for studio size operations.

Milling   The process by which ore is fine-ground in a mill.

Mill Jar   A studio-scale milling device consisting of a cylindrical container made of glass, stoneware, porcelain or metal that is partly filled with ore and grinding media and then rotated axially.

Muller   A heavy iron shoe equipped with a long handle. Used with a buckboard to fine-grind ore.

Nip angle   The angle subtended between a flat surface and a line between the points of contact of a crushing roll with the flat surface and with a lump of ore to be ground.

Ore   Rock with sufficient recoverable valuable mineral content to justify mining, beneficiating and processing it.

Panning   A concentration process using a hand-held flat-bottomed pan with straight, angled sides. The method is used for separating sand-size minerals having significant differences in specific gravity.

Pebble mill   Similar to a ball mill but using grinding media composed of hard pebbles such as flint or quartzite.

Polishing   A beneficiation technique designed to remove minor surface films of impurities from mineral grains by gentle abrasion in a mill.

Processing   The various operations performed on an ore to prepare it for use, these include crushing, grinding and screening.

Pulp   A mixture of finely ground ore and water.

Quartering   Dividing a pile of carefully mixed ore into four equal parts for sampling. Alternate quarters are saved as the sample, or for further rolling and quartering if too large. The other two quarters become "rejects".

Quern   An ancient Mesopotamian grinding device consisting of two flat stones, the upper of which has a central vertical feed hole and is slid back and forth over the lower, grinding the ore between them.

Recycling   The return of middlings in a flowsheet to a mill for regrinding.

Reducing   The removal of oxygen from an ore or ceramic material by heating in an oxygen-deficient atmosphere.

Riddle   A large, hand-held sieve, usually coarse mesh.

Roasting   Another term for calcining.

Rolling   Mixing ore samples by tumbling them back and forth on a square of canvas or heavy plastic preparatory to quartering.

Saddle stone   An ancient Egyptian grinding device consisting of two stones. The upper and smaller stone is slid back and forth over the gently inclined smooth surface of the lower stone, crushing the ore between.

Scram   An open-cut excavation, usually small, dug to mine ore.

Single jack   A short-handled sledge weighing about four pounds.

Slimes   Rock or mineral that has been over-ground. Usually difficult to recover since it remains in suspension.

Slurry   A thin watery mixture of clay or finely ground rock.

Stage grinding   A flowsheet in which ore is passed through a succession of mills, each of which reduces the particle size of the feed from the preceding mill before passing it on to the next.

Stripping ratio   The relative thickness of overburden-to-ore expressed as a ratio.

Tails, tailings   The unwanted fraction resulting from the beneficiation and processing of an ore. Also called waste.

Tramp iron   Bits of junk iron, or iron abraded from milling equipment, accidentally introduced into a mill and contaminating the ore.

Waste   See tails.

GLOSSARY III

List of terms used in geology

Alluvium   Sediments laid down by running water.

Argillite   A thick-bedded clayey rock.

Arenaceous   A term applied to rocks containing sand and having a sandy texture.

Bed   The smallest division of a series of stratified rocks. Also the floor of a stream or lake.

Bedding   The equivalent of stratification.

Crystalline rocks   Rocks composed of tightly fitting mineral crystals that have formed in the rock itself, such as granite, in contrast to rocks having grains cemented together, such as sandstone.

Dip and strike   Terms describing the attitude of rock formations and geologic structures. Dip is the angle between the horizontal and the slope of the formation. Strike is the compass direction of a horizontal line across the face of the formation.

Extrusives   Igneous rocks that have cooled and hardened upon reaching the surface of the Earth.

Fault   A large crack in the Earth's surface, often miles long and extending to considerable depth. Motion along the fault in either horizontal or vertical direction commonly offsets the rocks lying on the two sides of the fault.

Fluvial   Geologic features produced by running water.

Fold   A large wrinkle in the Earth's crust. Upward arching folds are anticlines, downward ones are synclines.

Formation   A large and persistent stratum of some one kind of rock. A group of strata having common characteristics. A related group of rocks.

Horizon   A particular stratigraphic position in a series of bedded rocks. Often used for defining the age of a bed or formation.

Hydrothermal   The alteration of sub-surface or near-surface rocks by the action of chemically charged hot water rising from deep underground.

In situ   In place. Deposits that have weathered or that have been hydrothermally altered in place are said to be *in situ* deposits.

Intrusives   Igneous rocks which have cooled and hardened beneath the surface and which, when molten, were forced up from great depths.

Lacustrine   Deposits laid down in lakes.

Laterite   A brick-red rock that has been weathered in a humid climate.

Leaching   The chemical attack on exposed or near-surface rocks provided by the agents of weathering which dissolve its minerals in the order of their solubility.

Metamorphic   A long-term geologic process involving rocks subjected to deep burial, intense heat, pressure and other factors. The process causes profound changes in the original rocks, transforming sandstones into quartzites, shales into slates and rhyolites into mica schists, for example.

Mineralize   To impregnate or supply with minerals, as in a vein or ore body. To petrify.

Pegmatite   An intrusive rock having extremely large mineral crystals such as feldspar, mica, and quartz. Also called giant-granite.

Plutonic rocks   Igneous rocks having a deep-seated origin such as some granites. See also intrusives.

Primary   Clay deposits which have been formed *in situ*, as compared to secondary deposits formed from transported material.

Residual   Roughly equivalent to primary and *in situ* deposits. The term refers to the least soluble portions of the original rocks, which, in effect, are clays.

Secondary   Deposits which have been transported from their original place to their present location by running water, wind, gravity or glaciation.

Sedimentary   A large class of rocks whose constituents have been transported to their present location principally by the geologic processes of running water and wind.

Stratification   The layering of sediments to form strata. Perfection of layering ranges from the extremely fine laminae laid down in deep ocean basins to the relatively coarse formations typical of lakes and bays, to the rude deposits dropped as the result of torrential flooding or glacial activity. The basic concept is that older beds are overlain by younger ones and missing layers indicate an erosional episode.

Stratum   A layer of rock that is more or less similar throughout. The plural form is strata.

Transported   Geologic material that is moved from one place to another by running water, gravity, wind or glaciation.

Weathering   The process that ultimately destroys surface rocks by the effects of rain, ground water, the atmosphere, and various organisms, Weathering is the chemical decomposition of the minerals in a rock, as compared to erosion, a largely mechanical or physical activity, which reduces solid rock to small pieces. See leaching.

INDEX

See also Glossaries
Italicized page numbers refer to illustrations and tables